GREAT LIVES IN BRIEF

A New Series of Biographies

ACCURACY
BREVITY CLARITY
MULTUM
IN PARVO

These are BORZOI BOOKS
Published by ALFRED A. KNOPF *in New York*

NAPOLEON I

Napoleon I

A GREAT LIFE IN BRIEF

BY

Albert Guérard

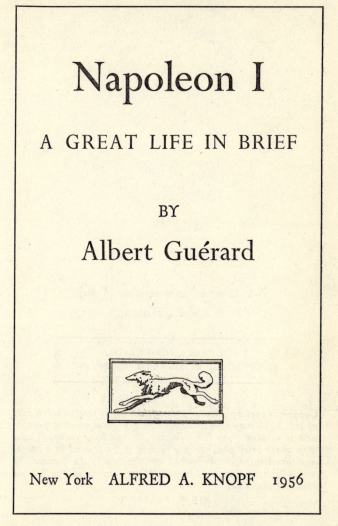

New York   ALFRED A. KNOPF   1956

L. C. catalog card number: 56–5803

© ALBERT GUÉRARD, *1956*

THIS IS A BORZOI BOOK,
PUBLISHED BY ALFRED A. KNOPF, INC.

84555

FIRST EDITION

FOR

my granddaughters

Mary Maclin and Lucy Lundie Guérard

To read when they are seven

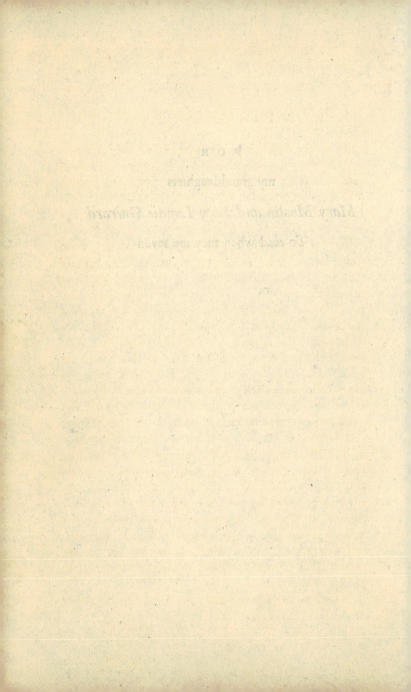

BIOGRAPHY, HISTORY, LEGEND

THIS will be the story of a *human* life. Of the multitudinous writings about Napoleon—over one hundred thousand, according to Kircheisen—many place him beyond our common humanity. For Victor Hugo, Léon Bloy, Dmitri Merezhkovsky, and Dr. McNair Wilson, he was *L'Homme, The Man*, in a messianic sense. In his lifetime, pious souls in England considered him as a fiend spewed from hell; and Pierre Bezúkhov, the hero of Tolstoy's *War and Peace*, spent laborious hours seeking to establish that his number was that of the Beast, six hundred and sixty-six. Even Taine, who posed as a realist and a positivist, tried to make our flesh creep with suggestions that Napoleon, under the semblance of a man, belonged to another race and another time: an aerolith from outer space, or, in Mallarmé's words, "a block fallen here below from some obscure disaster." For others, he was not a historical character at all, but undiluted myth, as he himself believed of Jesus Christ; J. B. Pérès and Archbishop Whately devoted clever little books to the proposition that Napoleon never existed.

After fifty years of study, Napoleon appears to me as neither angel nor beast, but as human, all too human: our brother—our Big Brother—a creature of strong but ailing flesh, lean and sulphurous in youth, paunchy and lardy in middle life; not a very good husband, who married two not very good wives; a martinet, an incomparable efficiency manager, with an addiction to gambling and gigantic dreams.

Napoleon belongs to history: it is through his career

that we know his personality. He made history; but first history made him. What would the tense Corsican boy have been, with the same passions and the same devouring energy, if he had been born a few decades earlier or later? Another Rousseau perhaps—that Rousseau with whom he once compared himself? Or a Balzac? Balzac had on his desk a statuette of the Emperor with the defiant words: "What he failed to accomplish with the sword, I shall achieve with the pen." [1] Who can tell? As indications, we have two admirable studies of the Napoleonic temper under totally different circumstances: Julian Sorel, the hero of Stendhal's *The Red and the Black*, and Rastignac, who in Balzac's *Father Goriot* challenges Paris to mortal combat. Archives provide only the incidents and the trappings, those things which were common to Bonaparte and Augereau or Masséna; the drama of Napoleon is in Napoleon's soul. And to that inner drama Stendhal and Balzac offer a better clue than Thiers or Madelin. For Napoleon is a hero of romance who happened to traverse history.

The relations between biography and history remain a baffling problem. Carlyle believed in "heroes," Emerson in "representative men," Napoleon III in "Providential men," Hitler in the Leader by right of divine election. On the other hand, Tolstoy, with painful elaboration, expounds his doctrine that there are no leaders at all. The strutting little figures are swept away by the flood they pathetically commanded to rise or to recede. Napoleon gave wrong orders, which were not obeyed; had they been obeyed, it would have made no difference. The greatness of Kutusov was that he gave no orders at

[1] I.e., to create a world. Napoleon looms enormously larger than Balzac; but the Balzacian world is more alive than the Napoleonic.

all. A willful paradox? It sounds less absurd in connection with the Russian campaign than with any other great
event in history. It does not make sense: it denies sense.
But the hypothesis that Napoleon, a political and military genius of unequaled magnitude, was, intellectually
and morally, in full control of the forces that carried him
to Moscow is an even more flagrant absurdity. We must
remember also that reputable historians—Adolphe
Thiers, Albert Sorel, Jacques Bainville—maintain that
the course of Napoleon, ascent and decline, was determined by the conquest of the Rhine frontier in 1795:
it would have been futile for the heir of the Revolution
to decree that "the Trojan War would not take place." [2]
Napoleon himself had a strange deep-seated belief in
"Destiny," a power beyond human computation and human will. This would not affect the appeal of his tragedy:
Œdipus also was the plaything of relentless fate.

On a less mystic plane, it may be asserted that history is made up of immense processes. Science can describe and explain them, for they are subject to laws;
but in their majestic sweep, the share of any individual
is infinitesimal. The Reformation is greater than Luther
or Calvin; the Enlightenment absorbs Voltaire and Diderot; James Watt stands only for an incident in the in-
dustrial revolution. Great men are not causes, but names
used as symbols for great events: just as Waterloo is
merely a village where the famous battle was *not* fought.
History is not a string of anecdotes. Again, Napoleon
saw deeper than some of his worshippers: he was conscious of that obscure power which he called *la force
des choses*, the irresistible might of things. On the proper
scale, it would be possible to record the advances and

[2] Jean Giraudoux: *La Guerre de Troie n'aura pas lieu*, written on the eve of World War II.

regressions of the nineteenth century without mentioning Napoleon at all. If this be the case, then let us admit that the present book is not written on the proper scale.

Finally, it may be contended that, as history is the collective memory of mankind, events and men are "historical" in so far as they are "memorable." Not because they are great: Mme Dubarry is better remembered than Condillac. Not even because they are true: most famous sayings on record are apocryphal. But because they are impressive, for the memory of the race is swayed by dreads and hopes. This factor, sentimental and æsthetic rather than scientific, constitutes the *Legend*. The legend may have a nucleus of solid fact: there actually was a Charlemagne, though the hero of the epic cycle, nearly three centuries later, was a very different personage. There may have been a King Arthur, though Tennyson did his best to make him incredible. There probably never was a William Tell—the only Swiss who lives in the hearts of men. Was there an earthly prototype of Prometheus?

In the case of Napoleon, the Legend is enormously more significant than sober history. Every study of the Napoleonic theme should begin with a thorough investigation of the Legend. Let this be done with no thought of "debunking," a process as vulgar as its name; but in order to disengage the plain palpable truth from the folk epic, the modern *Iliad* or *Nibelungenlied*. Because they have neglected this initial step, many painstaking scholars like Frédéric Masson, Louis Madelin, and Kircheisen have simply studded the Legend—unchallenged—with innumerable realistic facts. With the same method they could have written a learned monograph on Nicholas, Bishop of Myra, and retain untarnished their childlike faith in Santa Claus. Perhaps they would

not have worked so diligently if they had not been sus-
tained by that faith.

I have attempted elsewhere,[3] not to offer a survey of
that illimitable field, but to indicate a path of approach.
In the present book, which is pure biography, I pro-
pose to ignore the Legend almost entirely. The result
may at times appear disconcerting. What! A Napoleon
without the "whiff of grapeshot," a Napoleon who lost
six campaigns out of twelve, a Napoleon who botched
the Concordat and allowed himself to be hoodwinked by
Talleyrand and Fouché! I cannot, however, leave the
Legend out of account altogether, because Napoleon
was, deliberately and with magnificent success, the poet
of his own saga. The "glory" for which he craved and to
which he erected altars was an aura transforming drab
reality. That is why St. Helena, where with marvelous
skill he reinterpreted his personage, remains the most
successful of his campaigns. It was not for immediate
power that he was playing his part, but in order to impress posterity. He had his wish: his empire is dust, but
his fame has lost none of its splendor. A life of Napoleon
that would exclude Napoleon the Artist—*commediante!
tragediante!*—would be *Hamlet* without the Prince.

ALBERT GUÉRARD

[3] *Reflections on the Napoleonic Legend* (London and New
York, 1924).

CONTENTS

NAPOLEON I

Carlo Buonaparte (1746-1785)

Joseph
1768-1844
m. Josephine
de Beauharnais
1763-1814

NAPOLEON
1769-1821
m. (2) Marie-Louise
of Austria
1791-1847

Lucien
1775-1840

Eliza
1777-1820
m. Prince
Bacchioci

(Stepchildren
of Napoleon)

Eugène
1781-1824

Hortense
1783-1837

Napoleon II,
King of Rome,
Duke of Reichstadt
1811-1832

Pierre
1815-1881

Roland
1858-1924

Princess George
of Greece

THE
BONAPARTE
FAMILY

A Condensed Genealogy

m. Letizia Ramolino (1750-1836), Madame Mère

Louis
1778-1846
m. Hortense
de Beauharnais

Pauline
1780-1825
m. General
LeClerc
m. (2) Prince
Borghese

Caroline
1782-1839
m. Joachim
Murat

Jerome
1784-1860
m. Elizabeth
Patterson
m. (2) Catherine
of Württemberg

Napoleon-Louis
1804-1831

Charles-Louis-Napoleon
(NAPOLEON III)
1808-1873
m. Eugenia
de Montijo

Mathilde
1820-1904
m. Prince
Demidov

Napoleon
(Plonplon)
1822-1891
m. Clotilde
of Savoy

Louis-Napoleon
Prince Imperial
1856-1879

Victor
1862-1926

Louis
1864-1932

Louis-Napoleon
1914-
(present claimant)

CHAPTER ONE

YOUNG BUONAPARTE
1769–1795

ON Assumption Day, August 15, 1769, Mme Letizia Buonaparte was attending Mass at Ajaccio when she felt the first pangs of childbirth. She hurried home, had no time to reach her bedroom, and, on a sofa downstairs, was delivered of a son. No doctor was there to assist her, not even a midwife. She was nineteen, and in the five years of her married life she had already borne three children; only one, Joseph, survived. Little Napoleone —in the Corsican dialect Nabulione—was puny but well formed. He was entering life at a critical moment in the history of his country.

Corsica, which travel posters proclaim "the isle of Beauty": a tight little world, stern and wild like Caledonia, but under happier skies; harsh, mountainous, forest-clad; the flat eastern shore marshy and fever-ridden; the habitable valleys fertile enough, but isolated by abrupt ranges into distinct communities, especially in those days when highways were little better than mule trails. The untilled slopes were thickly covered with shrubs—arbutus, myrtle, thorn, laurel, and broom—the tang of which reached even to the sea. This wasteland was the *maquis* (*macchia*): a name which, through Émile Zola in 1898 and the *Résistance* in World War II, has become known through the world. After a *vendetta* or blood feud the outlaws would seek sanctuary in that aromatic wilderness. Gentlemen avenging their honor were at times hard to distinguish from cutthroats; banditry remained endemic in the highlands of Corsica until the very end of the nineteenth century. A little over three thousand square miles of ruggedness, poverty, and pride. Only fifty miles away lay the coast of Tuscany, then under the rule of Leopold, mild and liberal like his brother the Emperor Joseph II; a hundred miles to the north was Genoa, in resplendent decrepitude; a little farther, the France of the Enlightenment. The miles might have been centuries.

Aloof Corsica was invaded by all the peoples who ever sailed the Mediterranean: Ligurians and Etruscans in dim antiquity, Phœnicians from Carthage, Greeks from Phocæa, Romans, Vandals, Goths, Lombards, Byzantines, Saracens. It remained untamed, like its larger neighbor Sardinia, while Sicily was repeatedly a splendid center of culture. In the Middle Ages possession of the island was in dispute between Pisa and Genoa: the aristocracy of Corsica came from those two cities. At the end of the thirteenth century Genoa, farther away but stronger at sea, remained in uneasy control. The open fight for Corsican independence filled the whole of the eighteenth century. A Westphalian adventurer, Baron Theodor von Neuhof, made himself king and achieved immortality by figuring, with other deposed monarchs, in a chapter of Voltaire's *Candide*. The island might have been left to its fragrant primitiveness and to its medieval chaos—a loose confederacy of small cities or *communes*—but for the complex rivalries of Genoa, Sardinia, France, and Great Britian. The islanders did manage at last to achieve a rough unity under Pasquale Paoli (1725–1807), whose father and brother had already led them against the Genoese. With superb assurance the Corsicans created a "university" in the village of Corte, their inland capital, and requested Jean-Jacques Rousseau to draft their constitution. The

Republic of Genoa, long past its prime, could not cope
with the rebellion and called upon the French for assistance. For decades there was a fitful, ambiguous condominium. Finally, despairing of subduing the wild unprofitable country, the Genoese sold the shadow of their
rights to Louis XV (May 15, 1768).

In such a primitive country the few civilized families
stood out, though by Continental standards their posses-
sions and their learning might have seemed scanty. Carlo
Buonaparte (1746–85), Napoleon's father, attended a
Jesuit school at Ajaccio and pursued his law studies at
the "university" of Corte; but his wife, Letizia, *née*
Ramolino, though of good stock, never felt at home in
Italian or French; even after she had become the mother
of many kings, she gladly relapsed into her native patois.
Young Carlo was an ardent supporter of Paoli. He took
part in the last victory of free Corsica, at Borgo, and
perhaps in the final defeat at Ponte Nuovo (March 8,
1769). It was said that the intrepid Letizia was with
him, and the unborn Napoleon. The Paolists were over-
whelmed; the leader and some three hundred and fifty
of his followers, rescued by two British ships, sought
refuge in England.

The battle was lost; but for Carlo, only twenty-three
years of age, there was ample time to win another. He
refused to entangle his young destiny with a losing cause,
and wholeheartedly joined the French party. History
finds it difficult to pass judgment on "collaborationists."
The name is attached, opprobriously, to Laval and Quis-
ling; but it would fit also Marshal Smuts and Emperor
Hirohito. At any rate, Carlo showed no lack of decision.
He went to take his law degree at Pisa so as to qualify
himself for action on a larger scale; and, characteristically,
he spent a year's income in celebrating the event. Vanity

and shrewdness were combined in him: his fine presence, his taste for luxury, his knowledge of French and Italian, made him stand out among the uncouth local worthies. A welcome and convenient recruit for the new masters, he became the personal friend of the governor, Count de Marbeuf. He secured a position as assessor in the court at Ajaccio and managed to establish a private practice as well. Above all, he contrived to have his claims to noble rank officially recognized. This entitled him to the bene-factions of His Most Christian Majesty; several of his children—Joseph, Napoleon, Lucien, Eliza—were to be educated in various schools at the King's expense. Even Joseph Fesch, Letizia's half-brother, was not for-gotten: he went to Aix to study for the priesthood. His unobtrusive virtues and the grace of his nephew Napo-leon were to make him an Archbishop of Lyon, Primate of Gaul, and a cardinal.

The royal bounty was sorely needed. The Buona-partes, though "reputed nobles and patricians for two hundred years," had never been rich. The combined estate of the clan, ably and parsimoniously managed by Uncle Lucciano Buonaparte, archdeacon at Ajaccio, was modest; much of it was tied up in complicated and interminable litigations. If Letizia was thrifty—and thrifty she remained when her son was the new Charle-magne—Carlo was extravagant. His begging expeditions to Versailles were not fruitless, but he also brought back from Paris twelve embroidered suits for himself. The family was increasing faster than the means of support: eight of his thirteen children survived their father.

On January 1, 1779 Carlo Buonaparte took his two elder sons, Joseph and Napoleon, to the College of Autun, reputed to be among the best in France. Joseph, taller, handsomer, by no means a fool, but of an easy good nature that verged on indolence, was intended for an ecclesiastical career; Napoleon, who at the age of nine had already asserted his fiery temper, was to become a soldier. After a few months at Autun, improving his command of French, he proceeded to Brienne, where he had been granted a scholarship.

Brienne was one of the twelve schools recently selected by Saint-Germain, Minister of War, to serve as military academies for young noblemen. With a strong accent on *noblemen:* it was Saint-Germain who, in a famous ordinance, had hermetically sealed the officers' corps against commoners. Regimes harden as death closes upon them: under Louis XVI, Vauban could not have become a marshal of France.

In spite of its martial purpose, the school was run by a religious order, the Minims, with a few lay assistants. The curriculum was practical, free from the emphasis that for two hundred years the Jesuits had placed on Latin, rhetoric, and drawing-room manners. The material conditions were austere, but not unduly harsh. Only one feature strikes us as unnatural: for the whole six years of the course the boys were not allowed to go home. Napoleon was visited only twice: by his father and mother in 1782, by his father and his younger brother Lucien in 1784. He was no prodigy and no dunce. He gave a good account of himself in mathematics; his dancing was of the poorest; to the end his handwriting remained gloriously illegible.

Torn from all home associations, he found little solace in comradeship. He was not sent to Coventry; but, undersized, thin and sallow, speaking French with a ludicrous accent, he was branded as different. Boys can be cruel little snobs. Half the cadets were the sons of impoverished gentlemen and were supported by the

King's bounty; but they realized that, among the poor,
he was a pauper. Few of them belonged to the higher
nobility; but they did not conceal their scorn for the
"patrician" from a remote province recently bought like
a piece of real estate and rumored to be half savage.

The lonely boy became an ardent reader. He devoured the masterpieces of antiquity, particularly the
historians, and those of France's great century: his romantic, almost Byronic dreams were cast in a severely
classical mold. Throughout his career we shall find in his
style sonorous echoes of Corneille, and in his spirit the
long shadow of Plutarch. As he was not welcome among
the French, his boyish will-to-power took a Corsican
turn. He became a fierce island patriot; he hated the op-
pressors of his people, and worshipped the local demigod, Paoli. Perhaps there was in this attitude a secret
rebellion against the turncoat, the collaborationist, the
father whom, in all sincerity, he professed to admire and
love.

Napoleon had first been slated for the navy, but was
shifted to the army. He chose the artillery: in that highly
technical branch, brains had a better chance. After an
examination he and four others were selected to enter
the great military school in Paris. In keeping with Ga-
briel's stately architecture, the cadets were treated like
officers and gentlemen. They lived in a luxury that
Napoleon had never known, and was not to know again
for another decade. After only one year of study (October 30, 1784 to October 28, 1785) he was gradu-
ated, ranking forty-second out of fifty-eight. Just ahead
of him was Phélippeaux, another alumnus of Brienne,
who was to defeat him at Acre and perhaps deflect his
career. The boy, just over sixteen, was gazetted second
lieutenant in the regiment of La Fère.

Meanwhile Carlo Buonaparte, tortured by cancer of the stomach, had gone as a last hope to Montpellier, a medical center of ancient renown, and had died there on February 24, 1785. He left his family in a situation full of elusive promises and desperate embarrassments. The estate, in spite of Carlo's tireless solicitations and Uncle Lucciano's management, was tangled up as usual. Joseph (b. 1768) was changing his course from the Church to the army. Lucien (b. 1775), on the contrary, was giving up Brienne for the Seminary at Aix. Both moves were to prove abortive. Eliza (b. 1777) had the best prospects: she had been admitted to Saint-Cyr, the school created by Mme de Maintenon for the daughters of the impoverished aristocracy, whence she was expected to emerge at twenty with the accomplishments of a gentlewoman, a munificent dowry of three thousand francs, and a trousseau. Louis (b. 1778), Pauline (b. 1780), Caroline (b. 1782), and Jerome (b. 1784) were left under the care of the widow, on tenuous and problematic resources.

Although Napoleon, respectful of Corsican tradition, never challenged Joseph's right as the eldest, he had already assumed, *de facto*, the leadership of the clan. He disapproved of his brothers' changes of plans, speaking in the authoritative tones of a world-wise uncle. He took his responsibility seriously: within a quarter of a century, he had found thrones for most of the brood.

But, for all his family concerns, he was first of all, naturally enough, a spirited youngster entering upon the career that he loved. At the pinnacle, he was to remember with fondness the golden days when "he had the honor of being a second lieutenant of artillery." He was sent to Valence, on the Rhône, some sixty miles south of Lyon, where a detachment of his regiment was sta-

tioned. He had to go through the drill of the private, the
corporal, and the sergeant before he assumed his duties
as an officer: the old army believed in apprenticeship
rather than in theoretical learning.

Too earnest and too poor for social pleasures, he read
more avidly than ever. This time, in the sultry twilight
of the ancient regime, he absorbed the political writers:
Montesquieu, Mably, Raynal. He was, like most of his
contemporaries, steeped in Rousseau. Both young upstarts did reshape the world; both were conscious of
their native power, in contrast with their humble standing and the indifference of society; both felt the melan-
choly that is bred by moral solitude; in both tumultuous
minds there were vast dreams not fully under the control of classical reason. Napoleon, aware of the kinship,
once wondered whether it would have been better for
the world if he and Rousseau had never lived.

Napoleon was not to enjoy for long the studious leisure of a peacetime, small-town garrison. During the
next seven years his movements were complicated and
at times unaccountable. With revolution in the air, army
discipline had grown very lax. Napoleon was on leave
for longer periods than on active service. Much of his
time he spent in Corsica playing ambiguous politics;
part of the rest he was in Paris begging for an extension
of his furlough. Ill health, bad weather, anything would
serve as an excuse. As a rule, he managed to escape dis-
ciplinary measures and to collect most of his back pay.
He was not finally dismissed for persistent insubordination until the eve of his becoming commander-in-chief.
This is the most obscure and not the least paradoxical
chapter in his bewildering career.

He went back to Corsica in September 1786 for
the first time in seven years and nine months. On ac-

count of a war scare with Prussia (August 1787), all officers were recalled to their posts. But, without tarrying at Valence, Napoleon went on to Paris and was granted a new leave to attend the Estates of Corsica. He arrived in Ajaccio on January 1, 1788. Joseph, after taking his law degree at Pisa like their father, joined him for a few weeks. In June, Napoleon left to rejoin his unit, now at Auxonne in Burgundy; and for a miracle, he was to stay there for fifteen months.

The mob and the soldiery had caught the fever of July 1789: as an echo of Bastille Day, there was rioting in the placid little town. But by July 20 the officers had restored discipline. Napoleon's political opinions suffered many changes; but he never swerved in his horror of anarchy. Unruly at heart, he craved material order. As late as March 1815 he shuddered and shrank when he was deliriously hailed by the populace. In September 1789 he was off to Corsica again.

With the Revolution the political climate of the island had changed altogether. Corsica, like Alsace, had not grown French through a slow maturing process: although not disloyal, both considered themselves semi-alien. Both were born anew and made one with the French people, in the spirit of liberty. Napoleon, who, in his own mind, had always posed as a lover of freedom, accepted at once the Principles of 1789, while many of his fellow officers were hesitating, or even preparing to desert. In France, Paoli was hailed as a hero and a martyr of the people's cause. On the motion of Mirabeau, he was allowed to return from exile, and he was given the rank of lieutenant general. The National Assembly received him in triumph. But in his long absence he had learned nothing and forgotten nothing. He was for Corsica first, for Corsica alone. He was ready to accept membership in the French Commonwealth, but on his own terms. Rather than submit to orders from Paris, he would place his country under a British protectorate. Now the Revolution, in the name of "Liberty," was sweeping away all provincial "liberties" as survivals of the Gothic ages. There was from the first a misunderstanding between Paoli and the French Revolutionists: Napoleon and Joseph were mobbed as Jacobins. Soon after he landed at Bastia, the old hero, whom his people called Babbo (Daddy), was elected President. Pardonably, he welcomed with coolness the sons of the turncoat Carlo.

So, early in 1791, Napoleon, somewhat crestfallen, returned to Auxonne. This time, in order to relieve his mother, he took with him his brother Louis, of whom he was very fond and who was showing delusive promise. He tutored the lad, and for his sake had to deny himself every luxury. The regiment moved back to Valence. Incorrigibly, and over his colonel's opposition, Napoleon wangled another leave for Corsica. For him, as for the whole country, 1792 was a year of inextricable confusion. For outstaying his leave, he was regarded as an *émigré* and forfeited his French commission. In Corsica he got himself elected lieutenant colonel of volunteers; but he was openly at odds with Paoli, now full master of the island. On Easter Day he made a futile attempt to seize Ajaccio. In May he left for Paris, frustrated, his standing dubious, his outlook dim.

On June 20 he saw the mob invade the royal palace of the Tuileries. The King, who, since his abortive flight to Varennes, thought of himself as as prisoner and a martyr, offered no resistance; he even donned the red cap. *"Che coglione!"*—What a weak fool!—exclaimed

the young soldier. But the great war had started; it was
to last until 1815. All officers who had not emigrated
were welcomed back. No embarrassing questions were
pressed: Napoleon received his arrears of pay and was
promoted to a captaincy. He was still in Paris on August
10, when the Tuileries Palace was stormed again. This
time the throne collapsed altogether. Napoleon and
Eliza (Saint-Cyr had just been suppressed) lived through
the days of September, when bands of ruffians, drunk
with "preternatural suspicion," massacred the aristocrats
who had been rounded up in the prisons, a short, thorough way with security risks.

Back in Ajaccio by October 15, Napoleon was appointed commander of the National Guards. Two expeditions against Sardinia failed: French sailors and
Paolist soldiers came to blows. In April and May 1793
Napoleon made other attempts to capture Ajaccio. He
had not yet formally broken with Paoli; but the hero of
independence, fiercely denounced by the young fire-
brand Lucien Buonaparte, was outlawed by the Convention in April 1793. This time the breach was final.
Captured by the Paolists, Napoleon managed to escape.
The whole family fled to France after melodramatic
adventures. Their house was wrecked and looted by the
Corsican patriots.

Paoli, hard pressed, had to call in the British in 1794
and to acknowledge the sovereignty of George III. But
England was not deeply interested. Finding Paoli difficult, she did not leave him at the head of affairs. In 1796
the island was recaptured by the French. Babbo Paoli
was again a refugee in London, where he died obscurely
in 1807. The Corsican chapter of Napoleon's history
was closed. He saw his native shores again in 1799, on

his way back from Egypt, and he called a number of
Corsicans into his personal service. But he had out-
soared the small, fiery island.

Mme Letizia and her brood had reached Toulon, and
then Marseille, where, as French "loyalists," they received a small subsidy from the government. Napoleon
was reinstated in the regular army and promoted to
major. He seemed wholly committed to the party in
power, loosely known as the Jacobins. He wrote an able
pamphlet, *The Supper at Beaucaire*, in defense of their
policies. He took part in an operation against the coun-
terrevolutionists at Avignon. One of his protectors was
Augustin Robespierre, brother of the Dictator, Maximilien.

In that climactic year 1793, while France was struggling against Europe on every frontier, the west—Ven-
dée, Normandy, Brittany—was ablaze. Lyon, the second city, was in rebellion, and Toulon, the one great
naval base on the Mediterranean, welcomed the British
and Spanish fleets (August 28, 1793). Carteaux, a
painter of modest fame turned amateur strategist, was
feebly attempting to recapture Toulon. Napoleon served
under him with rage in his heart. Carteaux was super-
seded by Dugommier, a soldier who knew his trade. The
artillery was placed under General du Teil, a capable
officer whose brother had been much impressed by
Lieutenant Buonaparte at Auxonne; and so the young
major had his chance at last. He did not conquer Toulon
singlehanded; but he had an eagle's eye for key positions and he used his batteries to best advantage. There
is no reason to doubt the commendation of General du
Teil: "He has abundant knowledge, with intelligence
to match it; and bravery unsurpassed." "From the sublime to the ridiculous," to use a famous Napoleonic

phrase: while gathering laurels he also caught the itch, which was to annoy him for many years. Toulon was captured on December 19, 1793. There were massive reprisals: Napoleon, a subordinate, was not able to check them.

The path of glory seemed clear at last. The twenty-four-year-old was promoted to brigadier general, sent for a tour of inspection on the Italian front, entrusted with a secret mission to Genoa. His plan for an offensive in Italy, transmitted by Augustin Robespierre, was approved by the authorities in Paris, even though the best military heads were unconvinced. An important command seemed within his reach. Then came a sharp setback. He had been swimming with the Jacobin tide; and on the 9th Thermidor [1] (July 23, 1794), Maximilien Robespierre was overthrown. A few days later (August 9), Napoleon was suspended and placed under arrest.

He had not been compromised in political intrigues, however, and he was soon released; but the momentum of his ascent seemed broken. The Italian offensive was deferred. An expedition for the reconquest of Corsica (March 4–14, 1795) was thwarted by the British fleet. Napoleon was again without a definite job; and again, on May 2, he started for Paris, where so many of his battles were fought. He haunted the lobbies of the Convention and of the War Office: a disquieting figure, shabby, almost ludicrous, with flashes of impressive pride and with a record as mottled and disconcerting as his appearance

---

[1] By decree of the Convention, the year I of the Republic began on September 22, 1792. The months were named: Vendémiaire, Brumaire, Frimaire; Nivôse, Pluviôse, Ventôse; Germinal, Floréal, Prairial; Messidor, Thermidor, Fructidor. This calender remained in official use until January 1, 1806.

—many fumbling lunges and a single very creditable achievement.

He was given a stopgap assignment in the Topographical Section; but what he wanted was an active command, and in a field of his own choosing. Aubry, the man in charge of staff appointments, was himself a disgruntled old artillerist: he thought the ambitions of the fledgeling general preposterous. He offered him a brigade of infantry in the Army of the West. Napoleon had no stomach for that treacherous Vendean warfare: what glory could be reaped from obscure skirmishes with fanatical peasants? He declined the offer, at first under the plea of ill health. He was granted a short respite; when that expired, his name was struck off the list of generals on active duty. On the same day as the news of his dismissal, he received the official offer of a mission to Turkey to reorganize the Sultan's artillery. On the eve of the Revolution, he had thought of a career in India: this was a second glimpse of that fabulous East which held for him such a romantic fascination. The plan fell through; the dream remained.

Another will-o'-the-wisp flitted through Napoleon's life. When the Buonapartes were in Marseille they became acquainted with the Clary family: a solid fortune, made out of silk and soap. There was an exchange of services. Handsome Joseph won the hand of Julie Clary; and it looked as though Napoleon intended to claim her little sister Désirée as his bride. Her heart was his: we have touching letters from sweet eighteen to the hero of Toulon. How deeply the hero had committed himself we do not know. M. Clary is reported to have said: "One Buonaparte in the family is enough." The plain fact is that Napoleon, undaunted by his slender purse and dubious prospects, had made his way among the victors of Thermidor: a society not renowned for squeamishness, but dazzling to the young adventurer. In that glitter the endearing young charms of poor little Désirée faded from his memory. She married Charles Bernadotte, a vigorous, astute soldier whom Napoleon never liked or trusted, but whom he made a marshal of France and Prince of Pontecorvo. The Swedes, in 1810, chose Bernadotte as their Prince Royal; and Désirée Clary died as Queen of Sweden in 1860.

Then came Napoleon's supreme chance. Thermidor had left France in material and moral chaos. If Robespierre was the Tyrant, he was also the Incorruptible: with the reign of Terror, the reign of Virtue came to an abrupt end. Many of the Thermidorians had been terrorists—some of them out of terror. Most of them were corrupt; above all, their chief, Barras, *Roi des Pourris*, king of rottenness. That sorry crew tried to preserve its precarious power for safety and for loot against a resurgence of Jacobinism on the one hand, against a frank and thorough royalist reaction on the other. For their own protection, they added to the new constitution a clause requiring that two thirds of the representatives in the future assemblies should be chosen from the expiring and discredited Convention.

So Thermidor was to be saddled for years upon the new regime. The scandal was too great: the "Sections" (the forty-eight wards of Paris) were roused to violent protest. The opposition to the Thermidorian rulers was probably more royalist than republican; but party lines were not sharply drawn. The movement was "retching rather than insurrection." Yet Paris might experience another disastrous "Day": the masses, blindly marching against the Convention, might destroy the last shreds of

organized government. The insurgents were short of
arms; so were the loyal troops. The Sections had no
recognized leaders: the regulars had Menou, who was of
two minds, neither very good.

Barras, the natural chief of the Thermidorians, had
himself appointed commander-in-chief. But he was aware
of his limitations as a military man: he looked round for
a professional soldier. The best generals were at the
front. Fortunately, he thought of Buonaparte, hungrily
prowling for a job. He had met him in "society"; but
he had also seen him at Toulon. He turned the work
over to him.

The sympathies of Napoleon may well have been
with the insurgents: he, too, despised the profiteers of
Thermidor. But for him as for Goethe, disorder was
the worst of all evils. The government was beneath contempt: still, it was the only government. Besides, he had
received no offer from the amorphous discontent of the
Sections.

As it was in Toulon, as it was to be almost to the
very end, he saw at a single glance the key to the situation. Without guns the loose masses could win through
their sheer weight; but they would be powerless against
artillery. Guns were at hand, only a few miles away,
stored in the Sablons Plain: he dispatched Murat the
swift, who seized them in the nick of time. Meanwhile,
he posted the loyal troops at the right points to protect
the Convention—and waited.

There was no organized, concentrated fighting. Some
guns were fired on the quays. There was some shooting
on the steps of the Church of St.-Roch, but there is no
record that Napoleon was present at that point, that he
ordered the firing, or that he considered it decisive. The
"whiff of grapeshot" belongs to Carlyle rather than to

Napoleon. The insurrection was an enormous bubble that met the sharp point of an iron will. It was not defeated: it vanished (Vendémiaire 13–October 5, 1795).

Napoleon, "the Sword of Thermidor," was rewarded at once, and handsomely. On October 11 he was reinstated in the army as major general. On October 25 he succeeded Barras as commander in chief of the Army of the Interior. The greatest rewards were soon to follow: the hand of Josephine and, as a wedding gift the Italian command.

CHAPTER TWO

GENERAL BONAPARTE
REHEARSALS FOR EMPIRE: ITALY AND EGYPT
1796–1799

WHEN normal life was restored after the Jacobin orgy of Terror and Virtue, the center of society was the drawing-room of Mme Tallien. That superb creature, daughter of the Spanish banker Cabarrus and divorced wife of Count de Fontenay, was called, for her beauty and power, "Our Lady of Thermidor." She had—passively—contributed to the downfall of the Incorruptible. Young Tallien, sent by Robespierre to curb the royalist city of Bordeaux, saw Thérèse and was converted to more humane ways. He spared her, and thus incurred the dread accusation of *modérantisme*. He saved himself and his beloved by leading the attack against the tyrant. He married her in December 1794. But this was the climax of his meteoric career. Soon Thérèse became the chief ornament of Barras's extensive harem. Power as well as marital happiness slipped from Tallien's hands. His decline was steady and prolonged. He died, forgotten and destitute, in 1820.

Mme Tallien, the soul of mercy, helped many victims of the Terror. In her generous distribution of favors, she seldom forgot her rake-off: Queen of the Thermidorians, she was, like them, a staunch believer in the profit motive. When young General Buonaparte found his way into that demimonde—titles, glitter, luxury, and no moral armature—the boon he craved was a very modest one. His uniform was threadbare, and a parsimonious quartermaster refused to issue cloth for a new one. Mme Tallien smiled, nodded, and the quartermaster saw the light. It was in Mme Tallien's circle that Napoleon met Josephine. Like Tallien with Thérèse, he was subjugated: one glance, and the hungry young lion was in love.

Josephine Tascher de la Pagerie was born in Martinique in 1763. In 1779 she married Viscount Alexandre de Beauharnais. Both families belonged to the lesser nobility; both sprang from Orléanais; both had interests in the island: Alexandre was the second son of the governor. In Paris and Versailles the young pair enjoyed that "sweetness of living" which, in Talleyrand's nostalgic words, characterized the last years of the ancient regime. Their union, however, was stormy; and a formal separation was decreed in 1785. Beauharnais espoused the cause of the Revolution and rose high: as a civilian, to the presidency of the Assembly; as a soldier, to the command of an army. But aristocratic transfuges were constantly under suspicion. Beauharnais, selected as scapegoat for the fall of Mainz, was arrested and guillotined. Josephine also was imprisoned and sentenced to death: she was saved by the 9th Thermidor. She had two children, Eugene and Hortense, destined to play conspicuous parts in the grand drama of the Empire.

In 1795, she was among the merriest widows of the hectic Thermidorian world. She had had a brief affair with General Hoche; she counted for a while among Barras's mistresses. In his venomous *Memoirs*, Barras brands her as coldhearted, venal, and lascivious: impressive charges from such a Galahad. Her beauty could not compare with Mme Tallien's; but she combined to perfection languorous grace and aristocratic refinement.

The freshness of youth had already departed: in those days Creoles aged rapidly. But as the Huguenot poet Agrippa d'Aubigné puts it: *"Une rose d'automne est plus qu'une autre exquise"*: what so exquisite as an autumn rose? Like Queen Jezebel in Racine's *Athaliah*, she knew "how to repair the irreparable outrages of Time." Her dark eyes were lustrous and caressing. Because she had bad teeth, she affected a mysterious, tight-lipped, Mona Lisa smile.

Their meeting was Josephine's Austerlitz: Napoleon was at her mercy. It seems strange that a young man so self-centered and so confident should have been so utterly conquered by a woman six years older than himself, fading, with no solid position, and with a reputation that was not even equivocal. No doubt he was dazzled by her Old Court charm: she provided a link with the fabulous Versailles he had known only from afar. And she had a faint aura of that exoticism which Bernardin de Saint-Pierre's *Paul and Virginia* had made fashionable. Above all, in his austere youth and in his rough military experience, he had been starved of luxury and tenderness, and Josephine offered an admirable imitation of both. A Barras, with his blasé worldly wisdom, could see that both were flimsy and meretricious. But Napoleon was not of the same breed as Barras. There can be no greatness without a touch of naiveté.

How ardent his passion was, his torrid letters from Italy give irrefutable proof. Josephine's hold upon him was not merely that of an experienced harlot: his love for that shallow woman was deep. It withstood time and distance. It was she who first played false. While in Italy, he pretended to be half-blind; on his return from Egypt, he knew everything and forgave everything. This is the finest example of generosity in a ruthlessly egotistic career. Although the expression may sound irreverent, there is genuine sympathy in the Gallic phrase: "*C'est encore comme cocu qu'il est le plus grand,*" it is as a deceived husband that he best reveals his greatness. Nearly twenty years later, at La Malmaison, he could still evoke in the presence of Hortense the graceful phantom of his first and undying love: "My good Josephine! Certainly the most charming person I ever met . . . a woman through and through . . ." adding with a rueful smile: "But her debts! How I used to scold her about them!"

"My *good* Josephine!" Here is the key. She was loose, lazy, coldhearted, empty-headed: but she possessed the gift of easy kindliness, and she used that slender gift with consummate art. So there arose in France, as in the heart of Napoleon himself, a nebulous but indestructible legend: Josephine, the elusive, yet not wholly deceitful smile of a stiff and frowning regime, Josephine the Eternal Feminine tempering the rigor of the stern hero. In popular imagination it was she who brought Napoleon luck, innocent Marie-Louise who was his evil star.

They were married at night, on March 9, 1796: in sketchiest fashion, without any religious ceremony. They bridged the gap of years between them: she confessed to twenty-nine instead of thirty-three; he boosted his twenty-seven by eighteen months. She laid vague claims to the riches of the Indies; he proudly admitted that he owned nothing but his cloak and his sword. But, with his already imperial contempt for balanced budgets, he settled upon her an annuity of eighteen thousand francs. In spite of these "castles in Italy," she was not quite sure that Puss-in-Boots, as she had first called her ardent suitor, was a sound investment; but she was flattered by his

juvenile storminess; and Barras, who had an eye for
business, had advised the match. Three days later, the
bridegroom, still drunk with love, was on his way to
Italy.

The Italian command has been called a wedding
gift, but it was far more. The new five-headed execu-
tive, the Directory, had appointed Bonaparte (he had
discarded the Italian spelling of his name) without a
dissenting vote. He had applied for the assignment; he
desired it ardently; he had closely studied the Italian
theater of war, and had sent to headquarters volumes of
suggestions and plans. Above all, he had impressed
everyone with his coolness and decision in Vendémiaire.
Promotion did not wait on seniority in those days.

Highly as the Directors thought of the young general,
they were aware that he was untried in large-scale operations. But the Italian campaign was not intended to be
the major one. Napoleon's genius, and the luck that
followed him almost to the end of his career, completely
altered the original picture.

In 1795 Prussia, Spain, Holland, and Tuscany had
made peace with the French Republic. Genoa and
Venice were neutral. There remained England and, on
the Continent, Austria, with Piedmont (Kingdom of
Sardinia) as a minor ally. The master of strategy was
still Lazare Carnot, the Organizer of Victory. He was
the man who in 1793 had welded raw levies into a formidable host, fourteen army corps and twelve hundred
thousand men. He had evolved a new method of warfare, swift, tireless, and massive, with which his improvised officers could upset the meticulous chess game of
the old tacticians. Practically all of Napoleon's generals
were graduates of the Carnot school: he forged the instrument that made the imperial epic possible. Now

Carnot planned to impose peace in Vienna itself by sending two armies north of the Alps, one by way of the Main, the other down the Danube. These were entrusted to generals of established reputation: Jourdan, the victor of Fleurus and Wattignies; Moreau, known as a careful and efficient commander. The plan was so good and so obvious that Napoleon was to borrow it twice, in 1805 and in 1809. The Italian route on the contrary did not lead straight to Vienna: the eastern spurs of the Alps would oppose a formidable obstacle to invasion. This much Austria could guess: she put her best general, Archduke Charles, in command of the northern armies. To Italy she sent reinforcements piecemeal, always "too little and too late."

But Jourdan, who, after his two early victories, was invariably unlucky, was sharply defeated. Moreau, left unsupported, had to effect a retreat that has remained a classic: unbroken, he managed to capture guns and prisoners from his pursuers. When, after this disastrous setback, the Directory picked up Carnot's plan again and sent two armies over the same routes, one under Moreau, the other under Hoche, the campaign opened magnificently and came to an abrupt close: for Napoleon, acting as though he were a sovereign, signed an armistice that was almost a peace treaty; and the Italian campaign stood out as a unique and luminous achievement.

"Soldiers! You are destitute: I am leading you into the richest plains in the world." These famous words, though not apocryphal, were perhaps not uttered at the time; but they admirably express the spirit of Napoleon, his army, and his government. The Directory, suffering from a chronic state of bankruptcy, could not bear the cost of war; on the contrary, it relied upon war to refill its exchequer, a sieve of the Danaïdes. The Italian campaign was a *razzia* or looting raid on an epic scale. The government had misgivings about the airs the young proconsul was taking on. They sent Saliceti, Kellermann, Clarke, to keep watch on him or share the command with him; Napoleon shrugged them away and replied by assuming still more powers. But what could be done with a general who was shipping home gold, jewelry, art treasures, by the cartload? The army contractors grew fat—but they had to provide the goods; the generals were encouraged to line their pockets. Napoleon himself kept loftily clean: his quarry was higher. He merely attended to the needs of his family: Joseph made a fortune as commissary of the armies. The hero himself returned with a paltry three millions.

The details of the military operations have no place in this biographical sketch. But the merest layman is thrilled by the masterly game played by young Bonaparte. He was not to display the same unerring virtuosity again until 1814, in the wonderful and tragic campaign of France; and by that time, no skill would avail any more.

Starting from Nice in April 1796, Napoleon defeated the Austrians at Montenotte, Millesimo, Dego; the Piedmontese at Mondovi. Victor Amadeus, King of Sardinia, was compelled to sign an onerous armistice at Cherasco. Then, turning on the Austrian commander Beaulieu, Napoleon crossed the Po at Piacenza, the Adda at Lodi (there it was that his soldiers first called him "the Little Corporal"), and entered as a conqueror the queen city of Lombardy, Milan.

He was hailed by the Milanese as a liberator. Perhaps it was their enthusiasm that focused his destiny. He felt himself no longer a mere general, but a being apart, a demigod commanding the devotion of multitudes. He did not reflect—neither did posterity—that it was not his victory that the Italians were celebrating, but the defeat of the Austrians. We realize now that Napoleon was like a young heir coming into a vast heritage. He stood for France; the splendor of the Grand Monarch, the charm of the Paris salons, the exhilaration of the Enlightenment, the immense hope raised by the storming of the Bastille, the miracle of Carnot's victories. The coming of the French seemed to herald a new heaven and a new earth. That treasure of good will, so clearly manifested when, on May 15, 1796, Milan tumultuously cheered the victor, Napoleon was to grab as his own—and to squander. The victory, material and moral, was dazzling but precarious, as the greatest of Napoleon's victories were destined to be. Less than a fortnight after his triumphal entry into Milan, Lombardy rose against him; he ordered Pavia to be pillaged as a lesson.

By the end of May he had driven Beaulieu into the Tyrol; in June he laid siege to the key fortress, Mantua. Then he had to face a more redoubtable adversary, Field Marshal Count Würmser. For a while the situation looked ominous. But Würmser in his turn was hurled back at Castiglione; when he returned, he was routed at Bassano and had to seek refuge in Mantua, which, after a setback, Napoleon was besieging again. All sorties were repulsed, and on February 2, 1797 the renowned old marshal had to capitulate. Another army under Alvinzi was beaten at Arcola and Rivoli.

At last Archduke Charles assumed command against Napoleon. But by that time Austria no longer enjoyed numerical superiority. Charles had to abandon the line of the Tagliamento. He was pursued into the mountains

of Carinthia. An armistice was signed at Leoben on
April 17; it served as a basis for the triumphant peace of
Campoformio (October 17, 1797).

Triumphant, yet equivocal. It was only another move
in a protracted game. The French at Klagenfurt were
still a long, hard way from Vienna; and if Austria was
exhausted, so was France. But this was the cynical age
that had seen the three partitions of Poland. Prussia at
Basel and Austria at Campoformio yielded so much only
because they expected to recoup themselves at the expense of their lesser allies and of the neutrals. In dynastic
Europe the desires of the population counted for nothing: "souls" were neatly balanced in complicated deals.
Whatever may have been the early ideal of the French
Revolution—a crusade for democracy—by 1797 the
Directory and Napoleon were playing exactly the same
ruthless game as Frederick, Catherine, and Maria-
Theresa, a blend of force and fraud.

Only they played that game, like novices drunk with
their own luck, far more recklessly than their forerun-
ners. The pace grew furious. From 1797 to 1812, republics were created and abolished (it was in 1797
that Genoa and Venice ceased to be, two commercial
oligarchies stiff with age and tarnished splendor), grand
duchies and kingdoms carved out and suppressed—
Berg, Etruria, Westphalia, Warsaw—by a flash of the
sword and a stroke of the pen. It was a most exciting
game; only it never was quite real. The whole of middle
Europe was a teeming chaos of tiny principalities, bish-
oprics, free cities, which were medieval ghosts. The
people were bewildered and indifferent. The dynasties
stood for no principle, but gambled or fought for the
spoils. If Europe had not been such an array of obsolete

incongruities, the fantastic scene-shiftings done by the Directory and Napoleon would have been inconceivable.

Meanwhile the young conqueror had imposed his will on Parma, Modena, and the Pope. Resting from his labors, he was now holding court at the castle of Mombello, near Milan. The whole family was summoned to bask in the sunshine of his glory: Mme Letizia, Eliza, Pauline, Caroline, Joseph, Louis, Eugene. There the Corsican felt himself king, as Louis XVI had never been: king by the divine right of genius and destiny. The new Minister of Foreign Affairs, Talleyrand, wrote to him not as to a general of the Republic, but as to a prince whose favor was to be courted. Josephine graced the marvelous scene. She had offered many excuses for not joining him, but she had yielded at last to his ardent entreaties. To be sure, she brought in her train, with a vague staff appointment, young Hippolyte Charles, whom she found less heroic, but far more amusing, than her legitimate Puss-in-Boots.

Campoformio was to be followed by a congress at Rastatt for the general resettlement of Europe. Napoleon was appointed minister plenipotentiary; but it soon became evident to him that there was no genuine desire for peace on either side; and after a few days (November-December 1797) he returned to Paris. The Congress was to drag on uneasily for over a year and then break up when hostilities were resumed.

In Paris, Napoleon received a hero's welcome. Everything at home was confusion and corruption. Directory and Assemblies were plotting feebly and indecisively again each other. Coups d'état had become a routine political method. On the 18th Fructidor (September 4,

1797), the Directors had borrowed from Napoleon a sword, General Augereau, to cut their eternal Gordian knot once more. Napoleon's exactions in Italy had at any rate been profitable to France; in the miasmatic atmosphere of the political world his victories came with healing in their wings. Wherever he appeared, ministers and directors faded into insignificance. And—supreme coquetry of the victorious soldier—he affected to prize above all other rewards his election to the learned Institute of France as a mathematician.

But he did not see his way to power yet. As a general, in spite of his miraculous achievements, he was still only first among his peers. Hoche, the greatest of all, was dead; but Moreau, Masséna, Desaix, Kléber, or Joubert, guided by expert politicians, could have barred his way. He was bored and restless. He inspected the Army of the West, intended to strike at England; but he saw that the chances of a direct attack were slim. So he yielded to his dream and to his devouring gambling instinct: he would try his luck in the "gorgeous East," fountainhead of legends, religions, and empires.

He had already given the subject serious thought in Italy. He had wrested from Venice the Ionian Islands— Corfu, Cephalonia, and Zante—as stepping-stones to the land of wonders. He had sent the government a memorandum about Malta. The thought was in the air: on July 3, 1797, just before he became Minister of Foreign Affairs, Talleyrand had read at a meeting of the Institute a paper on the necessity for new colonies, and he had singled out Egypt as a favorable field. So the Egyptian campaign was decided, and the expedition set forth from Toulon on May 19, 1798.

The whole enterprise was so preposterous that it remains an enigma. The Directory and Napoleon must have known that they could not wrench permanent control of the sea from England. France had good sailors and ample materials for building a fleet; but the officers' corps had been practically destroyed by the Revolution. This was true also of the land forces; but there new methods had given France the edge, and there was nothing of the kind in naval matters. Privateering and occasional raids were still possible, not large-scale operations. Even if the French did reach Egypt, they would still be separated from India, their strategic goal, by three thousand miles of desert or sea. They could not throttle British trade: the main route was by way of the Cape. The blindest could see that the peace of Campoformio was precarious. How a government could send its best general and its best army overseas on such a wild adventure passes imagination. The desire to get rid of an embarrassing and all too popular hero would hardly justify such a suicidal move. In addition, the ever-indigent Directory could not afford such a costly enterprise: the treasury of Berne and the churches of Rome had to be rifled to meet the initial outlay.

If the consent of the Directory remains incomprehensible, Napoleon's decision is intelligible enough in terms not of strategy but of psychology. There was in his nature a strange dualism that explains both his repeated failures and his undying prestige. He was a blend of severe realistic common sense served by unequaled efficiency, and an untamable imagination. He stood, like his whole epoch, in the mingling lights of classical reason and romantic wonder. He loved mathematics and he reveled in Ossian. All great men must be guided by a dream. But in the case of Napoleon, there was a hiatus between his gigantic unsubstantial visions and the sharply practical means of execution. The Egyptian

campaign was swiftly and admirably organized. It included a notable team of scientists, scholars, and engineers. When it left Toulon—four hundred vessels, from
the stately *Orient* down, carrying fifty-four thousand
men— it offered a most imposing spectacle; and lo, from
the very first, it was a mirage.

Repeatedly Napoleon spoke of his "star," his miraculous luck. Nelson, the Napoleon of the sea, might have
defeated the French armada the moment it started out,
but a storm had compelled him to seek harbor. Once the
French caught sight of him, but he failed to see them,
and they slipped by. He was at Alexandria a few days
ahead of them, but sailed away again on a wild-goose
chase. When the inevitable finally happened and the
French fleet was destroyed in the bay of Aboukir (Battle
of the Nile, August 1, 1798), the French, who had
landed a month before, were already firmly established in
Egypt. On their way, they had captured impregnable
Malta from its knights without a fight: "thankful to find
someone there to hand them the keys."

Egypt, nominally part of the Ottoman Empire, was
governed, or rather exploited, by a loose military oli-
garchy, the Mameluke beys. France would claim to act
in the name of the Sultan, and to suppress the unruly
prætorians who had usurped his power. Talleyrand was
to go to Constantinople to secure the agreement of the
Porte; but he found it more sensible to remain at home.
The flimsy pretext, however, was duly invoked, and
when the troops landed, the Turkish flag was flown by
the side of the French. Turkey, unconvinced, declared
war on France, and struck an alliance with Russia and
England.

Alexandria fell, and then Cairo. The Mamelukes, a
medieval cavalry, were defeated; and "from the heights

of the Pyramids, forty centuries [rather *blasés* with the pageantry of invasion] contemplated the French Army." With his customary swiftness and energy, Napoleon organized a protectorate. It was intelligent, but it did not work. The population did not take very seriously his profession of Islamic piety. They soon found out that the old taxes, under new names and more stringently collected, were fully as crushing as before. After a few weeks of hopeful waiting, Cairo rebelled. The insurgents were mowed down with Napoleonic efficiency.

After the Battle of the Nile, Napoleon was trapped in his new conquest. He was sovereign indeed: if he was cut off from reinforcements and supplies, he was free from interference. He was Sultan of Egypt more literally than he had been King of Italy at Mombello. He was disenchanted: Egypt was his own, but a poor thing. Instead of fabled wealth, reality offered abject poverty.

Among the news that capriciously filtered in from France, the most indisputable related to Josephine's flightiness: Hippolyte Charles, among others, was in the ascendant again. Napoleon consoled himself with Mme Fourès, who had stowed herself away with the army under a man's uniform. For the sake of morality, the husband was shipped back to France. He was captured by the English, who, duly informed of the situation, returned him to Napoleon: there is a dry quality about British humor. Pauline Fourès ("Bellilote") was sprightly, and Napoleon would have made her his permanent sultana if she had given him a child. She failed, and disappeared from history. Her second husband rose to high positions under the Empire.

Napoleon decided to occupy Syria. The reasons are not clear; the results are unequivocal. He took El Arish,

Gaza, Jaffa; there he had twelve hundred prisoners of war shot because they were an encumbrance: not cruel by nature, he was free from squeamishness. He reached Acre; but Sir Sidney Smith had already landed forces there, including Napoleon's schoolmate Phélippeaux. The French had to give up the siege and trudge their painful way back to Egypt. A last ghastly touch was added to that nightmarish retreat: they were stricken with the plague. On July 14, 1799 Napoleon was back in Cairo. On July 25 he thrust back a Turkish army that had landed at Aboukir. He was Napoleon still, But what now?

So far as he was concerned, the game was up. To remain as the ever-threatened sultan of a poverty-stricken and beleaguered Egypt did not tempt him in the least. Kléber, whom he planned to leave in command, was not informed of his intentions. On August 22 Napoleon sneaked aboard the frigate *Muiron;* he set sail the next day.

His star was still with him: his nimble little ships— two frigates and a few smaller vessels—eluded the British cruisers. He stopped for a few days in Corsica, landed in the bay of Fréjus.

His sole justification for returning was the desperate plight of France, of which he had been apprised by the British themselves. Russia, which for seven years had been inactive in the west, had at last joined the coalition. It now included Great Britain, Austria, Naples, Portugal, and the Ottoman Empire, the most formidable array France ever had to face. By an ironical twist of fate, France had been saved just before Napoleon landed: through the victories of Brune at Bergen (September 19) and of Masséna at Zürich (September 26). This failed to affect public opinion: Napoleon was hailed with delirious joy, and his progress from Fréjus to Paris was a triumph. Others might win battles: it was believed that he alone could achieve peace. Above all, France wanted a strong man to sweep away Thermidorian misrule; and the Thermidorians wanted a strong man to consolidate their profits. It happened that the same man could serve both turns.

CHAPTER THREE

THE MAN OF THE HOUR
BONAPARTE FIRST CONSUL
1799–1802

NAPOLEON's seizure of absolute power on the 18th and 19th Brumaire (November 9–10, 1799) was not a mere *coup de force*, a simple, brutal act, but an imbroglio worthy of Figaro himself. As in Beaumarchais's comedies, the plot grew so tangled at one point that the protagonists must have wondered: *"Qui trompe-t-on ici?"* which side is being duped? At the crucial moment Napoleon broke down, and his triumph was a fluke. But there was more than mere luck in his sweeping victory. Blunder as he might, no other contender had so many trumps in his hands or up his sleeve. For fully two years he was literally the man of the hour. But after he had seized control, he managed to keep it for fifteen.

After a whole decade of revolution and seven years of war, conditions in France offered a sharp contrast. With a fertile soil and a long tradition of hard work the country had survived all convulsions. Much dead wood had been removed; many fresh energies released. Lafayette, returning from exile, was struck with the prosperity of the land. But the new society had not yet found its balance. The subconscious unity that comes from immemorial habit had been shaken even before 1789; the tense unity that is the result of a great common purpose had been shattered when Robespierre was overthrown. The people were not exactly dissatisfied with existing conditions; they wanted neither a return to the ancient regime nor a new social order; what they desired was a sense of permanency. The situation, political, economic, and military, was confused rather than desperate. France yearned for tranquillity at home and peace abroad. As the constituted authorities could achieve neither, the people saw no relief but in "the *coup d'état* to end all *coups d'état*."

Thermidor had been the triumph of plutocracy. Siéyès's dictum had come true: the Third Estate—that is, the moneyed bourgeoisie—was everything, the aristocracy very little, the common people nothing. The Revolution was ended, the rule of the middle class established. But thanks to five years of mismanagement, the new regime was still open to challenge. Socialism, which is implicit in Rousseauism,[1] had made its first appearance in modern politics with the conspiracy of Babeuf—Caius Gracchus Babeuf, for this was the age of pseudo-classicism. Radical measures had been proposed: a return to price-fixing, a levy on capital. The financiers were definitely alarmed; among them Ouvrard (1770–1846), who was to remain for many decades a power behind the scenes. For constitutional forms the moneyed interests cared very little; they were concerned with the essence: the divine right of property.

The instability of the regime was felt most keenly by those at the top. They knew that their fall was imminent; and eager to safeguard their own gains, the shrewdest among them were plotting against their own government. The Directors, in the last phase, were Barras, Siéyès, Roger-Ducos, Gohier, and General Moulins. The last two were honest republicans, and easy to hoodwink.

---

[1] "The earth belongs to none, its fruit to all" (*Discourse on the Origin of Inequality*). In Proudhon's blunter terms: "Property is theft."

Roger-Ducos was the partner, or shadow, of Siéyès. The key men were Siéyès and Barras.

Both had their origins in the old privileged orders: Barras was a viscount, Siéyès a priest. Both had abjured their former allegiances and were committed to the only realistic cause: money. There were great differences between them. Barras was first of all a voluptuary, Siéyès a theorist. Barras, in power for five years, had had his fill; Siéyès felt that his hour had come at last. In the early stages of the Revolution his famous pamphlet *What Is the Third Estate?* had won him renown for political profundity; a few oracular speeches and unplumbed depths of silence had confirmed it. During the Terror, he had ducked under. Questioned later, he answered: "*J'ai vécu,*" I saved my skin. Now he had emerged again; he had been successful in a mission to Prussia, and had been made a Director. It was time for him to give France the perfect constitution he had evolved in his years of silent meditation. For his great purpose, he needed an instrument, and one of higher quality than a rough soldier like Augereau. He had thought of Joubert, but Joubert was killed at Novi on August 15, 1799; and of Moreau, but that great and cautious strategist, hampered by a combination of loyalty and timidity, did not respond to his advances. Then Napoleon landed, and Siéyès understood that no one would have a chance against him. So, not without misgivings, he decided to employ Napoleon.

Napoleon had hopes of his own: he had been king in Italy, sultan in Egypt, and was ready, not to share power with others, but to grasp it for himself alone. As he had a vast, loose following, but no organized party; he needed a friend within the gates. His natural ally would have been Barras, as in Vendémiaire; but Barras was too skeptical and too weary for a bold adventure. Napoleon's best chance, perhaps his only chance, was to co-operate with Siéyès. Thus the theorist and the man of action, profoundly disliking and distrusting each other, struck a secret alliance. Their mutual hostility was outwardly preserved as a blind. In public, they met only to glare at each other; in the wings, they perfected their plans for a peaceful political comedy.

We find engaged in this conspiracy two fascinating characters without scruples, fear, or mercy, who were to work with Napoleon so closely and against him so effectively that they are inseparable from his destiny. These were Talleyrand and Fouché. It might be said that from 1800 to 1815 France was ruled by a triumvirate in which the splendid central personage was not invariably the most powerful. It was Talleyrand who, as an honest broker, brought Napoleon and Siéyès together. It was he also who secured the retirement of Barras. Rumor had it that he came to Barras with a heavy bribe, provided by Ouvrard; Barras was so eager to quit that he did not even sell out; Talleyrand, surprised and delighted, pocketed the money. Fouché, as Minister of Police, had a hundred eyes and closed them obstinately to the obvious Bonaparte-Siéyès conspiracy. In compensation, he invented a horrific Jacobin plot, which was to serve as a pretext for emergency measures. After the *coup d'état* had been effected, he helped manipulate public opinion, and he saw to it that order was not disturbed in Paris. It is odd to see the Man on Horseback force his way to power aided and escorted by three rather dubious ecclesiastics: Talleyrand had been Bishop of Autun, Siéyès an abbé, Fouché a tonsured and cassocked Oratorian brother.

The preparations proceeded with admirable effi-

ciency. Young Lucien Bonaparte, who loved political
strife as his brother loved the battlefield, was elected
President of the Lower House, or Council of the Five
Hundred, where republicanism, was still very strong.
With a show of bluff cordiality, Napoleon won over
General Lefebvre, commander of the Paris division.[2]
Lefebvre cried enthusiastically: "Let's throw those prat-
tlers into the river!" With Moreau, Napoleon used
deference and professions of republican orthodoxy. Moreau was so far duped that he agreed to keep watch on
Gohier and Moulins, the two Directors who were not in
the plot. According to plan, the Councils resolved that,
in view of the Jacobin menace, they would remove to
Saint-Cloud; and they entrusted General Bonaparte
with all necessary measures for the defense of the Republic. This was the 18th Brumaire, November 9, 1799.

On the next day the Councils met at Saint-Cloud, a
royal palace a few miles west of Paris, destroyed by fire
in 1870. No hitch so far; but it is a risk to let a night
intervene between the two acts of a *coup d'état*. The
Upper House, quaintly called the Council of Ancients,
was well disposed; but even there Napoleon's forcible
and incoherent ranting made a bad impression. When
he moved to the Council of Five Hundred, which was
meeting in the Orangery, he was hailed with violent
denunciations: "Down with the dictator! Death to the
tyrant! Outlaw him!" It was with these cries that Robespierre had been silenced and overthrown on the 9th
Thermidor. Napoleon had a cool mind and no lack of
physical courage; yet in that unfamiliar storm he lost his

[2] Lefebvre was an old trooper who had married a laundress.
In 1808 they were to blossom out as Duke and Duchess of
Danzig. The Duchess, vivid, fearless, with a gift of tangy pic-
turesque speech, remains a favorite character in French folklore as *Madame Sans-Gêne*.

nerve, stammered, and fumbled. The whole plot seemed in danger of collapsing. It was the civilians, young and old, Lucien and Siéyès, who retrieved the day. "They outlaw you?" said Siéyès. "Outlaw them!" Lucien, in his capacity as President, declared that the Assembly was terrorized by assassins (Arena was seen brandishing a penknife), and officially requested the troops, massed in readiness, to restore order. Murat came in first and gave the sharp command: "Throw them out of the windows!" Leclerc followed and mopped up. Leclerc was the husband of Pauline; Murat was soon to be rewarded with the hand of Caroline; with Lucien in the key position, the 19th Brumaire was a cozy brotherly affair. Soon the long red robes of the Five Hundred were seen flitting through the park.

The Directory had vanished, lamentable and un-lamented. The Ancients registered the fact. A few repre-sentatives of the Five Hundred—some fifty—were rounded up and gave their formal approval. Bonaparte, Siéyès, and Roger-Ducos were appointed provisional Consuls. The clumsy farce was over.

This outcome was not according to the plans of either Siéyès or Napoleon. Both were men of order, and they had expected to overthrow the government in a dignified constitutional manner. The irruption of Murat's grenadiers upset the precarious balance between the civilian element and the military. The Five Hundred had yielded to the force of bayonets: the fact was fraught with consequences. In a triumvirate of equals Siéyès, supported by Roger-Ducos, would have been supreme. But Napoleon, "the God of Fortune and of War," made himself First Consul and grabbed the sub-stance of power. Siéyès was shrewd enough to acknowl-edge defeat. He and Roger-Ducos gave up their consul-

ships, and were replaced by Cambacérès and Lebrun,
both decorative and discreet men. Siéyès was rewarded
with a seat in the new Senate and with a handsome estate
at Crosne; he was allowed to walk away with whatever
cash the Directory had on hand. He resumed his
thought-laden silence; but no one was impressed any
more. He died in 1836, a fossil long forgotten, eighty-
eight years of age.

But what of his cherished constitution? It is usually
taken for granted that it disappeared without a trace. It
was an intricate mechanism of checks and balances, and
its central pivot was the Grand Elector, a functionary
with a lavish civil list and no actual power. Napoleon
shrugged that conception away: "Just a hog being fat-
tened!" (Later he revived the title, with his brother
Joseph as the hog.) For that bloated shadow, he substituted a reality, himself. In the whole ninety-five articles
only two words mattered: Napoleon Bonaparte. Yet his
rule was not a pure military despotism; and although he
had the constitution ratified by a plebiscite, his ideal was
not Cæsarism either; for Cæsarism is democratic—or
demagogic—and Napoleon despised Demos. The Consulate and the Empire remained true to the Siéyès spirit:
they were governments by and for the Third Estate, the
bourgeoisie. Will-nilly, Napoleon, who spurned the
Thermidorians, was destined to remain the Sword of
Thermidor.

Siéyès and his class provided not only a spirit, but a
definite method, and above all a personnel. Siéyès had
always wanted a government of "notables" or prominent
citizens; and the surest sign of notability is wealth. According to his formula, authority must come from above,
confidence from below. So let the taxpayers choose one

tenth of their numbers, thus forming a communal list of notabilities. The next step of the pyramid, one tenth of the first, will constitute the departmental list; the last step, one tenth again, the national list. These notables had no power; they were not even consulted; but it was from them that the government picked all its function-aries at the various levels. The system was altered in 1802, with the creation of so-called "electoral colleges." But the spirit remained the same. Under Napoleon, there were no elections of genuine representatives until the Hundred Days. Louis XVI had been far more lib-eral in 1788.

Out of the four assemblies then created, the Council of State—an advisory legal body, a panel of experts, and a supreme administrative tribunal—was appointed by the ruler of the nation. The Tribunate, one hundred tongues who could discuss the proposed laws but not pass upon them, and the Legislative Body, three hun-dred mutes who could vote but not discuss, were at first selected by the Senate, the only institution that had even a semblance of authority. And the Senate was the pro-longed shadow of Siéyès and his group. He, with Roger-Ducos, Cambacérès, and Lebrun, picked out the first thirty-one Senators; these selected twenty-nine more; after that the Senate was to be self-recruiting, adding two members every year until the figure of eighty was reached.

The assemblies counted for little; the officials for much. They were recruited from the notables according to the criteria set by Siéyès. Napoleon, at thirty, away from France for the greater part of the preceding three years, would have been unable to improvise a civilian administration: he had to accept it from the hands of

experienced men. Gaudin, for instance, who kept the
finances of the Consulate and the Empire on a fairly
even keel, was a protégé of Siéyès.

On the whole, Siéyès and his friends did their work
well. If the grand phantasmagoria of the Empire was also
a solid, down-to-earth, efficient regime, it was chiefly
because of their appointment of moderate and competent
officials. These men ruled more wisely than the generals
would have if they had been entrusted with power; or
the émigrés if they had resumed their ancient privilege
of squandering the resources of the state; or the politicians
if, directly or indirectly, they had seized control of administrative functions. For a century and a half, France,
under a dozen regimes, has remained a bureaucracy with
strong traditions and a firm hierarchy. And this solid
armature, so necessary in a nation of incurable individual-
ists, assumed its present form on the morrow of Brumaire.

There have been in French history a few miraculous
dawns: in 1515, the accession of Francis I, the gay
young knight in whom medieval romance blended with
the early glow of the Renaissance; in 1661, the assumption of personal power by another young monarch, handsome and eager, Louis XIV. The first two years of the
Consulate have the same quality of confident, illimitable
hope. Each of these movements might be described as a
New Deal: not an upheaval, but a fulfillment of national
destiny.

Even the features of the First Consul seemed to respond to the auspicious climate. He was no longer the
tense, lean Puss-in-Boots of 1795, pathetic, ludicrous,
and disquieting. His face had filled, his complexion had
cleared, the daimonic fire had tempered to a glow of

quiet authority. For a fleeting hour, at the very summit, he remained human. And Josephine was smiling by his side. He had returned from Egypt determined to discard her. She, aware of the menace, had gone out to meet him, guessed the wrong route, and missed him. So his family caught hold of him first, bitterly unanimous in their denunciations. She forced her way into his house and sobbed all night before an inexorable door. Her children, Eugene and Hortense, joined in her supplications. The door opened: Napoleon had relented. After the storm they were happy. The First Consul was well worth having; but apart from self-interest, Josephine may have been moved by gratitude. And although his passion had abated and his illusions had been dispelled, he still appreciated her charm. She was an admirable hostess. She made old Jacobins and returned émigrés feel equally at home. The cynicism of the Barras-Tallien era was frowned upon; decency was the order of the day; soon Talleyrand was compelled to make an honest woman of Mme Grant. But the rigidity of imperial etiquette had not yet set in. There were happy days even in the stately and morose Tuileries, and particularly at La Malmaison, where the hero could still play blindman's buff.

The first acts of Napoleon confirmed the hopes of the people. On December 26, 1799 he wrote open letters to George III and the German Emperor, urging peace. On February 7, 1800 he declared days of public mourning in honor of George Washington. On February 13 the Bank of France was established. On the 19th the First Consul moved to the Tuileries. On the 20th he spurned an offer from the Bourbon pretender, Louis XVIII, to play the part of a General Monk and, as Constable of France, to become the first subject in a restored monarchy. Every one of these steps endeared him to public opinion: they promised peace and stability, with no return to the ancient regime.

In the euphoria of this political honeymoon, measures of less favorable omen received little notice. The prefectoral system was created on February 17, 1800, saddling France with a rigorous centralization that is still a curse. On the same day sixty out of the seventy-three political newspapers were suppressed; more were to follow, and censorship was clamped on the drama as well. French thought was to be absolutely free, provided that the fundamental dogma was not challenged—namely, that France and Napoleon were one, and that dissent was treason. Mme de Staël, who thought for herself and loved to think aloud, was snubbed as a public nuisance until she was exiled as a public enemy.

England and Austria had not responded to Napoleon's advances. Peace had to be won on the battlefield. On May 6, 1800 Napoleon left for the second Italian campaign. His troops crossed the Alps by way of the Great St. Bernard Pass: guns had to be hauled in hollowed trunks by teams of a hundred men. On June 2 Napoleon entered Milan. On June 18, not quite according to his plans, he met the Austrians at Marengo.

This time again there was an odd twist to his fate. Napoleon's troops were not routed, but they had decidedly the worst of the encounter. Melas, the Austrian general, had already dispatched news of his victory and turned the pursuit over to a subordinate. Napoleon's lieutenant, Desaix, at the head of a detached corps, rallied to the main body. His forces were exhausted by the march, but their spirit was unbroken. This was best expressed by the famous words: "The battle is lost: we have time to win another." A charge led by Kellermann, son of the hero of Valmy, clinched the victory. Desaix died in the hour of triumph.

The battle was not decisive: Melas could have resumed fighting the next day, and Austria refused to make peace. Yet Marengo was hailed at the time as a most brilliant achievement. Perhaps this was due to a feeling of relief. It was a bold gamble for the head of a new government to risk his all on the battlefield. He nearly was defeated; he might have been killed instead of Desaix. Already shrewd speculators like Fouché and Talleyrand had considered the possible emergency. They and their kind were all the louder in their praises of the returning hero. Napoleon was enough of a realist to read their thought. He knew that, in order to retain their loyalty, he was doomed to eternal success.

It took the great victory of Moreau at Hohenlinden (December 3, 1800) to break Austria's stubborn pride. On February 9, 1801, the peace of Lunéville was signed. In October, preliminaries were agreed upon in London; on March 25–7, 1802 they became the peace of Amiens. Other treaties were negotiated with Russia, Turkey, Prussia, and Bavaria. After ten years of incessant warfare the guns were stilled at last; and in the solemn hush there rose a hymn of gratitude to the genius who had so gloriously closed the tragic era.

Peace abroad, appeasement at home: France should be made livable for all law-abiding Frenchmen. Josephine and Fouché were particularly active in helping returned émigrés recover their legal status. Fouché, the regicide and former terrorist, was singularly gentle with them, provided that they did not engage in conspiracies; and the dread Minister of Police became, unexpectedly, a social favorite in the stronghold of the old nobility, the

Faubourg Saint-Germain. But he opposed a general amnesty. He found special measures of clemency politically safer and financially more profitable. Talleyrand, who belonged to one of the most ancient and most illustrious families in France, filled his drawing-rooms with members of the aristocracy. Under his courtly and ironical smile, men of proud lineage, bourgeois officials, profiteers, and plebeian generals jostled one another, with a smirk that barely concealed a snarl.

This eclectic policy, this deliberate blending of the élites, was intended to hasten the convalescence of French society. Other measures were to serve as the framework of a new France. Napoleon called them "masses of granite." They are even more impressive than his military exploits. The prefectoral system, the Civil Code, the Concordat, the Legion of Honor, the University of France, all had their inception in those two miraculous years, though some of them were not completed until 1807 or 1808. They worked; and they are so convenient to the central power that eight or ten regimes in succession have carefully preserved most of them. Whether they are as beneficial as they are imposing remains a moot question.

In 1799 the civil laws of France were a jungle. Written law in the south, custom law in the north, canon law as a model of procedure, the innumerable edicts and ordinances of the kings, a huge mass of revolutionary legislation, were confusedly struggling for survival. Several proposals had been made to clear up that legal chaos, in particular by Cambacérès (1753–1824). A noted epicure, and a most expert political trimmer, he was also a great jurist, born and bred in the "nobility of the robe." On the morrow of the Brumaire *coup d'état,* commissions were appointed to compile a code. The actual drafting was entrusted to four great lawyers: Tronchet, Portalis, Bigot de Préameneu, Maleville. They completed their work in four months: the project appeared in print on January 1, 1801. Then it was discussed in general sessions of the Council of State.

In the lull that followed Marengo, Napoleon frequently presided with his usual energy. "Wake up!" he told his assembly of sedate administrators, nodding at two o'clock in the morning. "We are here to earn the pay the Republic is giving us." Had he been an ordinary layman, some of his interventions would have caused a lifting of learned eyebrows: but he was the First Consul and not to be pooh-poohed. His influence, as a rule, was on the conservative side. The amended draft went, section by section ("Title") from the Council of State to the Tribunate and the Legislative Body. Differences were smoothed out in conferences presided over by Cambacérès. The Civil Code become law on March 21, 1804.

Three years later it was renamed *Code Napoléon,* and to this day the orthodox believe that it sprang verbatim from the hero's omniscience. It survived, not only in France, but in parts of western Germany; and it was adopted by the state of Louisiana. It confirmed the essential doctrine of the Enlightenment and of the early Revolution: the abolition of privileges, the equality of all French *men* before the law (women were kept in subjection). It also embodied the Thermidorian principle: the sovereign rights of the propertied classes. This was most tersely expressed in Article 1781, which it took sixty years to expunge: "The master's word is taken: as to the rate of wages; the payment of the salary of the previous year; and the advances on the salary of the current year." No civil equality between masters and men.

Nothing is more Napoleonic than the Concordat with the Pope: a swift and dazzling victory, swiftly followed by an irremediable breach, and a full century of bickerings. To clear away inveterate misconceptions, a fact and a few words should be borne in mind. The fact: within six years the Pope was a prisoner, and the Emperor excommunicated. The words—Napoleon's own: "The Concordat was my worst mistake."

The spasmodic attempts of fanatical minorities to root out the Christian faith had ended in 1794. The cult of Reason had been a brief local show; that of the Supreme Being, a form of "natural religion," had died with Robespierre. On September 18, 1794 all connections had been severed between Church and State. Under the Directory, Catholic worship was free; the Constitutional Church survived, somewhat languidly; Protestantism had at last a full chance; and new religious bodies appeared, such as the Theophilanthropists.

This regime of liberty was anathema to Napoleon's love of unity and discipline. He might have borrowed the ancient motto: *"Une foi, une loi, un roi,"* one faith, one law, one king, a curious anticipation of Nazi totalitarianism. He had excellent reasons for seeking an alliance with the Church. There was a strong reaction against the rationalism of Voltaire and Diderot. The sentimental, æsthetic, romantic return to religion, heralded by Rousseau, was to find its gospel in Chateaubriand's *Génie du Christianisme*.[3] The strongest argument, in Napoleon's own mind, was that society could not exist without economic and social inequality: religion

[3] Published April 14, 1802; fragments had appeared earlier.

alone could make that harsh reality acceptable to the masses. *"Il faut une religion pour le peuple"* (the common folk must have a religion) was a corollary of the Thermidorian belief in wealth. But the Thermidorians found an obstacle on their path to Rome: they had bought Church property at bargain prices, and the Church had never accepted the loss.

Pius VII, shrewd as well as meek, was ready for an understanding. His States were at the mercy of the French armies. He hated that arch-heresy, the separation of Church and State. He desired to end the constitutional schism, which refused to die of its own accord, and was a menace as well as a scandal. The prestige of the Holy See would be greatly enhanced if victorious France officially returned to the fold. And he saw the possibility of assuming over the French clergy a direct authority in matters of discipline which his predecessors had never possessed.

The negotiations were long and tangled. They resulted in the Concordat of July 15, 1801. But the spirit of the Enlightenment was still strong among the bourgeois, who were the mainstay of the regime: it was only on April 8, 1802 that the Concordat could be promulgated as a law. Ten days later, on Easter Sunday, a solemn *Te Deum* at Notre-Dame returned thanks for the restoration of religious peace. The schism was ended; the Catholic Church was officially recognized; the clergy were to receive salaries from the State; the Pope and the temporal ruler of France would in unison appoint the bishops; the purchasers of Church property would be left undisturbed. Napoleon had wrested from the royalists their strongest asset: the support of Rome. Henceforth he could boast of "My Prefects, my Bishops, my police. . . ."

Hardly had the incense of the *Te Deum* dispersed when the irremediable conflict surged up again. Napoleon was incapable of sharing power. To his mind, "the things that are Cæsar's" embraced all earthly things, particularly Church property and Church discipline. It was an ancient conflict, as ancient as Constantine: if associated, the temporal and the spiritual must fight for supremacy. The quarrel had torn medieval Germany, and the Emperor had to go to Canossa. But a French king had humbled the Papacy in 1303, and under Louis XIV Bossuet had drawn up the charter of Gallicanism: while remaining in spiritual communion with Rome, the French Church claimed the right to administer herself freely, under the protection of the anointed king. In the Pope's mind, the Concordat was to mark the triumph of ultramontanism, the Pontiff sole and absolute ruler of the Church throughout the world. In Napoleon's, it meant the confirmation of Gallicanism: the supremacy of the national sovereign even in the ecclesiastical domain. On his own authority, and without consulting the Pope, Napoleon added to the Concordat "Organic Articles" that boldly reaffirmed Bossuet's position. The Concordat, a disingenuous compromise, hampered the life of the Church for a hundred years, without strengthening the State. When it was denounced at last, the result was twofold: a great spiritual awakening among the Catholics and the waning of anticlericalism. The Concordat appeared as a brilliant tactical victory, but victory never is a substitute for wisdom.

Destiny, the coincidence of luck and genius, had served Napoleon marvelously well: in 1802 he was without question "first in war, first in peace, first in the hearts of his countrymen." Mme Letizia is reputed to have said: *"Pourvu que cela dure!"* If only it would last! It did not last: by the end of 1802, the honeymoon of France and the young hero was already over. What is to follow is an entrancing drama, but no longer solid reality; a titanic quest for the unattainable, a gorgeous and feverish dream.

CHAPTER FOUR

THE PARTING OF THE WAYS

NAPOLEON BONAPARTE: CONSUL FOR LIFE
1802–1804

ON August 1, 1802 Napoleon, at his urgent request, was proclaimed Consul for Life. His next birthday, on the 15th, was celebrated with elaborate rejoicings: a new glory was thus imparted to the Feast of the Assumption. The amended constitution was ratified by the usual perfunctory and slipshod plebiscite: out of a population of thirty millions, three millions expressed approval. The vote was taken on open registers; in the villages, there were long lists of names written in the same hand.

The discrepancy between labels and realities, of which we could quote many instances, is particularly striking in the case of the Consulate. The decisive change came, not in 1799 and not in 1804, but in 1802. The consulship for ten years entrusted to Citizen Bonaparte was still, and might have remained, a republican function. When in 1802 Napoleon Bonaparte, for thus he now styled himself, became Consul for Life, with the right of choosing his successor, the Empire was made. Its formal proclamation two years later simply involved stiffer and gaudier trappings. In 1802 a few men, of very different statures, realized the gravity of the change. One of them was Lazare Carnot, the Organizer of Victory; another was the enigmatic Fouché. They understood the principle at stake: it was indeed the point of no return. But for most of the contemporaries, and for most historians as well, 1802 was only a minor step. Power remained in the same hands, under the same institutions. True enough: but the power had changed its nature, and the institutions had become shadows.

From 1789 to 1799 the destiny of France and that of Napoleon had been converging. In 1799 they met and merged. For over two years it seemed as though the nation and the young leader were miraculously one. In 1802 their paths diverged. This moment marks the beginning of the purely Napoleonic saga, dazzling, tragic, and unreal. France was committed to the formidable adventure: not of her own volition, but because of bit, bridle, and spur.

When opinion has no free outlet, conspiracies become the only hope. A desperate remedy, for at that time every conspiracy contained the threat of civil war, with foreign powers intervening. The desire for rebellion was not unanimous, even when disenchantment had followed the glorious dawn of the Consulate. In 1802–4 Napoleon was not loved—he never was loved until after his death, and then only *against* his victors. But he was not purely and simply feared. His could be called a government by consent, if consent be equated with resignation. He was accepted by most Frenchmen, not as a positive good, but as the least of several assorted evils. The heirs of the Revolution saw in him a shield against a return to the ancient regime—an ancient regime aggravated by the bitterness of revenge. For the profiteers of the Revolution, the Thermidorians, he was a shield against social democracy. For all Frenchmen, he was a shield against foreign invasion.

The chief danger to his rule came, not from the Jacobins, but from the royalists. Robespierre and his

closest associates had been destroyed in Thermidor
(1794). The last Montagnards, defeated in Prairial
(May 20, 1795), had stabbed themselves to death,
passing the dagger from hand to hand. On December 24,
1800, as the First Consul was going to the opera
through the narrow rue Saint-Nicaise, a bomb or "in-
fernal machine" was hurled at his carriage. There were
many victims; he went unscathed. He at once affected
to believe, because he wanted to believe, that the "an-
archists," heirs of the Terrorists, were responsible for the
outrage. It suited his book: he was attempting to rally
the moderate elements to his cause, or rather to his person, and the red bogy had been effective on the 18th
Brumaire. So one hundred and thirty "extremists" were
deported on general suspicion. Later it was discovered
that the culprits were royalists: two of them, mere instruments, were duly executed on April 26, 1801. But
Napoleon thought it best to keep the radicals out of
harm's way; and they were left to rot alive in Guiana.

Out of that complicated series of intrigues—"tene-
brous affairs," to use Balzac's words—three names
emerge, and three men may serve as symbols: Cadoudal,
Moreau, and the Duke of Enghien. Georges Cadoudal
was a fit hero for an Alexandre Dumas romance. From
the very first, in 1793, he had fought in the west against
the Revolution. Captured, he escaped and fought again.
When organized resistance collapsed, he resorted to
plotting: he had a hand in the rue Saint-Nicaise affair.
Napoleon respected a man as determined and as ruthless as himself: in 1800, he granted him an interview.
After all, the new regime and the royalists were fellow
travelers. But Georges was a man of faith and could not
be snared. He fled to England and returned secretly, in
1803, with British gold. The plot involved the assassina-

tion of the First Consul, an insurrection in Paris, and—
the ever-frustrated dream of the royalists—the presence
of a royal prince. Cadoudal was thwarted, but for several months he managed to elude the police. He was
arrested in March 1804. A plea from Josephine obtained
a reprieve for those of his accomplices who were of noble
birth; Cadoudal, a commoner, was executed on June 4,
1804. He could remark with a bitter smile: "We have
worked better than we knew: instead of a king, we are
giving France an emperor."

The Moreau affair is more ambiguous. Moreau was
the only military man whose fame could balance that of
Bonaparte: Hohenlinden had been a more brilliant victory than Marengo. If Cadoudal was openly a royalist,
Moreau was no less decidedly a republican. His wife,
a Creole like Josephine, spurred his political ambitions;
not very successfully, for Moreau was exceedingly cautious and was at his best in a masterly retreat. He disapproved, and not simply out of jealousy, of Napoleon's
rise to absolute power. He certainly was approached by
Cadoudal: how he responded remains doubtful. Napoleon had him arrested and was hoping for a death sentence; by commuting it, he would reduce his one great
rival to impotence. But Moreau was acquitted. At a second trial, under extreme pressure, the court brought out
an equivocal verdict, with a penalty of two years' im-
prisonment. Moreau in jail would have been a greater
threat than ever: Napoleon made him accept banishment
to America instead, with a profitable liquidation of his
estate in France.

Most mysterious of all is the case of the Duke of
Enghien. The facts are plain enough; their motivation
still eludes us. A spy revealed that a young prince, a scion
of the great Bourbon-Condé family, was living at Etten-

heim in Baden. Napoleon must have come to the conclusion that he was the one the royalists expected to
appear when the Cadoudal conspiracy matured. He
sent Caulaincourt, a general and diplomat of aristocratic
birth, to arrest him. It was not Caulaincourt, but his
subordinate Ordener who actually captured the victim.
But his half-blind and reluctant participation in that
high-handed affair darkened the career and preyed upon
the mind of Caulaincourt, an attractive figure in an epoch
not notable for chivalric virtues. Enghien was taken to
the castle of Vincennes, near Paris; judged by a drum-
head court-martial, he was shot at half past two the next
morning.

Napoleon himself denied that he had intended to
send a last-minute reprieve: he would not indulge in a
bit of melodrama like the one that spared Dostoevsky's
life. He accepted full responsibility for the deed: were
not the Bourbons keeping sixty would-be assassins in
Paris? In fact, the breach of international law and the
secret trial were mere peccadilloes in Napoleon's heavy
record. Although Enghien was quiescent at the time, he
was Napoleon's declared enemy, lived a few miles from
the frontier, and was supported by English subsidies. It
was not so much a crime as an error. Enghien simply
was the wrong man. That error, however, turned into
a blunder of the first magnitude. For the death of Enghien roused feelings of profound horror among those
who believed in the sacred virtue of princely blood. It
caused Chateaubriand to quit the service of Napoleon
and gradually to turn into his implacable enemy. Inci-
dentally, the famous phrase: "Worse than a crime: a
blunder," so perfectly in the style of Talleyrand or
Fouché probably belongs to the very able but dimly remembered Boulay de la Meurthe.

Napoleon was not incapable of capricious and ruthless action. He gambled on intuitions, which in many
cases led him to triumph. But, although not shirking his
responsibility in this tragic affair, he repeatedly and publicly accused Talleyrand of having advised the step.
Certain it is that Talleyrand was fully aware of the facts.
He was present, with Cambacérès and Lebrun, when
the decision was taken; and it was he who gave Caulaincourt his instructions. Whether he originated the whole
scheme is a different problem. On the basis of available
documents, that problem is insoluble. Talleyrand did
not deny Napoleon's point-blank accusations; but he
could not have done so without exposing his life. Later,
he deliberately destroyed every particle of evidence in
the government's archives which might prove embarrassing to him; and his *Memoirs* are a vast quagmire of eva-
sions and deceptions. Had Fouché been Napoleon's evil
counselor in this case, the situation would be clear.
Fouché, a regicide and a Terrorist, would obviously
want to create a gulf between the First Consul and the
royalists. But Fouché's influence was not predominant
at the time. He was glad to let others—Murat, Savary,
Hulin—do the dirty work while he rubbed his hands
and smiled his bland and furtive smile.

This obscure affair evokes a wider and still more
baffling mystery: the relations between Napoleon and
Talleyrand. For seventeen years they were compounded
of fascination and hatred, of mutual appreciation and mutual contempt. Talleyrand, as early as 1797, saw in
Bonaparte the coming man and attached himself to his
fortune. He was also among the first to discover that the
Master was not "civilized," as he put it, not ruled by
common sense and a realistic view of the possible. By
1807, he was positive that Napoleon was no longer

sane. While still a great dignitary of the Empire, he plainly told Alexander of Russia that in the interest of France and of Europe the madman should be destroyed. Napoleon, who prided himself on his knowledge of men, was not fully aware until 1814 of Talleyrand's implacable enmity.

He suspected him, and could not bring himself to discard him. Why? He was no doubt impressed by the great name of Talleyrand-Périgord. What a triumph for the penurious petty "nobleman" from wild Corsica to be served by a man whose ancestor, eight hundred years before, had asked Hugh Capet: "Who made thee king?" He who had been dazzled by the meretricious graces of Thermidorian society was awed by the pure ancient-regime quality of Talleyrand's *savoir-vivre*, his lavish luxury that never smacked of the parvenu, his cool ironic superiority veiled but enhanced through his exquisite courtesy. Before Talleyrand, Napoleon felt uncouth. He hated him for it, as Nero hated Petronius Arbiter. But he never dared to crush him, for fear that the victim's last smile would mean: "What else could you expect of such a vulgarian?" He knew that Talleyrand was corrupt to the core; that, in any diplomatic negotiation, his first broad hint was: "How much for me?"; that he was an expert at procuring women for himself and for others, including Napoleon. But Napoleon's Swiftian misanthropy was baffled and fascinated by a depravity so much richer than his own. Somehow Talleyrand's impeccable courtliness brought out the foul-mouthed trooper in Napoleon. The Emperor publicly called his former Minister of Foreign Affairs, Prince of Benevento, Vice-Grand Elector of the Empire: *"De la merde dans un bas de soie!"* (s—t in a silk stocking.) But as he strode furiously away, he must have read in advance on Talleyrand's imperturbable face the avenging words: "What a pity that such a great man should be so ill-bred!"

As there is a Napoleonic legend, so there is a Talley-rand legend, hardly less indestructible. To the fairy tale of Napoleon's invincibility (remember that he lost six campaigns out of twelve), corresponds the inveterate tradition of Talleyrand's infallible sagacity. It would be instructive to list the major blunders of that supreme statesman and diplomat. His grand manner still impresses modern historians; his unadulterated corruption seems to them the very perfection of "realism." At any rate, he was free from the "virtue" that made Robespierre an abomination, and from the "chivalry" that made Lafayette a laughing-stock.

Cadoudal's complex conspiracies came to light, even though the light has a dubious quality. A few others, without attracting public attention, were fairly well known: in particular the first attempt of General Malet in 1808. But more important than the definite episodes is the secret history—the underground discontent, the quiet preventive measures, the thwarted plots. If on the surface the course of the Empire was untroubled at home, it was because Fouché was in power again from 1804 to 1810, and because, even after his dismissal, the redoubtable machine he had created still functioned, even in the clumsy hands of a Savary. Fouché was more than a chief of police: he had the prefects report directly to him, and this made him in fact a Minister of the Interior. Siéyès had dreamed of a republic with two consuls, one for war, the other for peace. This conception, though unacknowledged, prevailed almost literally under the Empire: Napoleon fighting the foreign enemy,

Fouché repressing disorder at home. Wherever two or three were gathered together, one at least was Fouché's agent; at any rate, he deliberately fostered that legend.

By definition, the arch-policeman should be the arch-villain: sinister of countenance, exuding cruelty and corruption out of every pore. Fouché was not prepossessing, but he was colorless rather than hideous. He was too clever a man to flaunt his iniquities; and in social relations he was curiously affable. His private life was happy and pure, almost a miracle in those days. He had principles: they happened to coincide with his interests, but that made them all the firmer. He remained loyal to the spirit of the Revolution, and he supported the Empire—not necessarily the Emperor—as long as the new regime remained true to its origins. He amassed a modest fortune—some thirteen million francs at a time when the franc went much farther than our present dollar.[1] Considering his opportunities—control of the underworld and judicious favors payable both in gratitude and in cash—he showed more discretion than many an army contractor or marshal. Talleyrand made forty millions out of diplomacy: the reorganization of Germany in 1803 and the Congress of Vienna were gold mines to him. Napoleon himself could boast that his purely private hoard amounted to more than two hundred millions. Even graft in those epic days was on a monumental scale: loot to match the Arch of Triumph.

The peace of Amiens had been hailed with joy on both sides of the Channel; perhaps with even greater relief in London than in Paris. In spite of three different Hundred Years' wars—or because of them—the two countries are linked by an ambivalent and undeniable

[1] 3 fr. 35 was a fair day's wage for a skilled worker.

mutual fascination: anglomania and anglophobia are both perennial in France, and so are their British equivalents in England. As soon as the treaty was signed, tourists by the thousands rushed to the Continent. The peace was reasonable—not dictated, not vindictive, it respected the vital interests of both parties. Yet it lasted only fourteen months.

French public opinion at the time, and for generations thereafter, made "perfidious Albion" responsible for the breach; and the willful lack of logic in British policy may easily appear as deviousness. England, of course, put all the blame on Napoleon's insensate and brutal aggressiveness. After one hundred and fifty years, research has not yet built up an irrefutable case for either side. The key to that problem is the central point in our study: the personality of Napoleon. Here history and biography are one.

As for England's irreconcilable opposition, the facts refuse to bow before the theories of historians. In 1802 England freely acknowledged the new boundaries of France. She had not been cudgeled into sullen acquiescence. She did not resent Amiens as a shameful peace. She received the news with almost unanimous joy. France held Antwerp for twenty years; and that "pistol leveled at the heart of England" never was a serious menace. The peril came from Boulogne. For centuries before Amiens, for a century and a half after Amiens, England accepted French rule over the vital Channel ports.

I firmly believe that it was as unnecessary as it was disastrous for England to join in 1793 the coalition against France. She should have preserved a friendly neutrality: Priestley was right and Burke was wrong. The Revolution stood closer to English principles than

did the Continental autocracies; and England too had
beheaded a king. With England's friendly support, the
Republic might have remained liberal, perhaps under a
Danton. It was England's unreasoning enmity that prepared the way for Napoleon. But in 1803 Napoleon
was a fact. The peace of Amiens became a scrap of
paper, because it failed to curb the conqueror's enormous
greed. For he was not satisfied with the "natural frontiers": he must keep control of Italy, of western Germany. "And tomorrow the world": Spain, Holland,
and their far-flung empires; Constantinople, India; even
North America, for the transfer of Louisiana back from
Spain to France and the Haiti expedition were manifest
signs.

I am therefore inclined to minimize the responsibility
of England in the resumption of hostilities. More paradoxically, I am inclined also to reduce her share in the
final victory. Thanks to her impregnability and to her
wealth, England provided a constant center of opposition; but she could not deliver the knockout blow. If,
supreme on land, Napoleon finally collapsed, it was
not through Mahan's "influence of sea power," but because he was unable to treat the conquered and the neutrals as his friends and allies. Their pride and interests
counted for nothing; his will, and his will alone, was
law; and that will was boundless. That is to say, it was
mad. But for Napoleon's incurable *Napoleonism*, Trafalgar need not have proved decisive, and the Continental Blockade might have been successful.

There is in French folklore a character, Joseph Prud-
homme, who has the gift of exaggerating truisms into
absurdities. He said: "If Napoleon had remained a
lieutenant of artillery, he would not have fallen from his
throne." Marshal Foch rose to the same height: "Napo-

leon was truly great: what a pity that he was so ambitious!" What the comic character and the great warrior
failed to acknowledge is that, with Napoleon, *greatness*
and *ambition* were identical. Ambition with him was that
flaw—it may be an excess of virtue—which, according
to Aristotle, drives the tragic hero into the abyss of his
fate, but also marks him as a hero.

Napoleon's ambition is unique because of its absolute purity. It was not bound by paltry aims. He had
ambition, not ambitions. He rightly said: "I am not
ambitious: at any rate, my ambition is so intimately
bound up with my whole being that it cannot be distinguished from it." Other great leaders have identified
their personality and their cause—Mohammed, Rousseau, Hitler, Franklin Roosevelt, Charles de Gaulle.
It is the messianic complex: "I, and I alone, am the
Way." Still, in all these cases, there was a faith, there
was a cause. Napoleon's creed is summed up in one
commandment: "Thou shalt have no other god beside
Napoleon." In him, personality was more than egotism,
more even than egomania; it reached the level of solipsism: in his eyes, he alone existed. He might have taken
as his motto the words of his favorite poet, Corneille:
"*Moi seul, et c'est assez*" ("I, myself, alone, and that
suffices"). A city welcomed him with a streamer, blasphemous and profoundly true: "*Sum qui sum*" ("I am
that I am"). This was felt from the first by people who
knew him well, admired him freely, but refused to fall
down and worship him: his brother Lucien as early as
1792, Mme de Staël in 1797: "For him, there is only
one person, himself; all others are ciphers." This raises
him immensely above the prima donna who merely seeks
applause: he felt the same contempt for praise as for
blame.

This formidable hypertrophy of the ego—one of the essential traits of romanticism—was, not created, but made possible by historical circumstances. He was so situated that there was no cause available for him to serve except his own. Not patriotism: the famous phrase: "I wish to repose on the banks of the Seine, among those French people I have loved so well," is outrageous propaganda. He was a Corsican patriot, and he hated the French: his little country disappeared as a political entity, and France became his instrument, but he never became a Frenchman at heart. He was not even a European: he would gladly have become a sultan, a rajah, best of all a Grand Mogul. He was attached to no class: by thin courtesy a patrician, he had no traditions in common with the French aristocracy; he hated the rabble; he despised the bourgeoisie. Even the army was not his family. For only a few of his generals—Lannes, Duroc, Junot—did he feel any genuine friendship. He loved his soldiers as his tools, not as his comrades. In Spain, when, ready to mutiny, they cried. "He treats us like convicts! Damn him! Shoot him!" he whipped them into submission: "Oh! You want to go back to Paris and enjoy yourselves! I mean to keep you with the colors until you are eighty!" To Metternich he said: "A man like me does not care a damn for a million lives."

He had no faith in human nature. He had seen the frivolity of the aristocrats, the shameful cowardice of the King, the ferocity of the mob, the brutality of the soldiers, the corruption of the profiteers; even love had come to him through a woman whom he could not respect. He had no philosophy: in his youth he had been devoted to Rousseau, and later he appreciated the acid common sense of Voltaire; but he came to despise all thought as "ideology," to consider thought as his personal enemy;

and rightly so, for thought is freedom. He had no religion. He was ready to use any faith—Islam or Catholicism—for political purposes, or as "an opiate for the
people." He professed at times a very commonplace
theism; but, more definitely, the coarsest materialism:
life is nothing but physics and chemistry. Beyond his
reach—for he was great enough to look beyond—he
acknowledged, not a Power that makes for righteousness,
but only blind Fate. When you tear off the trappings of
soldier and ruler, you find, not a frightened and shriveled
creature, not even a perverted soul, but a mystery, im-
penetrable because it is a vacuum. Napoleon is nothing
but Napoleon.

Honors and wealth: these he grabbed as he went,
roughly, abundantly, contemptuously, for his aim was
beyond them. It was even beyond power: power was
but his instrument, "his violin," as he put it. His sole
aim was *glory:* again a word he may have learned from
Corneille; and thirst for glory is another phrase for ego-
worship. His monuments of bronze or stone are altars to
glory—his own; and his institutions, his Legion of
Honor, his Code, were turned into so many Arches of
Triumph.

The very nature of such a thirst for glory is to be un-
quenchable. The morrow of every victory is an anticlimax: there must ever be new prodigies, each more
dazzling than the last. He was the eternal Don Juan of
politics and war. He put it himself with daring and
forcible humor: "God the Father's job? Not for me; no
future to it; a blind alley." [2]

[2] Lessing had said something of the kind: the truth in the
making is greater than the truth absolute; and Balzac, most
Napoleonic of romancers, shows in *Melmoth Reconciled* the
infinite weariness of omnipotence attained.

Hence also his wild gambling with fate. It was not in his nature to cash his chips and retire. To rest satisfied, to calculate on safe and modest profits, would seem to him craven and commonplace: the true hero stakes his all—world empire or downfall. So nothing with him could ever be final: material success, power, victory, were but stepping-stones to higher things. A power that is not boundless, that can be checked by a constitution or a treaty, seemed to him no power at all. This can be translated into very concrete terms. He was glad to sign the peace of Amiens because, as he saw it, it would open, not close, his way to further conquest. When the British reminded him that it was a curb, he accused them of wanting his destruction. A reasonable understanding with Alexander in 1812, a compromise with the Allies in 1813, would have been in his eyes stale and unprofitable. His destiny was the breathless unceasing course. Whosoever wanted him to stop, even though it were to rest in triumph, was his declared enemy.

Paradoxically, he faced without flinching, he almost welcomed, the idea of defeat. Better an epic defeat than a tame victory. The greatest heroes of mankind, in thought or arms, in fact or fable, have met disastrous ends: Prometheus, Socrates, Cæsar, Jesus, Roland. There is no triumph so pure and so lasting as martyrdom. On the epic plane he had chosen, Napoleon was right. There is no comparison between the hold he still has on our imagination, and the sober tributes we pay to Frederick the Great, Washington, Wellington, Bismarck. Had he played his cards more shrewdly, he would have won an honored place in history, but he would not be a demigod. The saga needed the *Götterdämmerung*, Moscow aflame, the Berezina choked with icefloes and corpses, Leipzig and the Battle of the Nations, the farewell to the Old Guard at Fontainebleau, Waterloo, St. Helena.

If Napoleon were but the martinet, the unscrupulous politician, the efficiency manager, the short and pudgy central figure in a stiff pageant, and, from beginning to end, the Sword of Thermidor, an indelible stain of vulgarity would cling to his fame. He was all that, and the vulgarity is there: but his heroic and lucid madness redeems and transmutes that thick worldly success. It lifts him, as he knew and desired, among the great myths of mankind, Alexander, Cæsar, Charlemagne; and more definitely, among the great romantic myths, his contemporaries: Prometheus, Faust, Don Juan. This place he coveted, strove for, conquered; and it cannot be taken away from him.

Insane asylums are filled with world conquerors. The cream of the jest is that Napoleon too labored under the delusion that he was Napoleon—and lo! he *was* Napoleon. For his crazy dream was served by such marvelous luck and such matchless efficiency, it had captured such an array of enormous forces, that even today it wins at least our willing suspension of disbelief. It has the degree of realism which marks the supreme fairy tales. It is too vivid and too consistent not to be, at least in the æsthetic realm, almost as good as true. After one hundred and fifty years we still love to imagine that but for an unkind trick of fate it might have become sober truth.

The career of Napoleon after 1802 is no longer hemmed in by factual history: it is poetry, a triumph of the imagination. It tallies perfectly with Kant's definition of art: *Zweckmässigkeit ohne Zweck*, adequacy to purpose without purpose, or, more tersely, art for art's

sake. To count the cost would be sheer philistinism.
Who cares about the death of one million vague human
beings? The gesture was beautiful. The dead are dead:
the glory is alive. And Americans, the most practical of
men and also the most romantic, still flock reverently to
His tomb.

CHAPTER FIVE

NAPOLEON EMPEROR
THE ASCENDING STAR
1804–1807

ON May 18, 1804 the Senate proclaimed Napoleon Emperor of the French. Lazare Carnot had protested again, in a noble and hopeless speech. This time Fouché was not on the same side. On the contrary, it was he who had steered the Senate to meet the desire of the Master; and he was rewarded with his favorite post, the Ministry of Police. As an old Jacobin, Fouché was reassured by the sacrifice of the Duke of Enghien: it looked as though Napoleon, Emperor of the Republic, had committed himself to the cause of the Revolution.

For the third time, there was a plebiscite: Rousseauistic democracy—the Will of the People, the Social Contract—was given this Platonic satisfaction. The result was impressive: again three million and a half ayes, in a country of some thirty millions, with a pitiful scattering of noes. It was also unconvincing. Louis Madelin, a staunch Napoleonist, gloats over this quasi-unanimity. But he also notes that during that very spring, Parisian opinion had been very restive; that the bar and the bench as well as many elements in the army had openly resented Napoleon's treatment of Moreau; and that, on the proclamation of the Empire, there was a sharp drop in government bonds. Only *sixty-six* people in Paris dared to register dissent; which proves that the plebiscite was either a miracle or a farce.

The Empire was declared hereditary; but the line of descent was not clearly defined. This greatly chagrined Joseph, who, as the eldest of the clan, believed in his own divine right, and who was encouraged by a small clique to think that he might be a more liberal ruler than his brother. All the Bonapartes, and particularly the great man's sisters, scrambled wildly for honors and prerogatives, "as if," Napoleon sardonically remarked, "they were fighting over the heritage of our father the king." Only three kept, or were kept, aloof: Mme Letizia, still shrugging her shoulders, unconvinced that "there ever was such an empire"; Lucien and Jerome, who had contracted unsuitable marriages. Jerome came to heel and gave up his American wife, Elizabeth Patterson. Lucien stood firm and remained in opposition until the Hundred Days.

All the Bonapartes were one in their hatred of the Beauharnais. The danger of their being passed over was very real. Napoleon was sincerely fond of Eugene: not a commanding personality, but loyal, talented, and above all tractable. Napoleon thought of adopting as his heir the son of his brother Louis and of his stepdaughter Hortense. It was Louis himself who rejected the plan with horror. He affected to believe in the atrocious scandal that the boy was actually Napoleon's son, and that Josephine had connived in the infamous scheme. So Napoleon's heir remained a shadow. It was this ambiguous situation that led, after six years of bitter feuding, to the divorce and the second marriage of Napoleon.

Although the word *Republic* survived for a while, and republican principles were still professed, republican simplicity was at once discarded for the gorgeousness of a brand-new regime. Grand dignitaries were created, with titles of Byzantine splendor. Joseph became Grand

Elector; Cambacérès Arch Chancellor of the Empire;
Lebrun Arch Treasurer; Eugene, Arch Chancellor of
State; Louis, Grand Constable; Murat, the dashing
cavalier, Grand Admiral; Duroc, a personal favorite,
sincerely devoted to Napoleon, Grand Marshal of the
Palace; Caulaincourt, Grand Equerry or Master of the
Horse. Sixteen generals were promoted to marshals. Four
years later most of them, and a few civil servants, had
dukedoms conferred upon them.

All this, according to Napoleon, was part of the "system": to impress Europe, to dazzle France, to reward
the loyal, to bridle the hesitant, to spur the ambitious.
And also to temper or dilute the pretensions of the old
nobility, which, in a thin but steady stream, was rallying
to the new sovereign. He welcomed the aristocrats of the
ancient regime—"Only those people make good servants!"—but he did not want them to swamp his court.

Princes of the Blood, dignitaries, marshals, had been
made rich by the Master's bounty and were allowed to
grow still richer. But that also was part of the "system":
they were expected to spend their new wealth like the
grands seigneurs of the old school. Mme Letizia refused
to play the game: Josephine played it only too well.
Titles and trappings, the improvised court had all the
glitter of a Shriners' convention. But not the uproarious
good humor. In spite of Josephine's graciousness—the
whilom *cocotte* had turned into a perfect Empress, dignified and charming—life at the Tuileries was stiff and
frigid. "Fossils" and "upstarts" were never fully reconciled. Everyone sneered at every glittering title—except
his own: for Cambacérès took himself seriously as a
Serene Highness, addressed by His Majesty as "my
cousin," and even Fouché rather fancied himself as Duke
of Otranto. "There is only one person more absurd than

Monsieur Maret: it is the Duke of Bassano": Talleyrand alone could raise his eyebrows impartially at them
all—even at the imperial crown.

Louis XIV had been the perfect host: the new Master
was curt as a rule, and not seldom rude. He treated
women with glaring discourtesy. He inspected them
with the baleful glare of a top sergeant, and publicly
criticized their looks, their dresses, their morals. His state
dinners were notorious. He might keep the company
waiting for hours, and when he rushed in, he bolted his
food in twenty minutes. Cambacérès the epicure could
afford to smile: he had amply fortified himself before-
hand.

Napoleon showed the same imperial egotism in his
brief encounters. He had Mlle Duchesnois, a great ac-
tress, summoned to the palace; through his valet, he
ordered her to undress; he forgot her for loftier concerns;
and when reminded of her presence, he sent word for
her to dress again.

Yet he could charm when he chose; not merely with
the condescension of omnipotence, which delights only
the snobs, but with the display of his vivid personality.
He won many of his *grognards* with a few words of
bluff comradeship (but they kept grumbling all the
same). Pope Pius VII, through the bitter storms of their
later relations, could never forget the enchantment of
their first meeting. Czar Alexander, unsteady, but intelligent and sensitive, was completely won over. And
when the Emperor of the West met the High Priest of
Western Culture, Goethe, each summed up his impression of the other in the same word: "Here is a man."
In this, the great play-actor was not a histrion: for the
part he played so well was Napoleon.

· · ·

The word *Empire* stood for many confused traditions and aspirations: vast dominion, military rule, supremacy. In assuming the imperial title, Napoleon was swimming with a strong if turbid tide. Public opinion accepted the change, if not with exultation, at any rate without demur. Few were the men like Rouget de Lisle (author of the *Marseillaise*), Paul-Louis Courier, Beyle (Stendhal), and Beethoven, who admired the republican leader and felt that when he reached for a crown, he was degrading himself: "He aspires to descend."

Of all the vast shadows evoked by the magic word *Empire*, the most substantial was that of Charlemagne. It was Charlemagne rather than Cæsar or Augustus whom Napoleon had before his eyes as a pattern and exemplar. He spoke with deep conviction when he referred to Charlemagne as Emperor of the French, and "our illustrious predecessor." It was the Carolingian precedent that made him desire to be consecrated by the Pope. In the case of Charlemagne himself, and of the German emperors until Frederick III (1440), that ceremony had taken place in Rome. Napoleon, more imperious, summoned the Vicar of Christ to his own capital, as if the Pontiff were his chaplain. The request was unheard of; the Roman Curia, extremely conservative, and violently hostile to a regime of revolutionary origin, considered it as preposterous. Pius VII decided to comply. No doubt he felt the pressure of French power on the frontiers of his States, and he was dazzled by the fabulous prestige of the new master; but his acceptance was dictated by less worldly considerations. In his eyes, the Concordat was still a miracle, and he thought no reward too high for the "man of God" who had accomplished it.

From the personal point of view, the voyage amply fulfilled the Pontiff's expectations. He was received with veneration throughout that France which he had believed lost to Christianity; Paris, the capital of Voltairian free-thought, was at his feet; the Emperor himself treated him with a unique blend of profound respect and filial affection. The four months of his sojourn were a delight; he returned to Rome laden with costly gifts and still glowing with his triumph, which for him meant the triumph of the faith. On a different plane, however, he came back with empty hands. He had not secured the return of the Legations (Bologna, Ferrara, the Romagna) to the Papal States. Catholicism had not been proclaimed, as he had hoped, the sole official religion of France. The divorce law remained on the statute book. The Gallican virus had not been eliminated from the Organic Articles. In the contest of wits between the two Italians, the *condottiere* had been sharper than the Holy Father.

Another disappointment: the Pope was not allowed to *crown* the Emperor. Napoleon was convinced that he ruled by the direct grace of God and the will of the people. The Church could anoint, consecrate, confirm him: but not assert any authority over him. Power unlimited was the first among "the things which are Cæsar's." Ultimately he was to chafe under the distinction between the spiritual and the temporal: "They— the priests—want the nobler part of man, leaving me nought but the carcass." He was beginning to feel himself the Vicar of God: the Pope was but his Imperial Minister of Public Worship, to be dismissed if need be like a Fouché or a Talleyrand. For every totalitarianism is theocracy, and the Napoleonic state was totalitarianism in absolute purity.

The eve of the coronation was marked by a scene of high comedy. Cunningly, Josephine confessed to the Pope that their marriage had been a purely civil one. Pius VII insisted on a religious ceremony. It was performed in haste and secrecy by Uncle Cardinal Fesch, with Berthier, Duroc, and Talleyrand as the sole witnesses. Napoleon, at the time, was not determined upon divorce; but the thought had crossed his mind, and he did not relish having another obstacle placed in his path. As the solemn historian Albert Sorel puts it, "the vigil of the new Charlemagne was enlivened by a shotgun marriage."

On the morrow, December 2, 1804, the long ceremony at Notre-Dame went off with the precision of a military parade. The Bonaparte princesses raged at having to carry the train of the hated Josephine, but they created no scandal. Napoleon himself placed upon his head the crown, which was a replica of Charlemagne's; and it was he who crowned Josephine, as may be seen in David's admirable (and inaccurate) painting. The face of the Empress had been carefully made up by a noted painter, Isabey; and for her robes Chevalier, the court tailor, sent his bill amounting to 74,346 francs 74 centimes. The winter day was comparatively fair and mild. The procession, on its way back from Notre-Dame, took a wide swing by way of the Boulevards. The good people of Paris, who dearly love a pageant, had their fill.

The ceremony at Notre-Dame had a brilliant and fateful aftermath. So far Napoleon had not been fully committed to the extension of his rule beyond the "natural frontiers." The hold of France on the satellite republics—the Ligurian, Helvetic, Batavian—could have been gradually relaxed. But he had made himself Presi-

dent of the Italian (formerly Cisalpine) Republic; now
he decided to be king of Italy (March 13, 1805), and,
like his illustrious predecessor Charlemagne, to assume
in Milan the Iron Crown of the Lombards (May 26).
Piedmont had already been carved into French departments, and the Ligurian Republic craved the privilege of
being absorbed. Thus Napoleon no longer was simply
the sovereign of a vastly increased France: he was manifestly heading for the Empire of the West, of Europe,
of the world.

Any permanent reconciliation with Austria was now
out of the question. And every new annexation was
another challenge to England; for although the Continental Blockade did not become a rigid system until the
following year, already every port that passed under
French control was closed to British commerce. Early in
1805 Russia, Austria, Great Britain, and Naples were
preparing a new coalition. Even Spain, misruled by the
Queen's favorite, Godoy, Prince of the Peace, was beginning to waver in her abject and ruinous subservience
to France. Prussia was Yea-and-Nay: Queen Louise was
ardently in favor of the Russian alliance; the weak-kneed
King preferred to wait and rush to the aid of the victor,
piously hoping it would not be Napoleon. The minor German states, technically Napoleon's allies, would
gladly have followed Prussia's example.

The only open enemies, however, were England and
her satellite Portugal. Against England, Napoleon made
gigantic preparations for an invasion. He had immense
forces gathered at and near Boulogne. It was there that
they received the name of Grand Army; there also that
the first decorations of the Legion of Honor were dis-
tributed. Thousands of flat landing boats were ready to

transport the mighty host. All that Napoleon needed was control of the Channel for three days.

Napoleon had won victories against heavy odds: why should not his admiral, Latouche-Tréville or, after his death, Villeneuve, show the same daring and achieve the same success? What Napoleon refused to realize was that Carnot had handed him a magnificent instrument: there had been no Carnot for the navy. Armies can be improvised and prove effective, especially against cumbrous and tradition-ridden adversaries; but at sea there is no substitute for seamanship and gunnery. With all his unrivaled power of self-delusion, Napoleon must have known that his naval forces were no match, in sheer mass, equipment, command or training, for the fleets of Great Britain, unchallenged since the close of the American war. And Napoleon's ally, the Spanish fleet, was in even worse plight: a ruin barely kept afloat.

The plan evolved by Napoleon was so gigantic, so hazardous, so completely out of touch with reality, that historians have come to wonder whether it was not a titanic bluff. It was, more probably, a titanic gamble: there was a chance in a hundred that it might succeed. The French were to entice Nelson to the West Indies, as though their sole purpose was to reconquer Haiti and protect their other colonies. There they would elude him, and while he was playing blindman's buff in the Caribbean, they would sail full-speed for Europe, collect the various French and Spanish squadrons in Spanish ports, force the blockade of Brest, and sweep into the Channel, in full mastery for a fateful few days.

The whole fantastic scheme had collapsed even before Nelson destroyed the French and Spanish fleets at Trafalgar (October 21, 1805). The Grand Army had

already left Boulogne. Napoleon received the news between two brilliant victories, Ulm and Austerlitz, and
affected the most perfect equanimity. Trafalgar was not
a decision, but a confirmation: the decision lay in the
utter disparity of the two instruments. It deepened England's sense of her invincibility; yet William Pitt was
soon to die in despair, and his successor Fox was a
partisan of peace.

At Boulogne, Napoleon had been poised between
two possibilities: a descent upon England, which was
becoming more and more improbable, and a Continental war, which was growing into a very definite threat.
In August the problem was decided for him: he received
definite information that the Third Coalition was formed
(it was signed on August 9), and, on the 23rd, that
Villeneuve was bottled up in Cádiz. On paper, the
coalition was formidable; and it felt confident of success. But Naples was weak, Russia was far away, Austria was slow, Prussia was hesitating: a single swift blow
could dislocate the loose and cumbrous alliance. One
word of command: the Grand Army, two hundred thousand strong, turned away from the Channel, and in
"seven torrents" rushed headlong toward Vienna.

This marks the beginning of the strictly Napoleonic
wars, which were not to end until nine years later, in
Paris, with a brief epilogue in 1815. It is a miracle that
such an unequal conflict should have been protracted
for a whole decade. The miracle was not altogether due
to the genius of one man. Marshal Foch said: "After
commanding Allied armies, I am less impressed with
Napoleon's victories." Napoleon, sole ruler, sole commander, imposed upon his own forces, civil and military, an artificial but redoubtable unity. The Allies,
richer in all resources, were divided, self-diffident, and

mutually suspicious. After a decade of failure they were barely beginning to hope anew, when their smashing defeat at Austerlitz stunned them for years to come. It was the shadow of Austerlitz that weakened Napoleon's enemies at Jena, Friedland, and even Wagram.

Napoleon affected to believe that military prestige was indispensable to his rule. But if he thought that France *demanded* victories, he was only transferring his own inner flaw to the whole nation, and *at the time* he was wrong. In the resignation of the French to his rule there is no proof that the great pageant of martial glory played an essential part. France, in 1805 as in 1799, was yearning for peace. Most Frenchmen believed that the Allies were thè aggressors; but the renewal of the war was received with dismay. Bonds fell again, though Napoleon confidently promised a brief and victorious campaign.

No doubt his contemporaries "cheered the team": Paris hailed him on his return almost as deliriously as New York greeted General Douglas MacArthur. But even with the tumult and the shouting went shrugs of increasing weariness: "Another victory: but where is peace?" The bourgeois, most careful to preserve the élite that formed the armature of France, bought themselves off from military service. Among the common people, the number of draft-evaders constantly increased; the "grumbling" of the rank and file rose at times to an ominous growl. It was only under Louis-Philippe (1830–48), a regime dedicated to peace at any price and to Business as the sole business of France, that the French, in romantic reaction, went on a wild spree of restrospective glory. At that time it was safe to quaff the heavy wine—as of thirty years before. But when Thiers, in 1840, engaged in a spirited and faintly Napoleonic policy, he was rejected by King, Parliament, bourgeoisie, and people. The proper place of an epic is in the storied past.

The army that turned so smartly from Boulogne to the upper Danube was indeed the Grand Army: not in numbers merely, but in fighting quality. It was an army led by young veterans: it had been fighting for ten years, and most of its marshals were under forty. The spirit varied with the ranks. The marshals themselves were sated with glory and eager for enjoyment. They felt themselves Napoleon's peers in age, origins, and ability; and they hated the thought of risking for his sake all their fabulous gains. Among those who served him best were many who were to betray him: Bernadotte, Ney, Marmont, Augereau. The common soldiers grumbled and were beginning to doubt. Pure Napoleonism was found, not among the marshals and not among the *grognards*, but among the officers. Some belonged to the aristocracy, the old fighting caste, for whom an army career was part of *noblesse oblige*. Others on the contrary loved the army because it was more democratic, truer to the spirit of the Revolution, than the stiff bureaucracy at home. For many, military life was the only way of escaping the infinite dullness, like a pall of lead, that the Empire was spreading over French society. To be an officer under Napoleon held the promise of gay adventure. It afforded full scope for the "triple talent" that the folk song ascribed to Henri IV: *"de boire et de se battre, et d'être un vert galant"* ("to drink, and to fight, and to be a very devil with the ladies").

We are told, and we easily believe, that Napoleon cherished his army: a craftsman loves his tools; and there is little doubt that he was a wonder of efficiency. Yet, to our surprise, even Napoleon-worshippers like

Kircheisen and Madelin admit that the administrative departments of the army—the service of supplies, the paymaster, the sanitary formations—were woefully and even tragically inadequate.[1] The troops, and particularly the Guard, were given resplendent uniforms, which are still the delight of historical painters. But these were not renewed, and halfway through a campaign they were soiled and tattered. The pitiful pay was constantly in arrears. For food each unit had to prey on the local population; and when several corps in succession passed through the same countryside, the peasants were driven to despair and the soldiers were starving. There were admirable surgeons like Larrey; but even in successful campaigns, the field hospitals were shambles. Posterity has chosen to ignore the seamy and nightmarish sides of Napoleonic warfare. So did the survivors: out of one million veterans, a few score wrote their memoirs, a whole generation after the events, at a time when the fashion was to revel in glory. Yet even in Coignet's artless *Notebooks*, the most engaging of all those documents, the grim reality appears under the grand parade.

Masséna, "the Darling of Victory," was holding Italy. The "seven torrents"—the corps of Bernadotte, Marmont, Davout, Soult, Lannes, Ney, and Augereau —were reaching the Danube; Murat's cavalry was dashing ahead; Napoleon himself was in reserve, with the Imperial Guard, "supreme hope and supreme thought."

In a few days the famed Austrian commander, Mack, was penned up in Ulm and compelled to surrender (October 17). On November 14 Napoleon was at Schönbrunn, the imperial palace near Vienna. The

[1] The authority on the subject, unchallenged, is J. Morvan: *Le Soldat Impérial* (2 vols., Paris, 1904–7).

Austrian and Russian armies attempted to organize themselves for resistance in Moravia. There, on December 2,
the three Emperors joined in combat. The winter mists
lifted at the right moment: it was "the sun of Austerlitz."

Austerlitz has been called "the most perfect battle in
history": it certainly was Napoleon's masterpiece. He
guessed every move of the enemies; he concealed every
one of his own. When the seven-hour fighting was over,
the Allies had lost 37,000 men, the French barely
8,000. In the snow that followed the brief outburst of
sunshine, the Russian and Austria Emperors were in
headlong flight, their troops in abysmal confusion. No
wonder the conqueror was wildly acclaimed by his
troops; no wonder he addressed to them a ringing proclamation, a classic of military eloquence. The anniversary
of his coronation could not have been celebrated with a
more magnificent festival of glory.

Napoleon granted the Russians a generous armistice—
too generous, in the opinion of some generals. Upon
helpless Austria he imposed a Draconian peace. Talleyrand had always advised moderation: he had long believed that only with Austria as a contented partner
could a durable settlement in Europe be attained. Napoleon swept the suggestion aside. No concessions; a heavy
war indemnity; territories for his German allies, for Italy,
for France. His Empire now extended to the Illyrian
Provinces, on the Adriatic, stepping-stones toward that
eternal mirage, Constantinople.

In 1805 Russia, still at war, had retired into her own
territory "to lick her wounds and weep for her dead."
England was incapable of effecting a landing: on the
Continent, Napoleon's fiat was law. Austerlitz intoxi-
cated him, as it crushed the spirit of his enemies. It

focused sharply in his mind the "Austerlitz complex," that one good battle could solve every problem. It was an Austerlitz that he kept seeking on his march to Moscow; and as late as 1814, when he had won a partial success in Champagne, he already imagined himself chasing the enemies, helter-skelter, into the Siberian plains. Was he not the victor of Austerlitz, "the god of Fortune and of War"?

For a few months reality seemed to anticipate his wildest dreams. As in an old-fashioned Christmas pantomime, wonders piled upon wonders. He could calmly decree that the millennial Holy Roman Empire had ceased to exist, and that the House of Bourbon no longer reigned in Naples. He could distribute thrones to his clan: Murat, Grand Duke of Berg, Joseph, King of Naples, Louis, King of Holland, Jerome, King of Westphalia, Eliza, Princess of Piombino and Lucca, later Grand Duchess of Tuscany. He could create a Confederacy of the Rhine, with himself as Protector. He could confer royal titles upon the ancient dynasties of Germany, titles that they accepted with gratitude and preserved proudly until 1918. He could shift as he pleased the medieval shadows that had survived the Enlightenment; he gave no thought to the underlying reality, the interests and the will of the peoples.

The position of Prussia was still uncertain. Outwardly she had preserved neutrality, and the Prussian envoy went so far as to congratulate Napoleon on his victory. To bind Prussia to himself, Napoleon had promised her the Electorate of Hanover, but he felt under no obligation to such a shifty partner. It looked as though peace with Russia and England were within reach: in that case, Hanover would be restored to the King of England. Prussia, attempting to dupe everybody, felt duped in her turn, and bewildered. Fox, who wanted peace, died; the anti-Napoleonic coalition revived between England and Russia; Prussia, this time, was compelled to decide; and the torrents of the Grand Army swept over her.

In her own conceit, Prussia was still the finest military power in Europe. Her armies had withdrawn at Valmy (1792) for reasons of general policy: they had not considered themselves defeated. At every victory of the Revolutionary troops, the veterans of Old Fritz smiled: "Ah! But wait till we, the real soldiers, get into this fight!" The outcome was Jena and Auerstädt; the complete annihilation of the Prussian forces; fortresses surrendering to a squadron of hussars; the King and Queen of Prussia refugees under Russian protection. The French entered Berlin in triumph, Murat in the lead, with twenty thousand francs' worth of plumes; Napoleon, in dramatic contrast, with his riding coat of sober gray and with a penny cockade on his plain black hat.

Jena and Auerstädt offer a good illustration of Napoleon's skill as a self-advertiser. They were twin battles, fought on the same day, October 14. At Auerstädt, Davout, with the smaller French force, defeated the main Prussian army. At Jena, Napoleon had the easier task. Auerstädt was unquestionably the more meritorious victory. Napoleon was not grudging in his praises of Davout: he made him later Duke of Auerstädt. Yet he contrived, for his contemporaries and for posterity, to create the impression that Jena was one of the decisive battles in world history, Auerstädt a minor engagement.

Russia was still unsubdued. The Battle of Eylau in East Prussia (February 7–8, 1807), in biting weather, was bloody and indecisive; the French held their ground, but they were too badly mauled to pursue the retreating enemy. Augereau, made the scapegoat, was sent back to Paris. Napoleon was held in check twelve hundred miles from his capital. The momentum of Austerlitz and Jena, however, kept up the spirit of the French and overawed the Germans: Napoleon could safely go into winter quarters in Warsaw and in the castles of Osterode and Finkenstein; and he managed gradually to replenish his army. Before Eylau, his supply system had broken down altogether, and the sufferings of the troops were indescribable.

Only on June 14, 1807, at Friedland, was he able to inflict a severe defeat upon the Russians and the remnant of the Prussian forces. It was not an Austerlitz; still, it led the Russian generals to advise an armistice. Alexander, engaged in wars with Persia and with Turkey, was ready to come to terms. So, for once, was Napoleon: he had sent Duroc to offer peace. The two Emperors met at Tilsit on a raft moored in the Niemen. The Imperial Guards fraternized in homeric banquets; the two autocrats embraced and swore eternal friendship. Alexander affirmed: "I hate the British as bitterly as you do." Russia was to join the Continental Blockade, which Napoleon had decreed in Berlin (November 21, 1806). So a personal meeting of the Big Two had settled the affairs of the world, with no regard for ideologies and sentimentalities. Napoleon could return to Paris in August, more than ever the conquering hero. He celebrated his victory in the most appropriate manner by suppressing the only institution where speech was still tolerated, the Tribunat.

It was during the winter lull before Friedland that Napoleon, in Warsaw, became acquainted with a Polish lady, Countess Marie Walewska. "Talleyrand," he crudely said, "got her for me." The episode, however, was far more creditable than these brutal words would indicate. She was eighteen, her husband seventy; both ardent patriots, they hoped that the Man of Destiny would resurrect their country, obliterated twelve years before. Napoleon and Marie sincerely loved each other. But Napoleon was not the man to let his tender feelings interfere with political problems, and he continued to play fast and loose with Polish aspirations. The lovers met again in Vienna in 1809; their son, Alexander Colonna Walewski, was to have an honored career under the Second Empire.

Meanwhile Napoleon was writing delightful letters to the Empress: "I love no woman except my little Josephine, good, sulky, and capricious." When she expressed the desire to join him, he put his imperial foot down: the place was cold, uncomfortable, barbarous, totally unfit for a delicate lady. Napoleon was by nature blunt; but even without Talleyrand's coaching he could also practice diplomacy.

CHAPTER SIX

DARK OMENS
1808–1809

AUSTERLITZ, Jena, Friedland: three decisive victories, three settlements imposed from a position of strength; and peace still a will-o'-the-wisp. A single voice heard; between outbursts of well-drilled applause, a vast silence, as if haunted by the ghosts of suppressed murmurings. The incredible adventure still incredible; yet the only actual, the only conceivable, reality.

England was now the sole enemy. Her Continental allies defeated, she remained impregnable. The Channel was a fact that Napoleon's imagination could not conjure away. So the Man of Arms, baffled, had to turn to an unfamiliar weapon, economics. It would be effective against "a nation of shopkeepers." On May 16, 1806 Fox had declared a partial blockade of the northern European coast. On November 21, 1806, in Berlin, Napoleon decreed that, in massive retaliation, all Europe be closed to British commerce. At Milan, on December 17, 1807, the prohibition was made stricter, and neutrals were compelled to take sides.

If political and diplomatic issues are still cloudy after one hundred and fifty years, economic problems remain veiled in darkness absolute. Realities are confused, and only hypotheses can assume definiteness—in the realm of the might-have-been. The Berlin Decree possesses the true Napoleonic style. It is still very impressive, but, like the elaborate constitution of the Empire, or the Imperial University, it was a façade, not "a mass of granite." Historians still affirm that through the blockade Napoleon *nearly* brought England to her knees: she suffered a severe economic crisis in 1811, with signs of mounting discontent. But the financial situation of France was even worse, and the discontent more profound.

Closing the Continent to British goods was bound to be a severe blow to a manufacturing and trading nation. Severe, but not fatal: Napoleon seems to have overlooked the fact that the rest of the world still existed. On the sea his fiat was not law. England maintained free intercourse with the Levant, India, the Far East. For a number of reasons her trade with America was hampered: Jefferson declared an embargo on December 22, 1807. Canada as yet was of minor importance. But England had now access to the former colonies of Holland and of France, and to the vast Iberian world, ripe for expansion.

If the *mutual* blockade had been effective, it need not have strangled continental Europe either. At that time a European *autarky* or closed economy was not inconceivable. With proper communications and no artificial barriers, Europe could have fed herself. She had all the mineral resources for her immediate needs. Only two vital articles came from beyond the sea: cotton and sugar. But wool, hemp, flax and silk were available, and the beet-sugar industry was created, which survived the emergency. No satisfactory substitute for coffee was discovered: the use of chicory is a lamentable legacy of those far-off unhappy days. But coffee-drinking in Europe was less than two hundred years old: Mme de Sévigné had pronounced it a fad. No proud nation will ever surrender for lack of coffee.

The economic cold war could therefore have been prolonged for decades without bringing disaster to either side. It represented simply the protectionist ideal carried to an extreme. Now protection makes the weak more anemic, but does not kill them outright; and it seems to strengthen the strong. England's maritime predominance was built up, for two centuries, through the Navigation Acts; and our infant industries throve mightily on pro- hibitive tariffs. One thing is certain: economic warfare *per se* could not have secured a clear-cut political de- cision. England and the Continent might have snarled at each other over the fence for ages and been only a little the worse for it. If Napoleon did fail, it was because he mismanaged Continental affairs.

But the fact we are liable to forget is that the block- ade, while by no means a farce or a mirage, was very far from being a solid reality. The Master of Europe issued commands with the majesty of omnipotence, and his im- perial gesture was duly recorded. But he did not con- tinuously hold that fatiguing Jove-like pose. Smuggling assumed grandiose proportions, and Napoleon winked at it. Furthermore, both he and the British granted a fantastic number of licenses to trade with the enemy. The conditions of that authorized illegal trade were debated in "open secret" negotiations. While the licenses alle- viated the hardships of industrialists and consumers, they brought profits to the hungry imperial treasury and to a long series of officials and financiers. For a license to trade was an asset that itself became an object of trade. It was because of his well-known connections with England that the speculator Ouvrard could be Fouché's agent in surreptitious peace feelers. There was an International of Finance, in Amsterdam, Hamburg, Frankfurt, in close contact with London and Paris. Hope, Labouchère, Par- ish, Baring, were among its leaders. And especially the

Rothschilds, whose empire came into being in those days: an empire *ære perennius,* more durable than Napoleon's bronze. *Homo economicus* is wiser than *Homo politicus,* and especially than *Homo pugnax.*

The Continental Blockade involved Napoleon in a series of highhanded acts. We should not believe, however, that he had a monopoly of brutality: England's treatment of Copenhagen, for instance, in 1801 and in 1807, was also an unscrupulous abuse of force. Both the British lion and the French eagle were beasts of prey. The blockade served as a last-minute pretext for intervention in the Papal States. It was to spell the doom of the short-lived Kingdom of Holland under Napoleon's own brother Louis. Ultimately, it led the Empire to stretch out absurd tentacles: the Hansa Towns, Bremen, Hamburg, Lübeck, became French cities. Yet these moves, at the same time irresponsible and logical, were of secondary importance compared with the repeated redrawing of the European map to suit the Master's interests, his fancies, or his whims. Although they caused severe hardships to certain commercial interests, they were not so keenly felt as the constant ubiquitous drain of gold and men which was the essence of the Napoleonic system. We may go farther: blockade, tribute, and conscription, heavy as they were, were secondary grievances compared with the humiliation imposed by the Master upon his allies, even upon his own brothers, as well as upon his enemies. Every word of adulation from reluctant lips, every benefit contemptuously tossed by him, would swell the treasure of hate in the secret of the hearts. Realists knew long before Sir Norman Angell that war never pays: the sole cause of war is wounded pride. And it was Napoleon's fate to wound the pride of all in order to prove to himself that he was the Great

Ruler of the Great Nation. It was his mad wager with Destiny.

The conflict with the Pope became acute in 1808. It was the first, perhaps the decisive sign that the imperial system was unsound. The quarrel was caused only in a small degree by the Continental Blockade: Civitavecchia was but a minor port. It had started earlier, at the very moment when the Concordat was promulgated. In fact, as we have seen, it started with Constantine.

This age-long conflict was complicated by an absurdity of long standing: the Holy Father was also an Italian princeling. As such, he had to play Peninsular and European politics on the most cynical Machiavelian plane. A Pope advised His Most Christian Majesty the King of France to seek the support of the Grand Turk against His Most Catholic and Apostolic Majesty the Holy Roman Emperor. This was in early Renaissance days: three centuries later the confusion still prevailed. So there arose from Rome four voices, seldom in full accord: that of the Holy Father in his spiritual character; that of the bewildered sovereign of the puny Papal States; that of Pius VII the man, meek, long-suffering, with a lingering affection for Napoleon; and that of the Curia, hating the usurper and all his works. And Napoleon was not a single entity either. There were in him the "Man of God" who had restored religion; but also the heir of the Gallican kings, the disciple of the Enlightenment, the soldier of the Revolution, and most of all the insatiable egotist who considered dissent a personal affront.

Thus, as Napoleon entered Schönbrunn in November 1805, he received from the Pope an ultimatum demanding the evacuation of Ancona. Napoleon shrugged the request away: Austerlitz was a sufficient answer. Then, in 1806, Pius VII refused to recognize Joseph as King of Naples: according to tradition, only the Holy See could bestow that crown. "But I am the Emperor of Rome!" Napoleon asserted. "There is no Emperor of Rome," the Pope replied. "The Pontiff wields full sovereign power in the City." Napoleon was already thinking of "withdrawing from the Papacy the donation made by his illustrious predecessor Charlemagne."

On November 12, 1806 Napoleon, from Berlin, ordered the Pope to join his Italian Confederacy: thus his Kingdom of Italy would be linked with his brother's Kingdom of Naples. The Pope demurred. In the summer of 1807 he was intimidated into joining the Continental Blockade. But Napoleon wanted more: a full promise that the Pope would in all cases make common cause with the Emperor. This meant undisguised vassalage; nerved to resistance by the Curia, Pius VII refused (December 12, 1807). Thereupon, on January 12, 1808, Napoleon ordered General Miollis to march on Rome. Every protest was met by another turn of the screw. A first excommunication (May 27, 1808) was not made public. On May 12, 1809 came the outright annexation of the Papal States; on June 10, a formal excommunication; on July 6, the Pontiff was wrenched from the Holy City and imprisoned, at Grenoble, Savona, Fontainebleau. Even though the climax was deferred, the essential facts were known throughout Europe; and they were to have a decisive influence on the turn of affairs in Spain.

The Spanish entanglement was to prove an incurable wound: while the Emperor was still winning victories and annexing far-off lands, his strength and prestige were slowly bleeding in the Peninsula. This tragic adventure, into which Napoleon seemed urged by the demon of self-destruction, was preceded by a sort of rehearsal, the conquest of Portugal. That expedition appeared logical enough, as logic goes in such affairs. England was inexpugnable; but she had two dependencies on the mainland which an enemy could seize as hostages. One was the Electorate of Hanover, the personal possession of the English King. The second was Portugal. Ever since the Methuen Treaty (1703)—in form a mere commercial arrangement for preferential tariffs on wines and woolens —Portugal had been in fact a most docile satellite of England.

Before the expedition could start, complicated negotiations were necessary with Spain, whose territory had to be traversed. Portugal was neatly partitioned on paper. There would be, as a commission, a principality for Godoy, the Spanish minister. Another slice would go to the Infanta Maria Luisa in exchange for the Kingdom of Etruria, which Napoleon had seized. The rest might be the booty of the French commander, Junot. Junot was a harum-scarum swashbuckler with a spotted record; but, a devoted retainer ever since the siege of Toulon, he was one of Napoleon's personal favorites. He had courted two of the Bonaparte princesses—perhaps a doubtful claim to a crown; and he had married into a family, the Permons, whom Napoleon knew and respected.

Junot's advance was a victory of luck over inefficiency. The Grand Army, in central Europe, was claiming the best in troops, officers, equipment: Junot was given only untrained recruits. The winter march through the mountains broke their fragile morale; soon there were more stragglers than combatants. Barely five thousand soldiers, starving and in rags, reached Abrantes, the fortified town that guarded the Tagus valley and the road to Lisbon. A show of resistance could have swept back that tatter-demalion host. But the royal House of Braganza had already taken flight to Brazil; Junot entered the capital a few hours after they had left. He was made Duke of Abrantès; but he never became King Andoche I; he never won even his marshal's baton. But for a while he strutted right royally in his good city, a duodecimo Napoleon. Six years later Junot, demented, jumped out of a window.

Napoleon accused Talleyrand of having trapped him into the Spanish embroilment: as in the case of the Duke of Enghien, no conclusive evidence remains. Melodramatic history would like to imagine Napoleon, whose thought was lightning and whose deeds were thunderbolts, suddenly deciding to establish his rule in Spain; and the Spanish people, with the same instant determination, rising at once in desperate resistance. Once again, plain history offers a more complex and blurred picture. The Spanish affair had been under way ever since 1795.

The Spanish Bourbons had been among the most ardent crusaders against regicide France. But the young Republic, after early reverses, had rallied on all fronts; beyond the Pyrenees, the French invaded Catalonia and the Basque Provinces. By the Treaty of Basel (1795), Spain had to pay ransom for her losses with her half of Santo Domingo. The royal house affected to be well satisfied with the outcome, and the all-powerful minister Godoy was created "Prince of the Peace."

In 1796 Spain joined France in the fight against England: as in the War of the Spanish Succession, as in the War of American Independence, a familiar pattern, almost a tradition. But in this ill-fated alliance, Spain was constantly the loser. Napoleon demanded Louisiana back —and sold it to Jefferson for a song. The miserable squadrons of Spain were buffeted in every encounter, badly mauled at Cape St. Vincent in 1797, destroyed at Trafalgar in 1805. Napoleon had a short way with satellites: they were taught to pay, and serve, and claim no rewards. How the Spanish people, famed for punctilious pride, could endure the French yoke for twelve aching years truly passeth all understanding. Evidently there were treasures of fatalistic apathy in that country capable of the fiercest reactions. And, although this very important element is hard to gauge, there were liberal tendencies in Spain willing to link their fate with the principles of 1789. Charles III had been an enlightened despot. He had expelled the Jesuits. This *afrancesado* or Frenchified element was not large, but it had vigor and intelligence. These advocates of renovation might sincerely have collaborated with a liberal France; but they had almost lost heart by the time Napoleon directly intervened.

The key of the situation was the royal family, Charles IV and Maria Luisa of Parma, his Queen. A caricatural pair: the King weak of mind and will, his consort a harridan. Goya seems to have caught their spirit in court portraits which might almost figure among his nightmarish *Caprichos*. The Queen imposed upon the realm her paramour, Godoy, a handsome guardsman, universally hated and despised. Godoy was no convinced Francophile: in 1805 he was ready to throw in his lot with the Third Coalition. But threats and bribes kept him in line. The horrible *ménage à trois* was a secret to no one except perhaps Charles IV. Ferdinand, the heir apparent, was aware of it. He became the center of a diffused opposition against Godoy, against his own parents, and against France, whose puppets they were.

This spirit of discontent was manifested in an uprising at Aranjuez (March 17, 1808) directed against Godoy. Finally the crisis broke out in the royal family itself. Mother and son hurled violent accusations at each other, and Charles IV, in bewilderment and despair, signed his abdication. Godoy could have been made the only scapegoat: the new King, Ferdinand VII, confiscated his property amid universal rejoicing. Ferdinand himself was no pattern of patriotism and dignity. In his rage against Godoy, he was eager to enlist the favor of the French Protector. He humbly begged for the hand of any Napoleonic princess. A daughter of Lucien was brought to Paris with that end in view; but as she was found tainted with her father's "Jacobinism," she was sent back to Rome.

The French were already in Spain, on their way to Portugal. Murat, with an "army of observation," was advancing into the distracted country, and reached Madrid on March 23, 1808. He had no authority to recognize the new King. He advised the royal family to seek Napoleon's arbitration; and the trio proceeded to Bayonne. The irrepressible Godoy was there ahead of them: he was to remain "attached" to his master and to his mistress until their deaths.

Napoleon welcomed father, mother, and son with gently smiling jaws. They were moved to tears by the kindness and courtesy of their glorious and omnipotent ally. After a family dinner on May 1, a reconciliation seemed to be effected. Charles IV would resume the crown, and Napoleon, the family arbiter, would more than ever be the actual ruler of Spain.

But on the 2nd of May, in Madrid, as two more

members of the royal family were preparing to leave for Bayonne, the mob rose in protest, with a rage that was a portent. On the Spanish side, there had been no preparations; Murat, sensing trouble, was ready. Indeed, he would have welcomed this occasion to impose his will. Had not Napoleon written to Joseph, King of Naples, two years before: "Shoot down those *lazzaroni* without pity. You can keep an Italian population in its place only through holy fear"? For "Italian," "Spanish" would read just as well. A few whiffs of grapeshot, and order reigned in Madrid. Only this chaotic, this abortive *Dos de Mayo* had long and tragic repercussions. It revealed to the Spanish people the fierceness of its own temper. On that day, war in the spirit was declared; and it was to be implacable.

The news infuriated Napoleon: somehow he made the Bourbons responsible for the (misguided) loyalty of their people. The epilogue of the tragicomedy was hurried through. Ferdinand returned the crown to his father, who abdicated in favor of Napoleon. The princes were sent to France as guests of honor, not as prisoners. Their host, at the Château of Valençay, was no less a personage than Maurice de Talleyrand-Périgord, Prince of Benevento, recently promoted to Vice Grand Elector. ("The only vice," Fouché remarked, "that he was still lacking.") The Princess of Benevento was expected to entertain her guests to the best of her well-known abilities. Napoleon was a most considerate jailer.

Murat, Grand Duke of Berg, expected to become king: he was on the spot, and a vigorous soldier. Napoleon hesitated. He offered the heavy crown to Louis, who wisely declined; then to Joseph, who accepted with reluctance. In a peaceful country, Joseph might have been an excellent constitutional sovereign: in the inferno of Spain his moderation was interpreted as weakness, and his lack of military talent made him the merest lay figure. Out of 120 Spanish notables summoned to Bayonne, only 40 appeared. They enthusiastically endorsed Napoleon's choice; and, for good measure, they ratified a constitution which was to remain stillborn. This was on June 6: the spirit of the *Dos de Mayo* had spread throughout the land. When he reached his capital, King Joseph was supported by a handful of *afrancesados* and at war with the rest of his people.

There were two main causes for this nation-wide, spontaneous insurrection. The first is best expressed in the homely phrase: "the last straw." For ten years at least, Spain had suffered from France's highhandedness; the farce at Bayonne brought the final revulsion. The second was the hold the clergy had on a fanatically Catholic population: even Belgium, Bavaria, and Rome were tepid in comparison. Had Napoleon presented himself with the nimbus the Concordat had given him, his chances would have been great: on December 2, 1804 he had become the Lord's Anointed. But in 1808, although the full details were not divulged, the masses felt, and the priests knew, that the Emperor was irremediably at odds with the Pope. So far Napoleon had fought dynasts: now he had to face both a faith and a people. The Spanish conflict assumed at once that character of somber ferocity which is inseparable from religious wars.

The French were not yet taking seriously that loose uprising of priests and peasants. Dupont, a commander with an excellent reputation, was sent to subdue Andalusia, in the far south. He reported at first that the operation was a mere military march. He must have proceeded with incredible carelessness; and it was said that he was hampered by wagonloads of booty. On June 19, at Baylen, he was attacked on two sides by insurgent forces. He thought himself surrounded, and capitulated at once. Furthermore, he included in the surrender his detached subordinates, who were in no danger. The French were to have been allowed to retire with arms and baggage. But the insurgents were not conventional fighters: they treated Dupont's troops as prisoners and huddled them into an island camp, where most of them perished of callous neglect.

The effect of Baylen was enormous throughout Spain and throughout Europe. Indeed, the disgraceful episode might be called one of the decisive battles in history. It was an Austerlitz in reverse: it pricked the bubble of French invincibility. The *Dos de Mayo* spirit received its confirmation on the battlefield. Portugal and England struck an alliance with Spain, represented by a junta operating from Cádiz. Sir Arthur Wellesley, the future Duke of Wellington, landed in the Peninsula. Joseph fled from Madrid in a panic. Junot, with his scarecrow army, found himself isolated in Portugal, and lost heart. He capitulated at Cintra (August 30). The British honorably carried out the terms of the convention; they shipped Junot and his men back to France.

Napoleon's rage may well be imagined. Baylen was not a mere defeat: he called it "a stain." Before he could proceed to Spain, he found it more essential than ever to strengthen his bond with Alexander of Russia. A meeting had been arranged at Erfurt. For nearly three weeks (September 27 to October 14) Napoleon displayed his power with deliberate ostentation. He appeared as the suzerain of the West, with kings and grand dukes in his train. Diplomatic conferences alternated with magnificent

parties. The Comédie Française played before an audi-
ence of crowned heads. When the line was uttered:

A great man's friendship is a boon from the gods,

Alexander effusively pressed Napoleon's hand. There
was hunting on the battlefield of Jena; and, in better
taste, a visit to Weimar, the capital of the German spirit.
Goethe and Wieland were treated with greater honors
than if they had been victorious commanders. The
Treaty of Tilsit was formally confirmed. Yet Napoleon
could feel a reticence that might easily turn into resistance and even enmity. Both autocrats were aware that
Baylen had blotted out Friedland.

What Napoleon did not know was that Talleyrand
was deliberately working against him. The great diplomat was no longer Minister of Foreign Affairs. This,
however, implied no disgrace. Talleyrand himself had
coveted one of the Grand Dignities of the Empire; and
Napoleon had made it a rule that such exalted titles
were incompatible with a cabinet position. But while
the colorless Champagny was holding the portfolio,
Talleyrand was still a trusted adviser, and he was brought
to Erfurt in that confidential capacity. He told Alexander in plain terms: "France is not interested in any conquest beyond the Rhine, the Alps, and the Pyrenees.
The nation is civilized: her ruler is not." And he adjured
the Czar to save Europe and France by not committing
himself irrevocably to Napoleon. It was the truth, and
it took courage to utter it. It would have taken heroism
to speak with the same definiteness to Napoleon. Talleyrand was no hero.

Napoleon rushed back from Erfurt to Paris, and from
Paris to Spain. He had now a large army in the Peninsula, and some of his ablest lieutenants. A charge of the

Polish light horse in the Somosierra Pass opened the way to Madrid. On December 4, 1808 the Emperor entered the sullen city, and subjected it to a most rigorous state of siege. As a gesture of liberation, he abolished the Inquisition, the very name of which filled the French with horror. Fifty years before, Spain might have accepted such a reform from her own Charles III; in 1808 it seemed as though the persecutor of the Pope, the Antichrist, were of malice prepense destroying the very bulwark of Spanish faith.

Never was Napoleon swifter, and never more ruthless. On December 22 he left Madrid to chase the British under Sir John Moore. He crossed the Sierra de Guadarrama in a terrific snowstorm; it was there that he heard curses from his hard-driven soldiers. Relentlessly he pursued the enemies toward Galicia; he was hoping to destroy them altogether. Abruptly, at Astorga, he turned the command over to Soult; and after a brief pause at Valladolid, sped to Paris.

Soult did not have Napoleon's daimonic drive; he gave the British time to embark at Coruña, where Sir John Moore fell. In the meantime Palafox was holding Saragossa against the French in one of the most heroic and most atrocious sieges in history. Priests and women were active in the defense and were mowed down in the house-to-house fighting. Lannes, a hard-bitten soldier, retched at the necessity of killing so many brave combatants. Finally, on February 21, 1809, the garrison gave up and was allowed to march out of the devastated city with the honors of war. Large-scale resistance was broken; King Joseph reigned in Madrid; but the *Dos de Mayo* spirit was not quenched, and the stain of Baylen was not effaced.

· · ·

The news that caused Napoleon to leave his army at Astorga was ominous indeed. He was informed that in Paris a conspiracy was afoot, involving the most powerful personages in the Empire; and that, three years after the crushing blow of Austerlitz, Austria was again preparing for war.

Parisian society had been amazed when, on December 20, 1808, Fouché and Talleyrand appeared arm-in-arm at a reception. Both knew the inner weaknesses of the Empire as Napoleon never did. Neither wanted—as yet —to destroy the regime; both had become convinced that the Emperor was rushing into self-destruction. They were "alerted." Their conjunction was rightly considered as a portent.

Their "conspiracy," however, was so far innocent enough. The same situation existed as at the time of Marengo. The whole state apparently depended upon one life, and that life precarious, at the mercy of dagger or bomb, stray bullet or germ. It was the duty of true statesmen to prepare for such an emergency. Joseph, who might have been a decent fair-weather head of the state, would never do in a desperate crisis. France was geared to military rule: Fouché and Talleyrand were in quest of a soldier whose stature would not seem comical by the side of Napoleon's. They thought of Moreau and of Bernadotte; at this time their choice fell on Murat. To what extent the *beau sabreur* King of Naples was aware of their preparations remains clouded. Certain it is that the ambition of his wife, Caroline, was as devouring as Napoleon's own.

All this was not openly disloyal: still, the fate of the Empire had been discussed behind Napoleon's back, and his disappearance coolly envisaged. Napoleon was an-gered by what he surmised even more than by what he knew. He chose to overlook Fouché's part in the plot: his threats to the Minister of Police were indirect, allusive. His wrath fell on Talleyrand alone, though he was still ignorant of the Erfurt betrayal. Cursing himself for his Spanish blunder, he made Talleyrand the scapegoat. The storm broke on January 28, 1809, when Napoleon, a master of vigorous language, called his Vice Grand Elector and Grand Chamberlain "S—t in a silk stocking." He attempted to cap this unforgettable phrase with a more unforgivable insult: "You did not tell me that the Duke of San Carlos was your wife's lover." With Old World courtliness, Talleyrand replied: "Sire, I did not think that this bit of information had anything to do with Your Majesty's glory, or with mine." He had stood his ground very well; still, he was sick with a fever all of the next day. Even then Napoleon was of two minds about Talleyrand. He deprived him of his court functions and of the handsome income they carried; but he did not destroy him, or even discard him. Talleyrand remained Prince of Benevento, Vice Grand Elector, an ornament to the Empire.

History is at times repetitious to the verge of the ludicrous: Austria was arming again. She would not have dared to do so if, as Napoleon had a right to expect, Alexander had exerted a restraining influence: Napoleon was forced to realize that Tilsit and Erfurt had lost their virtue. So, with quiet intensity, he made his own preparations. No easy task: for now some of his best troops were in Spain. On April 12, 1809 he was informed that Austria had declared war; within two hours he was leaving for Vienna. Within a month, after a short bombardment, he was entering the Austrian capital again.

But the Austrian army was intact in the field; and this time he had to face the best of the Austrian generals,

Archduke Charles. Attempting to cross the Danube, Napoleon's troops were sharply defeated at Aspern and Essling and compelled to retire to the Lobau Island (May 21). The collapse of a bridge had caused a fatal shortage of ammunition.

For seven weeks Napoleon was held in check and practically hemmed in, a thousand miles from his capital; with the Pope's curse on his head, England unsubdued, Spain smoldering, Russia enigmatic, his German allies wavering. The news of Aspern-Essling, greatly amplified, spread a wild surmise throughout Europe: could the end be near at hand? Both the spirit of the Revolution and the national sentiment, a form of romanticism, had wakened the politically slumberous mid-Continent. In that welter of ideals Napoleon's reckless despotism acted as a catalyst: *he* was the arch enemy of freedom in every form. The whole of central Europe was in a ferment. Andreas Hofer was rousing the Tyrol against Franco-Bavarian rule. Colonel Dörnberg attempted to overthrow Jerome in Westphalia. Major von Schill, a Prussian, led an attack on Magdeburg and, after wild forays, was finally captured at Stralsund. The dispossessed Duke of Brunswick formed a volunteer corps and, in connection with Austria, played havoc with Napoleon's German allies. He managed to extricate himself and to embark for England.

Napoleon was a gambler, but a cool-headed one. He knew that delay was hurting his prestige; but he also knew that a major defeat, so eagerly expected by all his enemies, would be final. So he perfected his preparations with masterly patience. By the 4th of July he had one hundred thousand men ready on Lobau, with over five hundred guns and, this time, ample ammunition. Five bridges had been built over the Danube. He had with him his stars, Masséna and Davout; and by their side Macdonald, Marmont, Oudinot, Bernadotte. On the 6th of July the Battle of Wagram was won. It had been as bitterly contested as Eylau: the French suffered greater losses than the Austrians. A notable victory no doubt, a masterpiece of tactics: still it was not an Austerlitz. On the 15th, Napoleon was again in *his* palace of Schönbrunn.

Napoleon was in no position to dictate. He was only too ready to listen to the propositions of Metternich, the Austrian Chancellor, just entering upon his forty years of rule. Considering the military situation after Wagram, the treaty signed at Schönbrunn on October 14 seems extraordinarily harsh: Austria lost more territory—she was completely cut off from the Adriatic—had to reduce her army, was made to pay a heavy indemnity. Metternich accepted those terms because he considered this merely as a move in a long game. Austria had already signed three treaties with France, at Campoformio in 1797, at Lunéville in 1801, at Pressburg in 1805; she was ready to sign a fourth "just as good." For the time being, at any rate, Austria chose to side with the conqueror. Wagram was a Friedland: the defeated had lost a battle, not the war. Why not a Tilsit, a reconciliation, an alliance? It is not certain that Metternich's game was then quite clear in his own mind. With inflexible tendencies—the dynastic state, a balanced cosmopolitan Europe, no democratic or nationalistic nonsense—he was in the conduct of affairs a thorough opportunist. He would play the French card, in tolerably good faith, or the Russian card, or the British card, provided that Austria would ultimately be the gainer. He preserved that poker face until 1813.

An epilogue to the great crisis was almost an anti-

climax. Three weeks after Wagram—at least six weeks
too late—the British effected a landing on Walcheren
Island, at the mouth of the Scheldt. It was a most ambitious enterprise: forty-two men-of-war escorted four
hundred transports carrying over forty thousand men.
The aim was to capture Antwerp. The danger was very
real: the strongly Catholic Belgian departments had become dissatisfied as a result of the conflict between the
Pope and the Emperor. They would offer little resistance
to invasion; indeed, an uprising was not out of the question. The regular French armies were either fighting in
Spain or watching an uneasy truce near Vienna.

The great personages of the Empire, the stately Arch
Chancellor Cambacérès first among them, did not lose
their heads, but declined to use them. Trained to passive
obedience, they supinely waited for orders. Fouché
alone proved capable of action. At the time, he was acting Minister of the Interior as well as Minister of Police.
He took hold of the situation with something of his old
Jacobin vigor. He issued proclamations in which patriotism had almost a republican ring. He mobilized
the National Guard, officered by men who were not
blind devotees of Napoleon. He reassured the country;
but he demonstrated thereby that France was more than
the Emperor and could save herself in his absence. This
was *lèse-majesté*, and a crime that Napoleon could not
forgive.

Fouché went farther. After some misunderstanding at
Wagram, Bernadotte had left in a huff. He had never
been manageable, and in politics he was an uncertain
factor. But Marshall Bernadotte, Prince of Pontecorvo,
closely connected with the Bonaparte family, had at
least an impressive name. Fouché placed him at the
head of the military preparations. The two formed an

able team. Nothing could be more displeasing to the Master.

By the time the Emperor returned, the danger had vanished. The Earl of Chatham and Marshal Berna-dotte were not to cross swords. As Leclerc in Haiti was defeated by fever, so Chatham on Walcheren was checked by a milder form of the disease. He had hoped at least to maintain a "pocket" at Flushing; but even this toe-hold had to be abandoned. By September 21 the last British troops had been evacuated. The fiasco was monumental and complete.

Napoleon was of two minds. He upbraided the dig-nitaries and ministers for their spinelessness. He duly commended Fouché's energy. At the same time he made light of the peril and hinted that the heroics of the Na-tional Guard had a touch of the ridiculous. He fully real-ized, however, how dangerous Fouché and Bernadotte could be. They might work with him, and work well; but not for him. They were not his men. In 1810 both of them were removed from the center of French af-fairs. But they had not surrendered, and both of them still had the power to thwart Napoleon.

CHAPTER SEVEN

SPLENDORS AND MISERIES
1810–1811

1810: never had the young Empire looked more impressive. What if it had received a severe wound at Trafalgar in 1805, a worse one at Baylen in 1808? It still seemed to be marching from strength to strength, from glory to glory.

A faith or a nation can stand crushing blows, for they live in the spirit. All regimes, however, are frail because they are machines; and a personal regime is frailest of all. Had Napoleon's miraculous luck held for a few more years, he might have found his Moscow in Samarkand, his Waterloo in Trebizond: by whatever name, the appointment could not be eluded. The Empire could not endure, because the Empire was Napoleon's dream, a dream that spurned every curb. At St. Helena, evoking the magic days of his early Italian victories, he said—magnificently, for his genius flashed in words of flame as well as in commands on the battlefield: "I foresaw what I might become: I could see the world moving under me, as though I were borne aloft in the air." A glorious vision: and lo, it was a vision. Napoleon constantly attempted to translate it into reality, to arrest its flight, to pin it down to earth. His institutions were meant to be anchors; he whose destiny was the insatiable quest yearned for stability.

So the great solipsist ("I, myself, alone, and that suffices!") was craving to perpetuate his name, his rule, his seed, for a thousand years. He refused to accept physical death: he wanted desperately to survive in the flesh. His own kin had disappointed him: the crowned Bonapartes, Joseph, Louis, Jerome, Caroline, could cease to be puppets only by opposing him; and when they did so, they became odious. He wanted a son of his own loins, the son Josephine had not been able to give him. He knew that the responsibility was not his. He had deliberately made the experiment; the chosen instrument was a reader in Caroline's household, Mlle Denuelle de la Plaigne. On December 13, 1807 a man child was born to him, that pathetic Count Léon who, after a raffish career, was to die obscure and a pauper in 1881.

The problem of his succession had haunted him ever since the creation of the Empire. Josephine was aware of it, but she could not avert the blow. It is in his relations with her that Napoleon appears at his most natural and best. If it had not been for dynastic reasons, he would have been content to keep her by his side. For years he resisted the thought of a divorce, urged not by the Bonapartes only, but by Fouché. When he told her of his decision, she fainted. Bausset, the secretary who carried her away in his arms, testifies that the swooning was a bit of play-acting: historical characters are constantly on the stage. But even though her grief was slightly touched up for effect, it was none the less sincere. So was Napoleon's. He behaved with the utmost consideration and generosity: he was no Henry VIII. She retained the title of Empress, and was granted a dazzling allowance, which, of course, proved inadequate. The Senate was officially consulted. Eugene, unswerving in his devotion to his stepfather, gave the only speech in favor of the Emperor's resolve. The august assembly, not quite unanimously, ratified it (December 16, 1809), and Josephine left for La Malmaison.

To persuade the Senate was easy enough. But there had been a religious ceremony on the eve of the coronation. Rome alone could pronounce an annulment; and the Pope was at war with the Emperor. Napoleon's power over the French episcopate was still so great, however, that a solution was devised: even canon law may yield a painful inch to the successor of Constantine and Charlemagne. On January 12, 1810, the *Officialité*, or Metropolitan's Court of Paris, declared itself competent. Cardinal Fesch and the witnesses, Berthier, Duroc, and Talleyrand, testified that the ceremony on December 1, 1804 had not been a proper marriage; and so the religious bond was declared nonexistent. Confident of the outcome, Napoleon had already gone a-wooing.

His choice was limited to the highest ruling families. He was not moved by the parvenu's desire to marry above his origins: he had reached the summit. Daughters of minor German royalties were considered and rejected: they were good enough only for the lesser members of the imperial connection—Jerome, Eugene, Berthier. One faction—Fouché and Caulaincourt among them—were advising a Russian marriage. Another favored Austria. Napoleon was won over to the Russian side. There was a formal alliance between the two states, and a personal friendship between the two rulers. No ideological gulf separated them. If Alexander was an autocrat, so was Napoleon; and the Czar was rather more open to liberal ideas than the French Emperor. Napoleon was ready to make heavy sacrifices in order to retain Alexander's friendship. He formally repudiated any intention of reviving Poland: Marie Walewska's immolation had been of no avail. Caulaincourt, the French Ambassador, was instructed to sue for the hand of the Czar's sister. At the news, which was not unexpected, the whole Russian imperial family was horror-stricken. In their eyes, the Great Friend and Ally was Antichrist. Moreover, Alexander had heeded Talleyrand's words at Erfurt. So he gave an evasive answer, which to Napoleon's ears sounded plain enough. A few days later Russia was courteously informed that the Emperor of the French had chosen an Austrian princess. The Romanovs, after all, were upstarts by the side of the Habsburgs.

To the Habsburgs, Napoleon's figure was even more horrendous than to the Romanovs. They had suffered more at his hands; and he was at the head of the nation that had martyred one of their own, Marie-Antoinette, never professing repentance. Young Archduchess Marie-Louise, in particular, had been brought up in the detestation of the monster. But the destinies of Austria were in the hands of Metternich. In the masterly game he was playing, he would sacrifice a princess as if she were a pawn. Using Hymen as an instrument of National policy was deep in the Austrian tradition. There was an oft-quoted Latin distich with the key words: *Tu, felix Austria, nube:* "Let others do the fighting: thou, lucky Austria, wed." On March 11, 1810, the marriage by proxy was celebrated in Vienna. Marie-Louise had been carefully brought up: she accepted her fate with quiet dignity. The classical-minded alluded to Iphigenia, to Jephthah's daughter; some spoke of "a beautiful heifer led to the sacrificial altar."

Beautiful she was not. As haughtily indifferent to all ideas as her great-aunt Marie-Antoinette, she possessed neither her spirit nor her charm. Yet this outrageous marriage of convenience was to take an unexpected turn. The Imperator, the incarnation of the state, the demigod, feeling the approach of middle age, desired passionately to be human at last, merely human. He was as impatient to be with his young wife as if he had been a second lieutenant. Throwing protocol to the winds, he rushed out to meet her ahead of the appointed place. He jumped into her carriage, kissed her ardently, and that same night, at Compiègne, claimed his marital rights. The strangely assorted pair were surprised and delighted with each other. Marie-Louise found that the Minotaur was a very affectionate monster. And Napoleon would gleefully tell his courtiers: "Marry German girls! Nothing like them: healthy, honest, wholesome, and fresh as roses!"

The wedding ceremonies were of unparalleled splendor. The civil one took place at Saint-Cloud on April 1, the religious one the next day in the Louvre; it was again performed by Uncle Fesch. There was one shadow in the rejoicings: out of thirty-nine stalls reserved for cardinals, twenty-one were left empty. The absentees were severely disciplined, exiled into remote provinces, deprived of their red robes (they were to be known as the Black Cardinals). But there was also a ray of auspicious light. At the wedding banquet Metternich, representing the Emperor of Austria, raised his glass "To the King of Rome!" This was the title that the Senate had adopted for the prospective imperial prince. It was reminiscent of the one borne by the heir apparent in the defunct Holy Roman Empire: King of the Romans. It seemed as though Austria, out of a millennial past, were acknowledging the supremacy of the new Charlemagne.

Marie-Louise was only nineteen; carefully educated —she could be insipid in five languages—she was wholly ignorant of the world beyond the rules of etiquette. She was devoid of that inner courtesy, that delicate, almost playful sympathy, which had been the key to Josephine's graciousness. She acted her part stiffly, correctly. She made no attempt to be a Marie-Antoinette: in politics, her influence was nil. But her very presence strengthened, if it did not create, certain tendencies within the Empire; and on the whole they were disastrous.

There is an aspect of Marie-Louise's influence that reputable scholars are strongly tempted to leave alone: its discussion might offend Victorian delicacy, and it is strictly incapable of proof. Marie-Louise, immature and innocent, turned out to be healthily sensual. The combination—*l'ingénue amoureuse*—had a piquancy that appealed to the forty-year-old veteran. A hero of legend, he was none the less a man. For months the supreme egotist had one guiding thought: to please his exacting young wife. He even attempted to learn dancing. Now, those months of conjugal dalliance were critical. He had to watch both the indecisive warfare in Spain and the growing menace in the East. The Napoleon of 1805 would have decided which problem to defer, which to liquidate; and by what means, force or negotiations. The Napoleon of 1810–11 remained in a haze. He knew the evils of hesitation, which had caused the downfall of Prussia; and now he, the master of energy, was among the drifters.

This paralysis of the will came with Marie-Louise; perhaps to some appreciable extent through Marie-Louise. It is far from certain that she should bear the sole, or even the chief, responsibility. Age offers a more obvious explanation. Napoleon was forty, and just reaching his prime. But he had lived with incredible intensity: some of his years were decades. We know what ravages a few years of war wrought on the physique, and perhaps even on the mental fiber, of Lincoln,

Wilson, Roosevelt. And even if he had remained the alert young leader of 1796, at ease in battle, administration, diplomacy, his task by 1810 had grown complex beyond human control. He was to be his masterly self again on the battlefield, in the German campaign of 1813, in the French campaign of 1814; in politics and diplomacy he was floundering. He had lost Talleyrand; he was soon to discard Fouché: even when he did not solicit their advice, the presence of these two men was an intellectual challenge. Without them, he gravitated to the level of a Champagny or a Savary.

The advent of Marie-Louise had another and more obvious consequence: it coincided with, and accelerated, a sharp reactionary trend in the regime. The change had been gradual but irreversible. The ideal of the early Consulate had been appeasement, fusion: but the Revolution was taken as a fact beyond dispute. The survivors of the ancient regime were welcome in the new, provided they accepted its principles and achievements. Such was, in particular, Fouché's attitude toward the returning émigrés. By imperceptible steps, monarchical forms were restored: even under the Consulate there was something of a court, subjected to an increasingly rigid etiquette. Old titles became assets. Nobles were preferred even in the officers' corps, hitherto overwhelmingly plebeian, and even in the bureaucracy, once the preserve of the middle class. Then an imperial nobility was manufactured: a handful of princes, some three dozen dukes, counts and barons by the score. A system of entail (majorats) was intended to restore the right of primogeniture among privileged families. From the throne down to the local gentry, the hereditary principle prevailed over Napoleon's great promise: irrespective of origins, a free field for all talents.

Now the nobles no longer crept back individually, chastened, accepting history: they were sought after. In December 1809, in preparation for his Austrian marriage, Napoleon "drafted" thirty men of high birth to serve as his chamberlains ("Only those people know how to serve"). Young noblemen were ordered into military schools so that the democratic taint might gradually be removed from the army.

The Empire of 1810 might indeed have been called "the Restoration." It was a Bourbon regime—with the Bourbons in exile. Napoleon himself was carried by this tide of reaction farther than he knew or desired. He was still attempting to preserve a balance. If he chose a Habsburg as his Empress, he believed that she would have to adapt herself to a court of revolutionary origin: "She will be playing whist with two regicides, Cambacérès and Fouché." But the logic of the situation was stronger than his middle-road intentions. Lebrun, once Third Consul, now Arch Treasurer, formulated the change with perfect clearness: to call to the French throne the great-niece of Marie-Antoinette was an act of repentance, an expiation. The Revolution was thereby sentenced. Napoleon, willy-nilly, accepted that view. He, the upstart of genius, became a legitimist. He referred to "my uncle Louis XVI" with apparent casualness. Now it was no longer the *émigrés*, but the regicides who were barely tolerated, and only if duly penitent. Cambacérès, shrewdest of time-servers, retained his ornamental positions. But Fouché had to go.

For Fouché's long-expected, ever-deferred disgrace, there was an obvious justification: he had been caught in surreptitious peace negotiations with England, in which King Louis of Holland had been innocently enmeshed. Those, however, who expected a sensational execution of the regicide, the former Terrorist, the butcher of Lyon, the unregenerate Jacobin, were disappointed. Napoleon's wrath spent itself in words. He staged one of his famous fits of towering rage (June 2, 1810). Fouché had to surrender his beloved Ministry of Police; but he remained Duke of Otranto and a Senator. He was even made Governor of the Papal States; but he was ordered to yield certain documents, and, as he attempted to elude the request, his appointment to Rome was canceled. He was sent, in dignified semi-exile, to his Senatorial seat at Aix. Napoleon took no further measures against him. Later, Eliza, now Grand Duchess of Tuscany, effected a show of reconciliation. In 1813 Fouché was made Governor of the Illyrian Provinces, an exposed outpost—indeed, a forlorn hope—where he showed competence and dignity.

The longanimity of Napoleon toward a man he so thoroughly distrusted is hard to explain. Fouché had been active on Napoleon's behalf in Brumaire; he had served admirably as the watchdog of the home front. But his manifest independence absolved Napoleon of any gratitude. It seems as though Napoleon himself were impressed by the "legend" of Fouché, the man from whom no secrets were hid. The greatest of these secrets may have been that Fouché, and Fouché alone, knew exactly the state of public opinion: a mystery the Emperor preferred not to probe.

Paradoxically, Fouché was regretted: not merely by the last Jacobins, who considered him as their shield, but by those aristocrats who, as early as 1800, had with some reluctance accepted Napoleon's rule. Fouché had dealt courteously with them, provided that they did not engage in conspiracies. The appointment of Savary as his successor created consternation; instead of a ripe statesman, a rough and witless soldier was to run the imperial police. Fouché, apparently resigned to his retirement, held himself in readiness to serve Napoleon again, but on his own terms; and if those terms were not met, to destroy him.

The situation in Spain and Portugal remained tragically confused. The masses and the clergy were passionately hostile to the invaders. But there were no more Baylens: in the field, the insurgents were no match for the French armies. Sir Arthur Wellesley, soon to be Viscount Wellington, was unable to make decisive gains. A precisian and a martinet, he was admirable in the handling of seasoned troops, but he had little use for the ubiquitous, disorderly, and heroic guerrilla fighters. He was not heartily supported by his own government: Spain was a heavy drain on the British treasury; the results, for many weary months, were not sensational; and the Cabinet grudged the cost. For two years Wellington, refraining from any lightning offensive, patiently watched the exhaustion and dissensions of the French.

Napoleon had large contingents in the Peninsula, with some of his most capable commanders. They should have been able, he thought, to drive Wellington out, as Sir John Moore had been driven, and at the same time to impose some kind of order upon the unhappy Kingdom. As a matter of fact, they almost did: there was a moment when only Cádiz and Lisbon were still holding out. Soult even inherited Junot's dream, and fancied himself for a while as King Nicholas of Portugal. The greatest weakness of the French besides their uneasy conscience was their lack of unity. For King Joseph and his military adviser Jourdan they had but scant respect. Most generals were thinking of booty first of all: Soult became notorious in this respect only for his lack of discretion.

Masséna was sent to take command. His pre-eminence among his peers should have been undisputed. He was the hero of Rivoli, the victor of Zurich, the stubborn defender of Genoa, the man who had saved the day at Aspern and clinched the victory at Wagram. But even Masséna was unable to curb the fractiousness of the French high command. His subordinates excused themselves by declaring that "he had aged." Soult at one time, Ney at another, refused point-blank to obey his orders. Masséna pushed Wellington back to the lines of Torres Vedras, which protected Lisbon: a triple defense of massive earthworks, with redoubts at the critical points, impregnable except at heavy cost. Masséna sent messenger after messenger to Napoleon: only the Emperor's presence could restore discipline among the generals and revive the fighting spirit of the troops. Napoleon, now unsure of grasp and flabby of will, gave evasive answers.

In despair, his lines of communication insecure, Masséna decided to withdraw. At first, Wellington simply let famine and discouragement destroy his opponents: whole companies deserted, irreplaceable ammunition had to be abandoned. When Wellington struck at last, he found there was fire still in the old lion of Rivoli: had Bessières properly seconded Masséna, the Battle of Fuentes de Onoro (May 5, 1811) might have been a resounding French victory. As it was, Masséna was forced to retire as far as Salamanca. He was, rather unjustly, made responsible for the failure of the whole campaign and was never entrusted with high command again. The fiasco was undeniable, and its effect immense throughout Europe. Baylen might have been an accident; Masséna's withdrawal was a defeat of the first magnitude.

Napoleon's desire to cut his losses in Spain was intelligible enough. He seems to have considered the right solution: to wash his hands of the whole mess, restore Ferdinand VII, recall the two hundred thousand men he so badly needed against Russia. But he no longer had the sharpness of vision and the moral courage to make such a decision. His troops remained in Spain, weakened by constant drafts for other fronts, at the very moment when they should have been either reinforced or withdrawn.

While Masséna was effecting his disastrous retreat, Napoleon's thoughts were absorbed by what seemed to him a far more momentous event. The young Empress was with child. On the evening of March 19, 1811 she suffered the first pains. Early the next morning Dubois, the accoucheur, told the Emperor in consternation that the delivery would be difficult. "Save the mother," Napoleon said. The forceps had to be used; the great Corvisart was called. At last, at a quarter to nine, the child was born. For a few anxious moments the frail life was uncertain. A faint little cry: the Emperor had an heir.

Cambacérès passed the word, and the guns started their solemn boom. Twenty-one salvos for a girl, one hundred and one for a boy. When the twenty-second detonation was heard, Paris went wild. For good or evil, Napoleon was still inseparable from France: the whole capital rejoiced with the man and the ruler. It was one of those instants of communion which are so rare in the history of any nation. The 20th of March 1811 appeared to be the climax of the Empire. As in Victor Hugo's great ode, the Master may have felt: "The future, the future, the future is mine!"

This outburst of loyalty was sincere; it did not prove lasting. The baptism of the King of Rome, on June 9, 1811, was an anticlimax. Nothing more gorgeous could be conceived. The procession was interminable and magnificent. Robes of office, mantles and coronets, gold braid and plumes vied in splendor. The imperial pair appeared in full court dress, a crushing mass of velvet, embroidered silk, and ermine, a glitter of diamonds and proud diadems. Yet the crowd wondered in their hearts: "Is this all?"

A last effort was made to restore the link between the new regime and its popular origin: the child was placed in the arms of old Kellermann, the veteran who at Valmy had won the first victory of the Revolution over absolutist Europe. But the Emperor himself remained aloof and stern. *Te Deum* and illuminations failed to revive the enthusiasm of December 2, 1804. In spite of pageantry and fair weather, there was a chill in that balmy June evening. Perhaps the good people of Paris had been kept waiting too long while their dinners were spoiling. There were deeper causes for anguish. The news from Spain could not be concealed; the rumors of war with Russia could not be suppressed; the economic crisis was more patent than the gaudy frippery of troops and courtiers. All that magnificence was oppressive and somehow ominous. At what should have been the zenith of the Empire, there was a shadow of foreboding.

CHAPTER EIGHT

DOWNFALL

THE RUSSIAN CAMPAIGN
1812

AS the crow flies, there are fourteen hundred miles between Paris and Moscow, seven hundred and fifty between the Rhine and the Niemen. Distance enough to
guarantee mutual safety. Not, however, when at either
end there stands an autocrat, drunk with power and pride.

France and Russia had no quarrel; Napoleon and
Alexander could not remain at peace. I shall list the
grievances that led to the actual conflict. They were real
enough, and of undeniable importance; yet not one of
them was such as to justify the enormous cost and the
fatal risk entailed by open hostilities. We should not
sweep aside the facts, as Rousseau taught; but we should
look behind the obvious facts. It was Bismarck the great
realist who gave currency to the word *imponderables:*
there are factors of a psychological nature that are more
potent than steel and gold. Even a Soviet academician
like Eugene Tarle could not make his book on *Napoleon's Invasion of Russia* an exercise in pure materialistic
determinism.

We must not be afraid of the trite and the repetitious,
for the romantic spirit is constantly alive within us, ready
to transpose reality into a realm beyond or below hard
facts and plain reason. For one hundred and fifty years
worshippers and detractors of Napoleon have agreed
upon the platitude that his ambition could brook no
limit. This is the sole cause of the Russian campaign, as
it was of the Spanish adventure. He wanted to impose

his solipsist delusion upon the universe: "The world is mine, and the fullness thereof; I can do what I please with my own." That there should be an independent power, even a friendly one, was to him an insufferable affront. This state of mind is *imperialism* in the simplest sense of the term: the craving to command and to be obeyed without demur, the refusal to discuss except from such a position of strength that discussion will be a farce. Such a state of mind is not uncommon; it exists, diffused and confused, even among the peace-loving masses of the most democratic countries. Stern patriots refuse to consider anything short of unconditional surrender— and this applies to friends as well as to enemies. That *dementia imperialis* ranges from coarsest "getting tough" to the grandeur that was Rome: *Parcere subjectis et debellare superbos.* "*Tout homme a dans son cœur Napoléon qui dort*" ("there is a Napoleon slumbering in every man's heart"). Napoleon was unique only in the intensity and absolute purity of that passion.

By 1812 the French had become immune to it. After two decades of war they were sated with glory. Even in 1799 they had hailed Bonaparte only in the hope that he would make peace. In the attack on Russia, Napoleon was rigorously alone: diplomats, army leaders, administrators, business men, all advised against it. The common people groaned; the veterans grumbled or cursed; many draftees took to the woods in despair. The whole titanic drama was the inflexible and therefore insane will of one man against the world.

Imperialism in this elementary sense—and in every sense—existed in England. But there it was not concentrated in the person of an autocrat. And England never had the power to coerce her satellites as Napoleon did. Her one singlehanded enterprise, at Walcheren, was a fiasco. Even in Spain, Wellington would have been powerless if the whole country had not been fanatically anti-French. England had to work with and through allies; so, compared with the French autocrat, she was moderate, reasonable, civilized. She was not impervious to the homely wisdom of "live and let live."

The case of Russia is more complex. In spite of violent inner contrasts, England was a well-integrated community. In Russia, the peasant masses, the aristocracy, the Czar, had not reached that degree of organic harmony which creates a nation. The muzhiks were inert and inarticulate; they had a vague horror of the Antichrist, the godless French Revolution, whose flag Napoleon had not discarded; and they nursed a hazy yet profound faith in Holy Russia. The aristocrats were unevenly divided. Superficially, most of them were Frenchified in manners and speech; but the France which had won their cultural allegiance was that of the ancient regime, the Paris salons of the eighteenth century. The men whose "Enlightenment" had survived the shock of the Terror were a dwindling minority; and even they did not allow their liberal ideology to interfere with their class interests. Like Catherine the Great, they were ready to agree with Diderot on paper, for "paper suffers everything." But on the realistic plane they had no thought of abolishing serfdom.

The Czar was, and remains, an enigma. The mystery of Napoleon's mind lies in its awful simplicity, which was also the secret of its greatness. Alexander's mind, on the contrary, was a chaos. He cannot be dismissed as a weakling and a fool: compared with Charles IV and Ferdinand VII of Spain, with George III and George IV of England, with Frederick William III of Prussia, with Francis I of Austria, he was impressive in mental and moral stature. He was an autocrat like Napoleon, but an autocrat by the whim of fate, not through strength of will, a buckram majesty, a hollow man; he felt the difference and attempted to bridge it. He craved for prestige as intensely as Napoleon, so as to catch up with his own destiny.

He had come to the throne under tragic circumstances: his father, Czar Paul, had been murdered. Even if Alexander's complicity was not open or even fully conscious, still he accepted the benefits of the crime, and at the hands of the criminals. The shadow of guilt haunted him: he had to "make good" as an atonement. And his father's fate was a grim lesson: in *old* Russia as in old Turkey, despotism was tempered by assassination. He had to be a great czar, a slave, or a corpse. He knew that he had lost face by his inglorious flight after Austerlitz. He was conscious that, not the defeat at Friedland, but the alliance with the victor at Tilsit had been considered by many Russians an intolerable humiliation. He was thus swayed toward opposing Napoleon even though he was aware that resistance might mean catastrophe.

Alexander was a man of good will without steadfastness. His Swiss tutor, Laharpe, had shaped him into an enlightened despot; but he was too fluid to hold the shape. Yet his "liberalism" toward Poland, toward defeated France in 1814 and 1815, was not wholly unreal. He was to turn into a mystic, and Mme de Krüdener inspired him with the noble dream of the Holy Alliance. He was at all times a sentimentalist. He had a romantic bond with the royal pair of Prussia: had they not sworn eternal friendship on the tomb of Frederick the Great? He and they formed a most virtuous *ménage à trois*, the charm of Queen Louise an excellent substitute for political wisdom.

With the same lovable capacity for love, he fell at Tilsit under the spell of Napoleon's personality. That the monster could smile so winningly, that the fabulous conqueror should seek the young Czar's friendship, struck him as little short of a miracle. He was *subjugated:* Napoleon chose to interpret the word in all its strictness. But Alexander's Napoleonism, though very real, was an infatuation, not a principle. A year later, at Erfurt, it had already lost most of its virtue. Alexander was not unprepared to heed Talleyrand's words of warning.

Napoleon called Alexander a decadent Byzantine, sophisticated and shifty. But it was his own policy, not the Czar's, that was tricky and unaccountable. On the face of it, Tilsit should have meant a division of the Continent: Alexander supreme in the east as Napoleon was in the west, with a vague condominium over the confused German world in between. But Napoleon could not conceive of yielding an inch. He had created the Grand Duchy of Warsaw; he swore that he had no intention of making it the nucleus of a revived Poland; then he took back his promise and chose to keep Alexander guessing. Poland, at that time as in the days of Pilsudski, might have reached out for Lithuania, for White Russia, for an indefinite share of the Ukraine. In Napoleon's hand, she would have constituted an instrument for containing and rolling back Russia which Alexander could hardly tolerate. Napoleon, against his promise, kept his troops in Prussia—at Prussia's expense. Alexander, a mottled soul, and generous in spots, deplored the continued enslavement of his Potsdam friends. Besides, outposts of the Grand Army right on the Russian border were far too "neighborly" for comfort. Napoleon dangled before his friend's eyes prospects of vast expansion in the Balkans: Moldavia and Wallachia were only a start; Constantinople itself was glimmering in the haze. But he was ready at a moment's notice to ally himself with the Turks or, given a chance, to seize Constantinople for himself. In the depths of his mind lurked the old dream: to strike at the root of England's wealth and power, to rival Alexander of Macedon by conquering India, with Russia as an auxiliary. Then, in bold anticipation of Sir Halford McKinder, he would control the Heartland, and the World Island and the World.

In the campaign of 1809 Alexander, Napoleon's ally, took care to avoid any decisive action. His attitude was rather one of neutrality, and not obviously benevolent at that. He declined to give Napoleon the hand of his sister Anna: the courteous, evasive answer could not conceal the horror with which the proposal had been received in St. Petersburg. By 1810 the exalted friendship which had been "a boon of the gods" had turned into a cold war.

In January 1811 Napoleon annexed to his empire the northern coast of Germany, as far as the Hanseatic port of Lübeck. The Czar did not like to see the tricolor permanently waving on the Baltic. Among the territories thus ruthlessly confiscated was the Duchy of Oldenburg. Now, Alexander's sister Catherine was married to the heir of that duchy; the airy promise of some compensation for the dispossessed ruler sounded like an insult. In May 1811 Napoleon recalled his Ambassador in Russia, Caulaincourt. Caulaincourt was an upright man whom Napoleon had treated with a peculiar blend of high favor and cruelty. An aristocrat by birth, a liberal by temperament, he was a loyal servant of the Empire as the recognized government of France. But he believed that Napoleon's policy toward Russia was aggressive, and he boldly stood for conciliation. This, in the eyes of

Napoleon, made him almost a traitor. At the same time young Colonel Chernishev, as aide to the Russian Ambassador Kurakin, was enjoying great social favor in Paris, won the graces of Napoleon himself—and took advantage of his position to secure secret documents on the situation of the French army. He escaped in time; his French accomplice was guillotined; and the situation grew steadily darker.

All this, however, was happening beyond the boundaries of Russia and might not have roused public opinion to fever pitch. It was the Continental Blockade that made the Russians feel the full weight of the French yoke. In France and in central Europe, the blockade was a mitigated curse; it might even be turned into an effective protectionist policy. But Russia, with rudimentary industries, needed to exchange her natural products—grain, hides, lumber, flax, and hemp—for manufactured goods. The Russian ports carried on a fairly active trade under neutral flags. But Napoleon was aware that those alleged neutrals were Englishmen in thin disguise. He insisted that Russia enforce the blockade policy in all its rigor. This meant intolerable hardships for the Russians, at any rate for the most articulate classes, and in a cause that they felt was not their own. Napoleon's stringent orders seemed all the more galling when it was known that France herself granted (or sold) extensive licenses to trade with the enemy. As the economic situation grew worse in Russia, the Czar imposed a high tariff on luxury imports such as silk and wine. It happened that these came mostly from France. So the economic front was bristling at the same moment as the diplomatic and the military.

Napoleon was tightening his alliances with reluctant Prussia, hesitant Austria, the subservient Confederacy of the Rhine, the vassal Grand Duchy of Warsaw; and French troops, far from withdrawing from Prussia, were moving steadily eastward. Alexander, on his side, stopped the war with Turkey, sought an understanding with Bernadotte, now Crown Prince of Sweden, and erected vast fortifications on the Niemen.

In this tense situation the last provocation, as might have been expected, came from Napoleon. With the familiar complaint that the blockade was not properly enforced, Napoleon seized Swedish Pomerania. Alexander then sent an ultimatum demanding the withdrawal of the French troops and also the long-deferred evacuation of Prussia. This document was handed in by Kurakin on April 25. Napoleon vented his anger on the trembling old diplomat: "You are behaving like Prussia on the eve of Jena!" He raged, but gave no answer. With an autocrat, even the hint of an ultimatum means instant war. Yet Napoleon hesitated on the brink. From Spain came nought but ominous news: he wanted to write off the miserable affair, and could not make up his mind to yield on any point. French opinion was visibly nervous, almost openly restive. The elaborate network of German alliances was fragile. Even the great gambler shuddered at the magnitude of the gamble. Yet to discuss tamely with Alexander meant the total destruction of the legendary character he had been creating: the invincible conqueror whose word could not be gainsaid.

It must come to a trial of strength, then, the path of reasonableness being barred. Napoleon had not so completely lost touch with reality as to desire an all-out war. Two hopes remained. The first was bluff: to awe Alexander into submission by a display of overwhelming power. If that failed, there remained the chance of a swift decisive victory, another Austerlitz. To Caulaincourt's warnings and objurgations, he had in readiness the soldier's reply: "One good battle will settle all that!"

It was part of his campaign, therefore, to show off his might so as not to use it. For days in May 1812 he held court at Dresden as Emperor of the West. The German princes rushed to his summons; they gave a splendid display of servility and even outshone their Erfurt performances. He had sent Narbonne to the Czar on a last-hope mission and waited at Dresden for the answer. Narbonne returned with empty hands—and empty pockets, for his papers had been stolen on the way. The Czar while professing his desire for peace, would not withdraw his ultimatum. The clash of wills was sharper than ever.

On May 29 Napoleon left Dresden. By way of Posen, Thorn, Danzig, Königsberg, he reached Wilkowiski (Vilkovishko), a small town a few miles from the Niemen. It was from there that he issued his proclamation to his troops: "Soldiers! The second Polish war has begun; the first ended at Friedland and Tilsit. . . . Are we no longer the soldiers of Austerlitz? Russia places us between dishonor and war: can our choice be in doubt? We shall go forward; we shall cross the Niemen; we shall carry the war into Russia's own territory."

The army he thus addressed was the largest ever gathered in European history. The exact numbers are still in dispute: the estimates vary from four to six hundred thousand massed on the Niemen. In addition, there were garrisons, depots, observation corps throughout the vast empire and a large force desperately struggling in Spain. Altogether, Napoleon may have had 1,200,000 men in his forces; as many as Carnot had raised and organized in 1793. There was a radical difference, however; Napoleon's host no longer was a *French* army. On the Russian front barely one half of the soldiers were even nominally French; and included under that name were men from the recently annexed territories. The rest were Italians, Poles, Germans, and even Spaniards generously lent by King Joseph. On the right flank Schwarzenberg led the Austrian contingent. On the left, the Prussians were incorporated with Marshal Macdonald's forces, which were to advance along the Baltic, through Mitau and Riga, in the direction of St. Petersburg.

Such was still the prestige of French arms that this unwieldy horde, without a common language or a common spirit, kept some kind of discipline for several months and fought with surprising valor. The Prussians, so soon to change sides, attacked their great friends the Russians with unexpected fierceness; they were nerved by the hope of conquering Kurland and Livonia, lands where the local aristocracy had been German for centuries, and was to remain German until recalled by Hitler. The Spaniards, of course, were hopeless in every sense. When a Spanish unit started sniping at its French officers, it was surrounded, disarmed, and every second man was shot. Napoleon was not cruel, but war is war.

For four days and nights the Grand Army, over four bridges, poured forth in mighty uninterrupted streams. The troops were in high spirit: it was the opening move in a fabulous game. For a moment, forebodings were stilled, discomforts cheerfully endured. Beyond the Nieman stretched mystery: a vast forest, dark and sullen; solitude and silence.

On June 28 Napoleon reached Vilna. Only four days before, Alexander had been there, gracing with his im-

perial presence a ball in his honor. He dispatched Bala-
shov, his Minister of Police, to meet the French
Emperor. The tenor of his message was studiously moderate; he even apologized for Kurakin's hastiness in demanding his passports. But the essential issue was clearer
than ever: no negotiation so long as a single French
soldier stood on Russian soil. In plain terms Napoleon
was requested to give up being Napoleon.

The conqueror was still undecided. He spent nearly
three weeks at Vilna, until July 16. He created a provisional government for Lithuania: that is to say, he
organized the squeezing of the country for the support
of his troops. But he was careful not to turn his conquest
over to the Poles, who were clamoring for it: for that
would have made the breach with Alexander irremediable. At this late hour, Napoleon was still working on
the hypothesis that the conflict which engaged one million men was merely a pique between friends. Let the
Czar get rid of his evil counselors, like that obnoxious
Stein, a refugee from Prussia, and the allies of Tilsit
would once again fall in each other's arms. Napoleon
was magnanimously resolved to forgive everything; only
Alexander would have to be more "loyal" in the future.
Let him take example from those perfect allies, the kings
of Bavaria and Saxony. Napoleon was merely waging "a
war of reconciliation."

One thing he made plain: he was not leading a crusade of liberation, either for the oppressed nationalities
or for the depressed classes. He was the Lord's Anointed,
one—the first, of course—in the great family of legitimate sovereigns. He claimed later that delegations came
to him urging him to free the serfs. The man who had
attempted to restore slavery in Haiti was not likely to
indulge in such democratic nonsense. He sent troops

to put down peasant revolts in Poland. Only in St. Helena was he to rediscover himself as the Soldier of the Revolution.

On the Russian side, there were advocates of peace at any price; and some were found in the imperial family. But the determination not to surrender was overwhelming. The methods, however, were not so clearcut, and the means at hand were very uncertain. The "Scythian plan" of luring the French to their destruction into the depths of Russia was not a deliberate policy. Rostopchin did tell the Czar (or claims he did): "Your empire has two powerful defenses: its vastness and its climate. The Emperor of Russia would be mighty in Moscow, terrible in Kazan, invincible in Tobolsk." But no one thought of retiring to Tobolsk or even to Moscow. What the Russians felt intensely was the shame of allowing the invaders to desecrate Holy Russia, and the ruinous cost of a scorched-earth retreat; what they desired was a crushing victory right on the border. Failing this, their immediate object was to escape encirclement and annihilation. The Rostopchin policy was forced upon them by Napoleon's initial superiority in numbers. They did not "trap" the French into Moscow any more than Joffre trapped the Germans into the Marne. Napoleon did not want to advance indefinitely, and the Russians did not want to retreat. But the crazy logic of the situation was stronger than their intentions.

There were good commanders on both sides, and moves deserving the stock epithet *masterly*. Yet the purely strategic aspect of this great campaign appears almost irrelevant. The objective was not to gain ground, but to break the opponent's will; and the will on either side was hardened by humiliating defeat as well as by elusive victory. The all-important factor was not epic massacre on the battlefield—Smolensk, Valutina-Gora, Borodino, were not decisive—but the humble problem of supplies. Not the climate, as Napoleon alleged in self-excuse. The army was decimated in scorching summer heat, grew anemic in lovely autumn weather, and the intense winter cold after the Berezina only added a touch of horror to its death-throes. The army perished because horses and men could not be fed. An immense service of supplies had been organized. But it was inadequate from the very first, to Napoleon's intense indignation. It could not keep up with the swiftly advancing troops; after the first rains it was bogged in the mire of primitive roads. The foraging parties had to push farther and farther to find a village not yet devoured. Oh, for the idyllic campaigns in Italy and Germany, when the armies were smaller, the countryside richer, and some of the inhabitants friendly!

Russia had two main armies in the field; the principal one under Barclay de Tolly, a Livonian of Scottish origin, the lesser one under Bagration. The two commanders hated and despised each other. Alexander's presence with the troops, far from restoring unity, was a source of confusion. Russia's first victory was scored when the Czar was humbly petitioned to save the country from far in the rear. So the Russian defense was uncertain. A great fortified camp had been created at Drissa, on the advice of a Prussian theorist, Phüll; it would have been a deadly trap, and was abandoned just in time.

Although Napoleon had with him some of his best lieutenants—Davout, Ney, the dashing Murat, King of Naples—his over-all strategy failed from the start. He had hoped to annihilate first Bagration and then Barclay de Tolly: thanks to the ineptitude of King Jerome, Bagration managed to extricate himself, and even Davout could not retrieve the situation; Jerome had to slink back to Kassel. The Russians could be neither bluffed nor thrashed into surrender. At Vitebsk, which he reached on July 28, Napoleon measured the abyss into which fate was luring him. He was incapable of taking counsel: still, he was impressed by the unanimous and desperate pleas of his closest associates. They were Berthier, the ideal Chief of Staff; Duroc, Grand Marshal of the Palace, and a devoted personal friend; Daru, a competent administrator, in charge of supplies; Caulaincourt, whom he was compelled to respect. To their immense relief, he decided: "Here we stop!" But this lapse into comparative sanity could not last. For a few days Napoleon was sullen and restless. Go into winter quarters in early August? Stop without a decision, checked, baffled, his Grand Army threatened with inglorious dissolution? On to Smolensk!

Barclay de Tolly, urged by Bagration and the other generals, made a stand at Smolensk behind antiquated walls. The first assault of the French failed (August 16). The Russians were finally dislodged from the flaming city; but they had lost only 6,000 men to Napoleon's 10,000, and they retreated unbroken. The same problem arose as at Vitebsk, but with more desperate urgency. It would be folly to go farther. This time it was Murat, old companion, brother-in-law, crowned head, who urged the Emperor to stop. He went down on his knees; and as Napoleon proved obdurate, he sought an exposed position, death the only alternative to disaster. His plea was not wholly unheeded. There was a moment of hope: the Emperor was heard to say: "The campaign of 1812 is over." Again his demon would not relent. "We need one earth-shaking battle right at Moscow. It will astound the world. Let the timorous shake their heads: I am through with their advice. . . . Our very peril urges us on." By that time the Grand Army had dwindled to less than one half of its original strength.

So the mighty opponents "agreed to have a battle." Their honor demanded it. Russian opinion, or rather Russian sentiment, would have none of the Scythian strategy. The "masterly" withdrawals of Barclay de Tolly seemed to court and people, as they did to Bagration, the evidence of a craven spirit: Barclay was not a true Russian. The old hero Kutusov, no favorite with the Czar, was made commander-in-chief. He had been one of the best lieutenants of the legendary Suvorov. To be sure, he had shared in the Austerlitz disaster, but the battle had been fought against his advice. Barclay de Tolly loyally accepted to serve under him.

The momentous encounter took place on the banks of the Moskva River, some sixty miles west of Moscow; the Russians call it Borodino (September 7). It was fought on either side with a savage valor unparalleled even at Eylau. Not once but three times Napoleon was urged to send the Guard into battle so as to clinch the wavering victory. He, the man of swift unerring decisions, hesitated. He could see that, without a stunning final blow, Borodino would not be the Austerlitz he was craving for. But the Guard was the backbone of the army, the one force kept in perfect condition: he could not make up his mind to venture it. The marshals resented his holding back the last reserve, thus almost nullifying their heroic endeavors.

As a result, Borodino was not even a Friedland, but an Eylau, an Aspern. Napoleon called it "the hardest and greatest feat of arms in the annals of the Gauls"; but Kutusov announced it as a victory and won his marshal's baton on that claim. He was boldly anticipating Tolstoy's

view of that fierce contest. In sober fact, Kutusov had to
retire, abandoning 45,000 dead, wounded, and prisoners
on the battlefield and leaving the road to Moscow open.
He still had an army unshaken in spirit, proud of having
shown its mettle, but so terribly mauled that it could not
stem the invaders' advance. But Borodino made it palpable that Napoleon could not win. From Smolensk on,
perhaps even from Vitebsk, the Grand Army was a huge
wounded animal, staggering ahead on momentum. In
numbers, equipment, and spirit, its life energy was oozing
out at every step.

Kutusov's army marched sullenly through Moscow.
The bulk of the population went with the troops. A vast
heart-rending exodus of a kind almost forgotten in civilized Europe: our own epoch, alas! was to see again such
human masses driven like frightened sheep. On September 12, at two P.M., Napoleon rode up to the Poklon-
naya Hill: thence he could see the golden cupolas of
Moscow glittering in the sun. The Guard, and the Emperor himself, broke into an exultant cry: "Moscow!"
Milan, Cairo, Vienna, Berlin, Madrid: how many capitals he had entered as a conqueror! But this culminating
triumph was different. No delegation to meet the victor;
no crowd, cheering or even sullen. A few foreigners, a
few stragglers; streets and houses were dead.

That same night, before he had pushed on to the
Kremlin, he was told that the center of Moscow was
ablaze. The fire raged for six days and nights. Most of
the houses were of wood, the weather was dry, the winds
fanned the flames, and no pumps were available. All
that the French could do was to salvage some loot from
the richer residences. The fire had been deliberately set:
the soldiers caught a number of arsonists and shot them
on the spot. It had been ordered by Governor Rostop-

chin. An equivocal personage, an aristocrat who spoke
French at home and tried at the last moment to turn
rabble-rouser in wretched colloquial Russian. Fond of
dramatic phrases and poses, he had sworn: "They shall
not pass!" and left the city with the rest. Later he was
to claim credit, then to deny the responsibility, for the
deed. There may have been moments in which the hero
and the histrion were almost fused in him. The grand
and costly gesture, like most gestures, was futile. About
one fourth of the houses escaped destruction: for nearly
five weeks the soldiers found adequate quarters in the
abandoned city. It was not lack of commodious billets
that compelled the French to leave Moscow.

The "victor" wrote to the "conquered" a strangely
gentle, almost sentimental letter: "I have conducted the
war against Your Majesty without animosity. A line
written to me before or after the last battle would have
stopped my march, and I would gladly have forgone the
advantage of entering Moscow. If anything of our old
friendship remains, Your Majesty will take this letter in
good part." To this touching effusion Alexander vouch-
safed no reply.

The invaders settled down, wearily at first, then with
mounting anguish, in the vast deserted city, gaunt with
the charred corpses of six thousand buildings. For a few
days Moscow was fairly well supplied: not a few peasants, indifferent to the clash of empires, brought their
produce to market. But the army grabbed the goods and
refused to pay, even in the forged currency that Napoleon had prepared; and the rustic carts appeared no more.
In his enforced leisure, Napoleon made pretense that
he was governing his huge empire as if he were at the
Tuileries. The French National Theater was long ruled
by a decree dictated in Moscow.

Again, as at Vilna, Vitebsk, Smolensk, Napoleon was of several minds. He knew that he could neither chase Kutusov's army through the illimitable plains, nor march toward St. Petersburg, nor even organize winter quarters in Moscow. The obvious solution was to consider his raid on the old Russian capital purely as a punitive expedition and a solemn warning that he wanted to be friends with Alexander. This purpose achieved, he could with some show of dignity retire to a less exposed place with a better chance of feeding and recruiting his army. He waited week after week, when every hour told heavily against him. A brief cold snap was a stern reminder: 1807 had taught him the rigors of a northern winter. Prudence at last won a belated victory: on October 20 he left Moscow. As a farewell gesture, he ordered the Kremlin to be blown up; but the fuses were damp and the damage was not irreparable.

The retreat started well enough. The weather was crisp and pleasant; the sole difficulty was the abundance of loot. But, apart from a couple of serious engagements —Maloyaroslavetsz, Vyazma—and of constant skirmishes, the same difficulties as in the advance harassed the return march. Horses and men could not be fed. The country had already been twice gnawed to the bone. Booty, equipment, ammunition, had to be dropped by the wayside. Even if there had been no Cossack patrols, no sharpshooters, no guerrillas, the army was disintegrating into a tattered mob. Four hundred thousand had crossed the Niemen: only one hundred thousand retired from Moscow.

At Dorogobuzh, Napoleon received ominous news. In the northern theater, Wittgenstein was driving back Victor and Oudinot; on the southern flank, the Austrian commander Schwarzenberg, instead of holding his ground against Chichagov, had, perhaps deliberately, allowed him to pass. Strategically, this was a disaster: Chichagov might cut off his retreat. Diplomatically, it was worse still: it was proof that the Austrian alliance, mainstay of Napoleon's policy, was the frailest reed.

What affected him most deeply was a mere episode, already closed, but a symptom he could not ignore. In 1808 General Malet had already plotted against the Empire. He had been confined in a sanatorium: perhaps, like many daring souls, he was in fact half-demented. On October 22, 1812 he escaped, donned a uniform, went to the Popincourt Barracks, announced the death of Napoleon, and showed a fake order from the Senate appointing him Governor of Paris. He liberated his former accomplices Lahorie and Guidal; the bold trio proceeded to arrest Savary, Duke of Rovigo, Fouché's clumsy successor, and Pasquier, Prefect of Police. All was going marvelously well until the conspirators struck General Hulin, hero of the Bastille, and "judge" of the Duke of Enghien. The tough veteran resisted; he was shot down, but his assistants disarmed Malet, and the farce was over. Slight as it was, the crazy plot revealed to Napoleon what Fouché had known since the days of Marengo: the whole fabric of his government would dissolve if it were not for the magic of a single name. It was then that he resolved to leave the army as soon as it was reasonably safe for him to do so, and dash for Paris.

At last Smolensk was reached, on November 10. The staggering and famishing soldiers were hoping for a breathing spell and a square meal. But the city had been destroyed more thoroughly than Moscow; the supplies had been eaten up by Victor's troops; the Russians were in relentless pursuit; it was impossible to pause and reorganize. So the men had to slog away again, now in bitterest cold. Eugene and Davout were forced to fight their way through; Ney, at one time, was completely cut off. Miraculously, he reappeared: never had "the bravest of the brave" displayed more indomitable resourcefulness. But he rallied the main body with only a handful of men. At Orsha, the Grand Army mustered 24,000 soldiers in formation, with some 14,000 stragglers painfully following.

It looked as though Chichagov, Wittgenstein, and Kutusov might unite on the Berezina and capture the last shreds of the once mighty host, the Emperor himself a part of the booty. The crossing of the Berezina, with scenes of incredible confusion and suffering, lives in folklore as the culminating disaster. On the contrary, it was a last despairing victory. For Eblé and Chasseloup-Laubat, chiefs of engineers, managed to build two bridges on the icy river and rebuild them when they broke down. The troops crossed them in ranks to the sound of bugles and drums, an army still. Only the stragglers, who the day before had refused to move, rushed to the bridges in a belated stampede and were killed or captured by the Russians. Ney, in command of the rear guard, managed to hold off Kutusov's attacks. It was then that winter struck with deadly rigor. The thermometer fell to seventeen degrees below zero Fahrenheit. The plain was strewn with frozen corpses. At last, on December 4, the army reached Smorgoni, a few miles short of Vilna.

It was a wonder that even a few should escape in formation, tortured but unsubdued, and their Emperor with them. A wonder of Russian ineptitude? Many thought so at the time and upbraided Kutusov for failing to deal the death blow. His unwillingness to sacrifice

Russian lives did not sound very convincing. Perhaps the old man was as his admirer Tolstoy describes him: sluggish, somnolent, and fatalistic. Perhaps, a Russian of the Russians, he thought too exclusively in Russian terms: the French were leaving and would never return: so why strain yourself in that devastated winter waste where the pursuers suffered hardly less than the pursued? Europe would have been spared three costly years of uncertainty and strife if the Cossacks who once surrounded Napoleon had managed to capture him.

The Emperor thought, or barely hoped, that it would be possible to make a stand at Vilna. At any rate, from there on there could be an orderly retreat. There would be regular supplies, and reinforcements would stiffen the shattered army. So at Smorgoni Napoleon felt he could leave his troops. In the peculiar logic of the imperial system, he was fully justified. Others could guide the tragic return. But Napoleon was France; he alone could hold the regime together, raise new levies, keep his allies in line, create against Europe a still formidable front. The same thought explains the famous Twenty-ninth Bulletin, in which, frankly admitting the disaster ("An act of God; a victory of winter alone"), he calmly concluded: "Never has His Majesty been in better health." To the last, the single article of his creed was: "I, myself, alone, and that suffices."

He had left the army in charge of Murat instead of the abler and more dependable Davout. But King Joachim had caught something of the Napoleonic virus. He too thought that his presence was indispensable in his threatened realm, and he abandoned the army in his turn. It was Eugene, self-sacrificing and modestly competent as was his wont, who brought the army back across the Niemen. The army? Berthier—Marshal Berthier, Chief of Staff, Prince of Neuchâtel—wrote in despair: "There is no army any more."

Meanwhile Napoleon was dashing along, with a small escort of Polish lancers. Through Vilna, Kovno, Warsaw, Posen, Dresden, Leipzig, Erfurt, he rushed unrecognized, Caulaincourt his constant companion. He poured forth a stream of memories, imprecations, and dreams, for he was none of your strong silent men; and Caulaincourt's notes on that tragic journey are to my mind the most fascinating of all Napoleonic documents. On December 18, 1812, at night, an ordinary postchaise deposited its fare, the Emperor of the French, at the Tuileries.

CHAPTER NINE

THE GERMAN AND
THE FRENCH CAMPAIGNS
1813–1814

SO complete was the disaster in Russia that we feel it should have been followed by the immediate collapse of Napoleon's power. Yet it took fifteen months and the combined efforts of all Europe to force him into uncon-ditional surrender.

There is no single solution to this great historical puzzle. The many causes overlapped and at times con-flicted; and Bismarck's *imponderables* must be evoked once more. When the separate traditions, aspirations, selfish interests, and complicated intrigues of twenty states are thrown together, the result is a confused mass. The single will of one man at the head of a single highly organized system enjoys an enormous advantage.

Europe could not overcome all at once the tremendous momentum of French prestige. For two decades—nearly a generation—the French had lost not a few battles, but they had won every war. Not a treaty, from Basel in 1795 to Schönbrunn in 1809, that did not mark a new extension of their imperium. I have already stated that this long series of victories, from Valmy to Wagram, had not created, but had only enhanced the vast and complex glamour that surrounded France. Louis the Great, the French classics, the Paris salons, the *Encyclopedia,* the Rights of Man, had their share in that incomparable treasure which Napoleon appropriated, coarsened, and squandered.

In material terms, it took time for the magnitude of

the disaster to be fully realized. Napoleon could still boast that he had defeated the Russians in the field and captured their capital. Other countries could not rely on grim General Winter to destroy their enemy; and the logistic problems that had proved the undoing of the invaders were far more manageable in central Europe. Napoleon still held strategic positions: Stettin, Danzig, Torgau, Glogau, Küstrin, Magdeburg, Wittenberg, Hamburg, Erfurt, Marienburg. Most of these he kept, like the Nazis their "hedgehogs" and "pockets," until late in 1813; some until 1814. He had lost four hundred thousand men: but ruthlessness is an effective mask for diminished power. He wrote to Eugene: "Hold Berlin as long as you can. Make examples to preserve order. At the least insult from a Prussian village or city, have it burned down; even Berlin, if it does not behave properly." Bluff is a milder method, not to be despised. The Emperor ordered that "the Duke of Ragusa [Marshal Marmont] will pass through the city [Dresden] tomorrow at noon, his troops in parade uniform, taking his guns, and marching in the strictest order. He will send his baggage with everything that does not look well around by way of the pontoon bridge." The Napoleonic army was the finest show on earth, and the Imperator had to be something of an impresario. In the diplomatic field, as 1813 dawned, the whole of Germany—Austria, Prussia, the Confederacy of the Rhine—was nominally on Napoleon's side: York's surrender, to which we shall revert, might have been an isolated act of insubordination. Beyond their borders, the exhausted Russian troops would be powerless. Even Goethe was impressed: in his eyes, the stricken Titan was still invincible.

Napoleon was not doomed in advance except by the inner law of his being. If, early in 1813, he had *boldly* retired within the "natural frontiers" and allowed Europe to dispose freely of the vast spoils, the result would have been a fantastic scramble, during which France, an ironic spectator, would have had time to recuperate. Who knows? Napoleon might even have been called upon to arbitrate. This was to be the policy of Talleyrand at Vienna; carried out by Napoleon a year earlier, it would have saved the Rhine for France, and myriads of lives.

The inescapable fact is that Napoleon was Napoleon. To yield at any point was beyond his capacity: he must dictate. He believed—and posterity, not infallibly wise, has endorsed his belief—that his prestige was due entirely to his military glory, of which his conquests were the tangible signs; whereas it was as a peacemaker and as an administrator that he had established his power. If he abandoned Spain, Italy, Germany, and returned to the frontiers of 1795, he felt, his fabulous halo would pale, and with it his autocratic power at home. Freed from the incubus of war, France would have insisted on liberty, which to him was another word for disorder. He was well aware that the French were craving peace; so he had Maret read in the Senate a declaration of his pacific intentions. But in the same breath he asserted that "none of the countries joined by constitutional ties with the Empire could be the object of negotiations": this would have made it impossible to barter away even the Hanseatic cities or the Illyrian Provinces, which now belonged to the sacred soil of France. So Napoleon's concessions, grudging and belated, were even less sincere than the offers of the Allies. The Allies, being of many minds, might have muddled into moderation: Napoleon's mind was adamant.

The Russian armies were depleted and weary before

they reached the Niemen. Many Muscovites, Kutusov among them, were doubtful about pushing farther. It was Prussia that struck the decisive blow. Prussia, after Jena, had been humbled, disarmed, dismembered, ransacked, oppressed more ruthlessly than any of Napoleon's other victims. And the wounds cut deeper, for Prussia had lived for fifty years on the glorious memories of Frederick the Great; her aristocracy was an officers' corps; her Queen embodied the proudest Prussian spirit. It was from Berlin that Fichte gave his rousing *Addresses to the German Nation*. The Rhinelander Stein had come to serve Prussia because, even in her humiliation, she was the last hope of a resurgent Germany. Hardenberg seconded him. The army had been drastically cut down by the victor. But Scharnhorst, Clausewitz, Gneisenau, gave it a new spirit and, through the training of large reserves, made it capable of rapid expansion. Early in 1813 Prussia, in her reduced state, was able to place as many soldiers at the front as enormous Russia.

The turning from groveling ally to crusader of liberation came, not dramatically, but in a manner that was hesitant and almost furtive. In 1812 the Prussians, under the high command of Marshal Macdonald, fought on Napoleon's side; and, as we have seen, they fought hard. But the French and their auxiliaries were compelled to withdraw after failing to capture Riga. A Russian force managed to separate the Prussian contingent, now under York, from the main body. York desired ardently to go over to the Russians; but he had to consult the King; and the King instructed him, evasively, "to protect Prussian interests." Whereupon York signed an agreement with the Russians at Tauroggen (December 30, 1812) which opened to them the road to Königsberg. Frederick William III feigned indignation: a "beautiful soul," he could not dream of being disloyal to his liege lord Napoleon. The drab truth back of this shining virtue was that Eugene still occupied Berlin. An unwary French ambassador allowed the King to slip away to Breslau (January 22). It was not until March 17 that he struck a formal alliance with the Czar. Three days later he addressed a stirring appeal to his people and to his army. The great German campaign of 1813 had begun.

A lull of four months. A lull? Never, not even in Italy, had Napoleon been so formidably active. He was fighting for his glory alone, against the interests of Europe and of France; but the spectacle of that daimonic energy is awe-inspiring, like that of a great cataclysm. Vanished was the sluggishness that had weighed him down after he turned forty. One would forget that his short figure had grown fat, that his features, once as sharp as a newly minted medal, were now puffy and blurred. He was every inch the Imperator.

He won a last victory. Cajoling and browbeating (*commediante, tragediante,* as Alfred de Vigny would have it), he persuaded the Pope, now his prisoner at Fontainebleau, to sign a new Concordat far more favorable to Cæsar. But the Pope, while yielding, reserved his final assent until he had consulted his Curia; and that last triumph of Napoleon, though it was celebrated with a *Te Deum,* proved illusive.

But his one great concern was to create a new army: for arms were still his *ultima ratio.* He had to call in anticipation the contingent of 1814, to recall discharged soldiers, to draft many who so far had been exempted. The bourgeoisie, his mainstay, watched his efforts with misgivings. As we have seen, their most cherished privilege was that of buying themselves off from fighting, and

Napoleon was coming dangerously near taking it away from them. Among the people, he could not and would not rouse democratic patriotism of the 1792 brand: that would have been akin to Jacobinism, the enemy he had been attempting to crush for ten years. So there were no volunteers flocking to the colors, eager to defend "the nation in her peril": on the contrary, draft-evasion and desertion were rife. The proportion of new recruits to veterans was larger than ever, and the conscripts were sped untrained to the battlefield. Worst of all was the spirit of discouragement among the officers, and especially among the marshals. Napoleon did score one striking success, which might have been symptomatic: Lazare Carnot, the staunch Republican who had refused his advances, rallied to him in this hour of need. He was made Governor of Antwerp, a key position that he defended admirably until the end of the war. On the other hand, Bernadotte and Moreau had now joined his enemies, and Murat, while he joined the Grand Army again, kept negotiating with Austria in order to preserve his throne.

In Germany, Stein, restored to office, was rousing the new, still uncertain national sentiment against the oppressor. Arndt, Körner, Rückert, Schenkendorf, Uhland, with their impassioned addresses and poems, were far more effective than the traditional diplomats. The German princes, still hesitant, were requested by Russia and Prussia to leave the Confederacy of the Rhine or take the consequences. Mecklenburg was the first to secede. The King of Saxony wavered with the tide of battle.

On April 15 Napoleon left Saint-Cloud for the front. The first great encounter was at Lützen, on May 2. The French had a marked numerical superiority, and the Allies, under the nominal command of Wittgenstein, were loosely organized. It was a French victory, and in his proclamation to his troops, Napoleon ranked it higher than Austerlitz, Jena, Friedland, Borodino. He spoke in terms that sound strangely modern: "We will hurl these Tartars back into that fearful clime from which they must never sally forth again. Let them remain in their frozen steppes, the abode of slavery, barbarism, and corruption, where man is reduced to the level of the brute." But the enemies had been pushed back, not shattered. Although Bautzen, on May 20–1, was another sharp defeat for the Allies, it was not the "good battle" of Napoleon's dream.

The raw army had fought well, but it was in poor condition. There was a cruel shortage of ammunition, and a disastrous lack of cavalry for reconnaissance work and sudden blows. Napoleon had to give up the hope of an immediate and triumphant military decision. He had to resort to diplomacy, not fully realizing that time was inexorably working against him. On June 4 an armistice was signed at Pläswitz.

This was the opportunity that Metternich had been awaiting. Austria, if she chose Napoleon's side, could keep the minor German princes in line. She had no trust in Russia or Prussia, and even less love for either. But she was in position to exact her price. Beyond mere rectification of boundaries, what she wanted was the complete withdrawal of the French from Germany and Italy. Austria would then be supreme in both areas, and the peer at least of France in the European field. To make such concessions while still undefeated seemed to Napoleon the height of absurdity. On June 28, at Dresden, the French Emperor and the Austrian Chancellor had a nine-hour discussion, tête-à-tête, one of the stormiest, most dramatic, and most pregnant in history. We

have to rely on Metternich's account, published long
after the event, and manifestly touched up in his favor.
Still, there are few documents in which Napoleon's voice
reaches us so sharp and clear, commanding, angry, vulgar, and sublime, with odd half-sincere drops into famil-
iarity and cordiality. "My honor first, and then peace.
You have no inkling of what goes on in a soldier's mind.
A man like me cares nothing for a million lives. . . .
If it costs me my throne, I'll bury the world under its
ruins." To this magnificent roaring, Metternich *may* have
icily replied: "Sire, you are lost."

The armistice was to expire on July 20; it was prolonged until August 10. When hostilities were resumed,
Napoleon had increased and tautened his forces; but
now England, Russia, Prussia, Sweden, and Austria were
united in a firm alliance. Bernadotte, head of the Northern army, and chief strategic adviser to the coalition, laid
down an excellent rule: always yield ground whenever
Napoleon himself is in command; strike hard at his lieutenants. This was a well-deserved tribute to the Emperor's genius; it was also dictated by the fact that the
Master, naturally enough, always kept the best troops in
his own hands. So Oudinot, Macdonald, Ney, were defeated piecemeal; while the stoutest of them all, Davout,
was holding Hamburg and could take no part in the
main operations. Dresden was still a notable victory for
the French. But it had a tragic epilogue: Vandamme,
rushing to cut off the enemy's retreat, was captured with
seven thousand men.

The French army was dwindling at an appalling rate.
After so many marches and countermarches, the countryside was bare: bread and meat were not available. The
unseasoned recruits, ill-fed and overworked, fell by the
wayside. There were ninety thousand on the sick list.

Numerical superiority was now heavily on the side of the Allies. Bavaria had already gone over to the coalition. The Saxons were to change sides in the course of the coming battle. Against 320,000 men, Napoleon had barely 160,000.

Blücher, Schwarzenberg, and Bernadotte were closing in on Leipzig. The fighting raged for three days. Napoleon won his own victories: his defeats were "acts of God." This time, Providence—or improvidence?—denied him a proper supply of ammunition: "Twenty thousand rounds, and I should have been master of the world!" He could not make up his mind to retreat in time. The premature blowing up of a bridge sacrificed the whole rear guard. Leipzig became known as the *Völkerschlacht*, the Battle of the Nations. It is commemorated by a huge monument of Wagnerian pseudo-barbarism. The German campaign was lost.

The French were in headlong retreat. The Bavarians, under Wrede, attempted to intercept them; but at Hanau the fleeing herd had momentum enough to push aside its former allies. Early in November, out of 300,000 men Napoleon had mustered in midsummer, 60,000 had reached Mainz. On the 7th, Napoleon contemplated the Rhine for the last time and hurried for Paris.

A brief pause. There were three armies on the eastern front, ready for the kill: the Northern, under Bernadotte; the "Silesian," under Blücher; the "Bohemian," under Schwarzenberg.

If he had had all the troops scattered in the German fortresses, and those which Eugene *might* have saved from Italy, and those that Suchet, an admirable soldier, was bringing back from Catalonia, Napoleon would have had enough solid veteran troops to stiffen his raw

levies, those pathetic adolescents who were to be called
the *Marie-Louises*. But all these elements of strength
failed him: for many years the great realist had built on
wishful thinking. Augereau, who was to operate inde-
pendently in southeastern France, never was a great strategist, and never fully loyal to Napoleon. Meanwhile,
the southwest was morally lost. In October 1813 Wellington had crossed the Pyrenees; and Bordeaux was
waiting for a chance to welcome the English and the
Bourbons.

Meanwhile the Emperor liquidated—how belatedly!
—his two worst mistakes: he sent the Pope back to
Rome, Ferdinand VII to Madrid. With his assemblies
he was as curt as ever. If the war was to be fought at
all—and he refused to consider any other solution—the
situation demanded a dictatorship. The Legislative Body
had dared at last to raise its voice: Napoleon declared
the session closed. On January 1, 1814 he vented his
indignation in a typical speech, colloquial, with sudden
flashes of poetry. The pompous Roman mask is torn off;
the man appears in his elemental fierceness: "What is a
throne? Four bits of gilt wood, a scrap of velvet? What
makes the difference is the man who sits on it. . . .
I picked up the crown in the gutter with my sword. . . .
We must wash our dirty linen in the family. . . . You
are but the representatives of local interests: in my hands
alone rests the destiny of the nation."

On December 2 Schwarzenberg had entered France
from Basel and Geneva, in violation of Swiss neutrality.
The main French defenses thus turned, Blücher was
able to cross the Rhine on January 1, 1814, at Coblenz
and near Mannheim. The two generals thus operated according to an over-all plan, but were independent in their
respective zones, a situation fraught with difficulties.

Schwarzenberg, in the grand Austrian tradition, was punctilious and slow. Old Blücher was impetuous: he was to be remembered as *Marschall Vorwärts*. This lack of perfect co-ordination gave Napoleon a series of chances: he could rush from Blücher to Schwarzenberg and inflict a sharp reverse on each. And he was on familiar ground: his first success was scored at Brienne, the site of his old military school. Then came Champaubert, Montmirail, Château-Thierry, Vauchamp. At each of these sharp and fragile victories against adversaries who outnumbered him at least three to one, he ordered triumphal salvos to be fired at the Invalides: the Parisians shrugged their shoulders and the funds fell a few points. From the military point of view this short campaign has remained a classic: it rivals Napoleon's finest achievements in Italy. As sheer drama, this indomitable defiance of the great fighter at bay is magnificent, even though it was criminally futile: the æsthetic realm extends beyond the safe and sane.

There were diplomatic flutters, talks of an armistice, a shadowy and delusive congress at Châtillon. Caulaincourt, the advocate of conciliation, had been called in at last, but far too late, and with no power. The aim of the Allies was now clear: Napoleon must be removed. His heroic obstinacy doomed him: it was evident that he could never learn the ways of peaceful intercourse. And that aim was now within their grasp. Talleyrand, still Vice Grand Elector, sent word to the Allies: "You are crawling on crutches. Fly to Paris: you are awaited." Six years after Erfurt, Talleyrand's prophecy was fulfilled and his hour had come. The Sword was to yield to the Silk Stocking.

Checked at Laon and Craonne, Napoleon was planning a bold counteroffensive in the rear of the Allies,

combined with an uprising of the peasants: a people's
war. France might yet be the tomb of the invaders! He
saw with amazement that his grand strategy was not
countered, but simply ignored. In plainer terms, his bluff
was called: while he was threatening to cut off their
retreat, Schwarzenberg and Blücher were hastening toward Paris. Marmont and Mortier had fallen back to
protect the capital. But their forces were inadequate, and
they could not count on the spirit of the population.
Throughout the country the French were going on strike.
They refused to join the colors and to pay the taxes. Napoleon, especially after 1810, had appointed many royalists to administrative positions: these men could hardly
be expected to nerve the population to resistance. Without a final battle, Napoleon was becoming an isolated
adventurer in his own empire.

Leaving the army in Berthier's hands, he arrived at
Fontainebleau on March 31. He was still urging Marmont and Mortier to resist, were it only for a couple of
days: in what despairing hope we cannot even surmise.
But he learned that they had capitulated the day before,
after a token resistance that was spirited enough at the
Clichy Gate to win Marshal Moncey a statue. Marmont,
a great favorite with Napoleon, had even gone over to
the Allies. On April 2 the Senate voted that the Emperor
be deposed. It justified its action with a full, damning,
and woefully belated indictment of his aggressiveness
and tyranny. Napoleon summoned his marshals to Fontainebleau for a last council: Ney, Lefebvre, Oudinot,
Macdonald, Moncey, Berthier, with Maret, Caulaincourt, and the devoted Bertrand, Duroc's successor. All
urged him to abdicate in favor of his son.

Senators and marshals have been accused of disloyalty

and even of treason. If we accept the dogma that Napoleon was France and could do no wrong, the charge is justified. But there was no treason if they believed—and the fact was palpable—that Napoleon had become the sole obstacle to European peace. There was no disloyalty either: they were not, as is so constantly repeated, his creatures. On the contrary, the Senate still represented the Siéyès element, which had made Napoleon. Most of the marshals had won their spurs before Napoleon became absolute. They accepted their batons from him as the reward of their services, not as a personal favor. They had thought all the time that, in the common enterprise, the lion's share had been exorbitant; and now he was gambling away the fruit of their common efforts for the sake of his personal glory. The first allegiance of senators and marshals was to France, not to an upstart sovereign: it was Napoleon who had betrayed his trust. Their "crime" was not to have rebelled at last, but to have waited so long. At what moment is a man justified in turning against the established government of his country? There is no sure criterion: each historical crisis, each individual case, must be examined on its own merits.

Again Napoleon had waited too long: his abdication in favor of his son was spurned. Nothing would do but complete surrender. At last, on April 12, he signed away that power which had become a shadow. The same night he tried to poison himself. That episode was long shrouded in doubts. The reports were contradictory, and the attempt was not consonant with Napoleon's invincible lust for life. Caulaincourt's testimony, however, is not open to challenge. A Catholic in name only, Napoleon had been brought up in the Roman tradition, which exalts heroic suicide: a great man remains to the last the sole arbiter of his fate. The poison turned traitor: Napoleon was merely sick. On the 13th he was again not merely resigned, but eager to live.

This bleak twilight of a glorious reign was prolonged almost beyond endurance. Napoleon had to wait at Fontainebleau for a whole week, until every detail of the settlement was properly ratified. That his treatment at the hands of the Allies was so mild—indeed, so generous—was due entirely to Alexander. The Czar had followed the armies; he enjoyed, not without cause, a unique prestige among the Allies and even among the French. There were elements of chivalry in his strangely compounded nature. Prussia or the French royalists might have meted out to Napoleon the fate of Pius VII, of Toussaint l'Ouverture, of the Duke of Enghien. Instead of the dungeon or the firing squad, Napoleon was given an estate, the Island of Elba, with a princely income of two million francs per year. He was to retain his imperial title; he could keep a token guard and a miniature court: Cæsar was given Sancho Panza's island to play with.

On April 20, in the court of the White Horse at Fontainebleau, Napoleon bade farewell to a detachment of his Old Guard, kissing the flag and General Petit. No maudlin-ness in that pathetic scene: next to his own glory, the Guard was perhaps the thing he had most genuinely loved.

On his way to his derisory kingdom, he had to face the hostility of his whilom subjects. Lyon, Aix, shouted: "Down with Napoleon!" Augereau issued an insulting proclamation. At Orgon, beyond Tarascon, he saw himself hanged in effigy, and a surging mob made him tremble for his life. For safety, he had to borrow the hat and cloak of the Austrian commissioner. At Fréjus he was courteously received with a royal salute of twenty one guns by the English man-of-war that was to transport him. He boarded the ship, the *Undaunted*, on April 28. On that very coast, only fifteen years before, he had landed from Egypt. On May 3, after a stormy passage, he reached his Lilliputian empire.

Marie-Louise had been given the Duchy of Parma, and Metternich had committed her to the care of General Count von Neipperg. This dashing one-eyed hero and diplomat fulfilled his task to Marie-Louise's perfect satisfaction: after Napoleon's death they contracted a morganatic marriage and had three children. When Neipperg died, the Duchy was administered by a handsome if severe French aristocrat, Bombelles, who was duly promoted from majordomo to morganatic Prince Consort. The King of Rome, become Duke of Reichstadt, lived in Vienna with his doting grandfather. For Marie-Louise, her four years on the French throne were hardly even an unpleasant memory.

CHAPTER TEN

ELBA AND THE HUNDRED DAYS
1814–1815

THE RETURN from Elba is the most spectacular episode in Napoleon's amazing career: one man, alone, reconquering an empire. Our purpose is not to belittle, but to understand. What kind of regime was it that Napoleon swept aside with such contemptuous ease: granite or pasteboard?

Napoleon's rule had lasted so long only because the dissatisfied could not agree on a substitute. A republic? But the name still evoked the Terror, and Thermidorian corruption; it was smeared with mire and blood. The Duke of Orléans? It was the solution to which Talleyrand and Lafayette were to rally in 1830: "a French Revolution of 1688." The prince, forty-one when Napoleon tottered, was shrewd, and tempered by adversity. But during the twenty years of his exile he had lived in isolation, at times in poverty. He had no organized party; he was profoundly unknown in France. A man fighting under a foreign flag, like Bernadotte? Preposterous! To give Napoleon an acceptable successor would have required long and laborious preparations. As early as 1808, Talleyrand felt convinced that Napoleon must be removed. But the chief characteristic of Talleyrand was his lazy opportunism. He was farsighted, but not courageous enough to venture out and meet trouble. He was first of all an epicure: wine, women, and whist. His most memorable advice to his subordinates was: "Above all, be not zealous." So he drifted into Bourbonism because, although it was the worst possible solution, it was the only one that was ready-made.

The Bourbons had to be rediscovered. They were as forgotten as the Stuarts. Aimée de Coigny laughed in 1812 when a friend suggested a Bourbon restoration. Yet a few months later it was through her that Talley-rand came into contact with Vitrolles, the daring and pertinacious agent of the Pretender. In 1802 the ex-Bishop of Autun had reached a sort of winking peace with Rome. Now he received assurances that he would be *persona grata* with Louis XVIII. So he started pre-paring the way for a return of the Bourbons. But without zeal.

To prepare France for the Bourbons was the lesser half of the work: Chateaubriand, the only great writer of the age, was an effective propagandist.[1] It would have been wise to prepare the Bourbons for France. Louis XVIII, after his quarter of a century of exile and ob-scurity, was eager to return. Selfish and frivolous, he was no fool and no bigot. He had little desire to play the part of an autocrat. Approached in time, he would have ac-cepted intelligent terms: a constitution frankly acknowl-edging the principles of 1789 and, as a symbol, the tri-color flag. As a matter of fact, these were the stipulations of the Imperial Senate when it deposed Napoleon and recalled the Bourbons—adding, with dignified effron-tery, special guarantees for its own honors and emolu-ments. England and the Czar would undoubtedly have favored such a moderate solution. In the enthusiasm

---

[1] In his essay *On Buonaparte and the Bourbons, and on the Necessity of Rallying to Our Legitimate Princes for the Happi-ness of France and of Europe,* written in October 1813, an-nounced for publication on March 31, 1814. "Worth an army of a hundred thousand men to the Princes." At least, Chateau-briand thought so.

of the moment, the King's brother, the Count of
Artois, nodded approval to everything: "Nothing is
changed in France: there is only one Frenchman the
more."

But by that time the Bourbons, thoroughly unde-
sired, had become the only practicable solution. They
need not submit to terms. The King was surrounded by
émigrés whom their long years of impotence had nar-
rowed, warped, embittered. Of them it was said that
they had "learned nothing and forgotten nothing." So
they rejected, as Rousseauism and revolution, the idea
of a contract between sovereign and people. The King
ruled by right divine. He only consented to "bestow" a
charter on his subjects: a free gift of his grace, and
freely revokable. 1814 was "the nineteenth year of his
reign": the Revolution and the Empire were expunged
from the record. And as a sign of this uncompromising
return to the ancient regime, royal France tossed away
the tricolor that Louis XVI himself had accepted, and
returned to the white flag and the golden lilies. This
disastrous turn could have been averted with a modicum
of foresight and energy. Talleyrand refused to cross the
bridge until he came to it, but it turned out to be the
wrong bridge.

In the diplomatic field, at any rate, the disowning,
not only of Napoleonic imperialism, but of the Revolution and its great principles, had the anticipated result:
the treaty between the Allies and the restored French
monarchy (Paris, May 30, 1814) was remarkably
mild. France retained, not only her boundaries of 1792,
but Avignon, Savoy, and a few strongholds on the
northeastern frontier. No war indemnity, while imperial France had exacted so much. Even the works of
art looted for twenty years were not reclaimed. And the

restored Bourbons resumed at once their place in the councils of Europe, a place second to none. Talleyrand represented Louis XVIII at the Congress of Vienna with unbowed head—indeed, with his familiar touch of princely insolence. After all, Louis was the only sovereign who had never made peace with Napoleon. As a balm to dynastic vanity, this policy was an incomparable achievement. The French people refused to take it seriously.

Unfortunately, because Talleyrand had been forced to accept the Bourbons on their claim of legitimacy, not on the basis of national consent, he was compelled to play the same card at Vienna, and the results were disastrous. He was right in abandoning without haggling all the fortified places still held by French troops: they were not genuine assets. He might have secured Belgium; and he might have installed some friendly sovereign like the King of Saxony on the Rhine, instead of the inimical and insatiable Prussians. In the confused Europe of 1814, now that sheer military adventure had been ruled out, three forces were at work: the national and democratic, still inchoate and frankly revolutionary; the bourgeois liberal, seen at its best in England; and the traditionalist, legitimist, or absolutist, represented by Austria. We may easily forgive Talleyrand for not anticipating Woodrow Wilson and his principle of self-determination; but if he had not capitulated to circumstances, he might have worked for genuine constitutional liberty, the Enlightenment without revolution. Instead, he constantly harped on legitimacy, in which he himself had no faith. Legitimacy fastened upon central Europe thirty years and more of the Metternich regime, as dull and heavy as lead. It gave his clients, the Bourbons, a temporary advantage, but it created a gulf between

them and modern France. It must be noted that Talleyrand was soon to be discarded by the Bourbons, and
that he turned against the regime he had done so much
to create. His many apostasies are the signs of his repeated blunders.

It was not the Bourbons as men that France resented:
it was *legitimacy*. As Napoleon had prophesied, when
he disappeared there was a universal *Ouf!*—a sigh of
immense relief. France would have been satisfied for a
while with a humdrum government, but the white flag
was a provocation. It made twenty-five momentous
years of French history *illegitimate;* it definitely por-
tended reaction without a check. Imponderables again:
the acts of the monarchy were moderate enough. At its
worst, the Restoration was more liberal than Napoleon
at his best. But behind Napoleon there stood the principles of 1789, much as he had attempted to whittle
them down. Behind Louis XVIII there loomed a
clerico-feudal regime, Spanish rather than French, from
which France had escaped with Henri IV two hundred
years before. A phantom? But if you believe in it, what
will strike more terror than a phantom?

Apart from this fundamental discord, there were many
causes of discontent. The veterans were sent home with
scant pay and less praise; from heroes they were turned
into beggars and treated little better than bandits. Many
officers with a splendid record were put on half pay,
while popinjays from the emigration filled the new Royal
Guard. Peace had come, but the most objectionable
taxes were not lightened. The end of the great blockade
flooded the market with British goods: the industries
built up under protection were threatened with bankruptcy. While the aristocracy—including Josephine—
were entertaining the Allies, the masses, and even part

of the bourgeoisie, looked upon the new regime with a contemptuous indifference tinged with dread.

All this is general history; but it is also an indispensable part of Napoleon's biography. A destiny is not sheer creation: it is energy molded by circumstances. Obviously a lesser man—and a saner man—could not have taken advantage of the opportunity. On the other hand, even a stronger man would have been stopped at the first move, had Louis XVIII been a Henri IV, had not the whole Restoration been a senile ghost, at the same time frightening and impotent.

The Congress was dancing in Vienna when the news burst like the trump of doom: "HE has escaped!" Thereupon the assembled powers solemnly declared him an outlaw. No compromise: to maintain himself, he would have to defeat Europe singlehanded.

For ten months Napoleon had been pretending to busy himself with his tiny domain. Pathetically, he had passed reviews and held court. More sensibly, he had explored every nook and cranny of the island and attended to the iron mines. His letters to Marie-Louise went unanswered; perhaps unopened.[2] But Marie Walewska came to visit him, with their little son. Mme Letizia, whom he revered, and Pauline, the irresponsible and seductive, whom he loved, joined him. His bruises were healing. His spirit—he was only forty-five—was soaring again.

He knew that the Fontainebleau settlement that had given him Elba was precarious. The French government—pardonably—refused to pay the pension that had been promised in its name. His guard was an expensive

---

[2] On January 3, 1815 she sent him a curiously dutiful and coolly affectionate letter. It was the last.

toy, and his funds were running low. The Allies had misgivings about his living so close to Italy, which was in ferment. They were considering a safer place of seclusion, and St. Helena was already mentioned. Above all, the Emperor received news from every visitor that the Restoration, imposed by the victors (this was not quite the truth), had no inner strength. Now that the foreign troops had been withdrawn, it would collapse at a push. Napoleon remembered his return from Egypt and took heart. This would be the most daring of his gambles.

The watch over the island must have been extremely lax. While the British Commissioner, Colonel Campbell, was on a trip to Leghorn, Napoleon could do as he pleased. Elba had a "navy," the brig *Inconstant*. A few smaller craft, fishing smacks and ore-carriers, were chartered or commandeered. On February 26 the Emperor, with twelve hundred men, left Porto Ferraio. On March 1 the diminutive armada reached the bight of Juan, near Cannes. The landing was unopposed.

As soon as he trod French soil, Napoleon issued a proclamation in his best martial vein: "Soldiers! We were not defeated! Your general, called to the throne by the voice of the people, is back among you. . . . Put on the tricolor cockade: it was the one you wore on our great days. . . . Victory will rush charging ahead. The Eagle, bearing the national colors, will fly from steeple to steeple until it rests on the towers of Notre-Dame."

Napoleon avoided the obvious route, the valley of the Rhône. His experience ten months before had been a warning. And Masséna was in command at Marseille, a determined soldier who had served him well, but who had no love for him. So he went through the Alps, and for days vanished in that grand and lovely wilderness. The villagers, delighted with the excitement, came out to meet him and marched for a while with his little column. The test was Grenoble, the first city with a garrison. General Marchand, in command, sent out a battalion to arrest him. Never was Napoleon seen to better advantage. He went alone ahead of his own troops, opened his coat, and called out: "Soldiers of the Fifth Regiment! Do you recognize me? If anyone wants to kill his Emperor, let him do so." The royal officers gave the order to fire; the soldiers rushed in a frenzy of devotion to hail the risen demigod. Here the heroic and the histrionic blended to perfection. Napoleon loved to pose as a realist and professed to despise all men: yet he could also gamble on their chivalry. Young Colonel Labédoyère was sent against him with the Seventh Regiment: he too went over to his old chief, and five months later was to pay for his defection with his life. Grenoble opened its gates and illuminated its streets. General Marchand and the royalist officers had fled.

To the government, basking in its "legitimacy" and unaware of its own fragility, the enterprise, at first, appeared preposterous. When, after Grenoble, the affair appeared in a more serious light, the Bourbons did not take instant flight. The royal princes, Artois, Angoulême, Berry, went out to face the menace. The Duchess of Angoulême, "the only man in the family," attempted to hold Bordeaux. They were heartened by the support of some of the most glorious among the marshals. Soult, who thought he had drastically purged the army of dangerous Napoleonic elements, declared: "The man is an adventurer!" Ney vowed that he would bring him back to Paris in an iron cage.

Meanwhile, on March 10 Napoleon had reached Lyon. The response of the populace was enthusiastic and at the same time ominous. What Napoleon could read in the thunderous applause and on the vociferating, passionate faces was not loyalty to him, but intense hatred of the Restoration. It was the Revolution rising up again, and Napoleon recoiled. We know that he hated democracy, which he chose to confound with mob rule. An aristocrat of sorts, and a soldier through and through, he would never consent to be the Emperor of the Jacobins.

Three days later he resumed his march. Ney now had misgivings about that iron cage. He felt that his troops were wavering: in spite of Soult's efforts, there had been no total transfusion of royalism into the veins of the army. Ney received a message from Napoleon: "Come to me, and I shall embrace you as I did after the battle of the Moskva!" The marshal assembled his command, and gave the word: "The cause of the Bourbons is lost forever!" And they shouted the logical answer: "Long live the Emperor!" At Auxerre, Ney fell into Napoleon's arms.

With a chosen band, the Emperor hurried on to Paris. Then he left even those few behind, and went ahead almost alone in a postchaise. He reached the capital on the evening of March 20. All day the city had been tense with surmise. Thousands of horsemen, waving their sabers, formed an improvised escort. The six hundred officers and dignitaries who were waiting for him at the Tuileries received him with tears of joy. France had been granted a crowning miracle. As for Louis XVIII, he had ponderously skipped away twenty-four hours before.

For nearly one hundred days, wherever he went, Napoleon was hailed with delirious enthusiasm. Just beyond that pageantry of triumph he could feel the void and the cold: France was not with him. His terrible solipsism, his lonely pride, raised him above vanity: he alone could deceive himself, and this time he was not deceived. There were in him a madman, a poet, a supreme technician, and a morose realist. The realist had the last word: he said: "They allowed me to return as they allowed the Bourbons to depart." France had been reconquered in three weeks without a shot. But this most glorious of his campaigns was only a luminous, evanescent streak. The implacable reality was infinite weariness, skepticism, and gloom.

No more "legitimacy" for Napoleon. He could no longer pose as "the nephew of Louis XVI": Louis XVIII had spoiled that game for him. No democratic uprising either: the one constant note in his career was his refusal to be the Emperor of the Reds. His sole concession to democracy was the plebiscite: a question from on high: "Myself, or chaos"; no discussion; and a thundering assent: *Vox Populi.* As it was in the beginning of his power, so it remained to the very end: Napoleon had to seek support in the middle class, the Believers in Property. But he complained that Louis XVIII had spoiled his bourgeoisie for him. Pale, equivocal, vaguely threatening, the Restoration was none the less a constitutional government. Dissenting opinions could be voiced in the chambers and in the press. The bourgeoisie had recovered their power of speech after ten years of imperial silence: they could not be hushed again. If Napoleon was to remain on the throne, it would have to be, not as the victor of Austerlitz, but as an amended version of Louis XVIII—at least until he had won another Austerlitz.

The thought was highly distasteful, but he acknowledged the necessity. His solipsism was not unmitigated madness: he could bow to "the force of things." And boldly, since people wanted a liberal constitution, he went straight to the Mother of the Liberal Church, the Fifth Great Power, the indomitable bluestocking Mme de Staël—his pet aversion. He could not appeal to her directly. But he called on her disciple and more than friend Benjamin Constant. Constant had sworn a mighty oath that he would never have any truck with the tyrant. Now he and his friends worked on the desperate hypothesis that the leopard could change his spots. Constant produced a standard parliamentary constitution with a strong British accent: two chambers, with ministers responsible to them. This British pattern implied a sovereign placed above politics—that is to say, above action: a gilded figurehead. Napoleon winced at every article: "You are binding my hands. No one will recognize me in that garb." But he yielded with his fingers crossed. Give him his "one good battle," and how soon would the constitution find its way into the scrapbasket! As the only sop to his vanity, he insisted that the new document, so flatly contradicting the spirit of his previous reign, should be modestly called: *An Additional Act to the Constitutions of the Empire.*

He gathered at once a surprisingly good team. Caulaincourt, a good Frenchman, a good European, a true liberal, ready to serve Napoleon loyally, was put in charge of Foreign Affairs. His many virtues were of no avail, for Europe held him incommunicado. Lazare Carnot was entrusted with the Interior, a guarantee that the

Bourbon reaction would be checked and even reversed. Davout was Minister of War. And there was another star of the first magnitude, even though a baleful one: Fouché. He was on hand when Napoleon returned. With a mixture of fascination and loathing, Napoleon offered him his old portfolio, the Police. And Fouché performed his task well: the scattered uprisings in the west petered out. Fouché had passed the word that it would be wiser to wait.

The Chamber, elected by indirect suffrage, represented, as Napoleon thought it should, the notables, the interests, the well-to-do. But they would no longer consent to have power snatched from them, as it had been in 1800, when their leader Siéyès was shoved aside. They watched Napoleon's conversion to liberalism with undisguised incredulity, and they were not slow to manifest their independence. Napoleon wanted his brother Lucien to be President of the Representatives: Lanjuinais was elected instead, with Lafayette as Vice-President. Both were committed to making the Constitution a reality. A plebiscite to ratify the new regime was ordered. The vast majority of the nation took no part in it. Whether the million and a half who took the trouble to vote were endorsing the liberal Constitution or the anti-liberal Emperor, history will never know. Everyone felt that all this was shadow-play. The one reality was the coming war.

It could not be averted: Napoleon's oaths of pacific intentions fell upon deaf ears. Fouché, more successful than Caulaincourt, did manage through his agent in Basel to establish contact with the enemy. His desire was to gauge realities: if there had been a chance of negotiating on behalf of Napoleon I, or at least of Napoleon II, he would have done so. Nothing would have suited his book so well as a regency of his own making, in which he would have had the substance of power. But Napoleon had men spying on his own police. He was informed of the transaction and roundly accused Fouché of treason: "You are a traitor, Fouché! I ought to have you shot!" "Sire," the great police chief replied, "I beg to disagree." The same scene had occurred in 1810. Again Fouché kept his temper, his life, and his job.

A great ceremony had been planned to announce the results of the plebiscite. It was called the Field of May, a Carolingian reminiscence, but did not take place until the 1st of June. It was held in the historic Champ-de-Mars, then a vast sandy waste. Napoleon appeared in a gorgeous court costume that struck a false note: the legendary green uniform, the plain hat with the penny cockade, would have been truer to the spirit of the hour. For this was no idle pageant: it was a solemn vigil before the ordeal of war. The reading of the Constitution was boring: who cared for legal phrases? The thrill came when the troops passed in review and Napoleon gave them new eagles. He asked each unit to swear allegiance to the restored Empire; and they shouted back: "We swear it!" Then they marched into the gathering night, after this supreme salute to Cæsar.

Napoleon did not dare to order a *levée en masse*. He called for 700,000 men, including the soft and shaky National Guard. Davout managed to get him 400,000, of whom 200,000 were available for action, 125,000 ready for an immediate offensive. It was a far cry from Carnot's 1,200,000 in 1793, but it was far more than he had had in Italy. And it was a good army: wholesale draft-evasion had purged it of the less reliable element, and it had a large proportion of veterans. The command was the weak point. Of the marshals, only Soult and Ney, who had turned their coats as the Bourbons fell, were available. Mortier was willing, but sick. Davout was kept in Paris at the War Office. Grouchy, just made a Marshal, had the reputation of a good cavalry officer, but he had never commanded an independent corps.

The nearest enemy forces were in Belgium under the supreme command of Wellington. One army, composed of North German, Dutch, and British troops, was under Wellington's direct orders. The other army was Prussian, and led by Blücher. As usual, the Allies had failed to gauge Napoleon's rapidity: he was upon them before they had established close contact. Napoleon's plan was to destroy Blücher first, and he detached Ney to seize Quatre-Bras so as to hold off Wellington. But Ney, bewildered by his sudden conversions, had lost his nerve, and fumbled. The contest with Blücher took place at Ligny on June 16. The Prussians were routed; Wellington put it bluntly: they got "a damn'd good hiding." They lost 12,000 men; the old Marshal himself, thrown from his horse, was nearly killed. Had Ney secured Quatre-Bras in time and rallied to Napoleon, Ligny might have been another Jena-Auerstädt. Napoleon ordered Grouchy to pursue the fleeing army and complete its destruction. Then he turned to Wellington.

Wellington withdrew his troops from Quatre-Bras after a sharp encounter and took his position behind a ridge on Mont-Saint-Jean (Waterloo was his headquarters, far in the rear, and played no part in the battle). His one hope was to hold until Blücher could re-form and join him. It was a curiously elementary battle: Wellington, his lines once drawn, could not maneuver, and Napoleon, in Henri Houssaye's terms, "disdained to maneuver." There was no intuition, no sudden grasping

of a miraculous opportunity. Even his daimonic activity
failed him at the supreme moment: before the battle, his
generals were dismayed by his puffy, lardy face and lack-
luster eyes. Waterloo was a contest, not of skill, but of
courage. Two brands, equally precious: the fury of the
attack, the tenacity of the defense. Ney, in particular,
in mental confusion and welling-up despair, repeatedly
sent admirable troops to senseless destruction, and kept
clamoring for more.

As the afternoon dragged on, it looked as though the
slogging match would end in a costly French victory.
But both armies knew that the decision would come from
outside. Napoleon hoped that Grouchy and his 30,000
men, after scattering Blücher's troops, would rally the
main forces in time for the kill. But the Prussians, under
the temporary command of Gneisenau, were able to
elude pursuit, reorganize, leave Grouchy wandering.
They made straight for the main battle. Several detach-
ments reinforced Wellington in the course of the afternoon. Finally Blücher himself, all bandaged up and, as
he ruefully said, "somewhat stinking," arrived just as a
desperate assault of the French had failed.

The news immediately spread through the fighting
lines; hope changed camps. Wellington ordered the
attack; the French resistance collapsed. After hours of
heroic tension, the sudden Gorgon face of disaster created a panic. There are few such headlong routs in the
annals of France. Among the troops which, in square
formation, protected Napoleon's retreat, there was no
disordered flight, but a somber unbowed withdrawal.
The Guard fought well to the end, though Cambronne
avers that he used neither of the historic phrases ascribed
to him.[3] Grouchy, whose corps was intact, managed to

_____

[3] "The Guard dies but never surrenders." "*Merde.*"

rally some of the stragglers. On the morrow of Waterloo, there still was a French army.

There were many errors and many elements of chance
in his brief campaign. Things need not have happened
exactly in this fashion. So innumerable writers, Robert
Aron and H. A. L. Fisher among them, have wondered:
"What if Napoleon had won at Waterloo?" The answer is plain: Waterloo would have come a few weeks
later and gone by another name. For Europe was roused
and united. One million men were on the march. The
France of 1793 might have met them, but the France
of 1815 was not with Napoleon.

On the 18th, Paris had been filled with rumors of a
great victory; on the 19th, official silence, and a rising
flood of anguish; on the 20th, the truth was known. On
the 21st, at eight in the morning, the now familiar postchaise brought Napoleon back to Paris.

What was to be done in this collapse of a world?
Lucien, Carnot, Davout, an impressive trio, urged Napoleon to seize a Dictatorship of Public Salvation (here
Public Safety would be too tame a term). He rejected
their suggestion. Not that he had lost his nerve: he was
full of energy still, even of bluster, and was neither penitent nor resigned. But now we find in him again the
same coexistence, or rapid alternation, of mad gigantic
dreams and sharpest realistic vision. In whose name
would he seize power, the people's or his own? Pure
Napoleonism, blind faith in the invincible hero, was a
dead horse. And, we must repeat, he would not become
the Messiah of the Mob: that would have been the
negation of his whole career. Nothing could be done
without the bourgeoisie; that is to say, without the
Assemblies.

The Chambers made it plain that he would have to give up the throne. Two days were wasted in shilly-shallying, with some eloquence as a by-product. On the 23rd he signed his abdication in favor of his son. The Chambers ratified the act; there were cries, numerous and hearty enough, of *Long Live Napoleon II!* Yet all must have felt that these solemn and momentous decisions were meaningless. The Allies were far more determined against the Napoleonic dynasty than they had been in 1814; they were more powerful; they would have been more ruthless. But the Chambers, if they were not Napoleonist, were bitterly opposed to the Bourbons. They raised the frail obstacle of Napoleon II against the threat of the White reaction. In confusion and despair, they did not even follow the twisty logic of their own policy. They acclaimed Napoleon II, but they failed to proclaim him.

Realism is a word that stands for no single reality. As a rule it denotes selfishness and cowardice. But it can also mean the courage to follow plain common sense. Then its first axiom is: "Do not break your skull against a stone wall." Napoleon was realistic in the best sense of the term when he refused to seize a senseless dictatorship. The politicians were not: their thought was an uneasy blur. Then Fouché took hold of the situation, and posterity branded him a villain for his pains.

Historical condemnations are based upon might-have-beens. A sober republic with Carnot, a constitutional monarchy sponsored by Lafayette, a regency guided by Fouché, would have been excellent solutions. But in June 1815 they simply were not available. Retrospectively, we may conceive of a Provisional Authority, rejecting Napoleon, condemning his latest aggression, requesting immediate peace, but at the same time maintaining the right of the French people freely to choose its own form of government. It did not happen. The only decision arrived at was to maintain the Empire with Napoleon II; and that decision would not stand against the first blast of Prussian guns.

The problem was to have a government that the Allies would recognize before Blücher reached Paris, and Blücher was marching fast. Not that the Prussians were barbarians—modern Huns, to revive William II's unforfortunate phrase. But the return from Elba had caused among them a recrudescence of "Holy Wrath." In that mood they might easily have yielded to the temptation to give the incorrigible French a taste of their own medicine. Remember that Napoleon, as a farewell gesture, had attempted to blow up the Kremlin; and that he had instructed Eugene to burn down Berlin, if it did not behave. What if Paris "did not behave"? The men who sang Luther's choral on the battlefield of Waterloo might later, like Luther in the Peasants' War, have shrieked: "Kill them all!" Wrath is all the more terrible for being holy. Against this very real, this now forgotten peril, the Bourbons, who had kept in close touch wtih Wellington, were the only possible shield.[4]

Everyone felt, without acknowledging it, that Fouché was the man of the hour. In working for an unpalatable solution, not of his own choice, he was no doubt attempting to save his skin, his title, his wealth. This is not irrelevant, but it is secondary. He had to maneuver, for the Chambers were committed to the impossible; and he maneuvered with his well-tried skill. He sent La-

---

[4] History affords a miniature indication of the danger and of the remedy. Blücher, after entering Paris, was determined to blow up at least the Jena Bridge. Louis XVIII sent word: "Wait till I have reached the bridge; then you will blow me up with it." The bridge was saved.

fayette on a diplomatic wild-goose chase: a congenial assignment for the Hero of Two Worlds. He managed to get himself instead of Carnot elected as Chairman of the Provisional Commission, which he deftly turned into a Provisional Government. His agents had never lost touch with the English and with Louis XVIII.

The immediate difficulty was the presence of Napoleon. To arrest him might have caused a revulsion of feelings, perhaps an insurrection or a military coup: some of the Napoleonists, having ventured all, were in a desperate mood. He must be urged to depart, with gentle but unrelenting insistence.

He had retired from the Élysée (his Tuileries days were over) to La Malmaison, where Josephine had died a year before. There fate granted him a few days of bittersweet repose. The young summer was perfect; the rose gardens were lovely beyond compare. La Malmaison had seen his honeymoon with power and glory in the magic early days of the Consulate. It was still fragrant with the memories of Josephine, who, in spite of all, had been his first, ardent, and enduring love. "Ah!" he told Hortense, "how happy we could be if only they would allow us to live here!"

But General Becker, his appointed escort, was becoming urgent. Rumors were spread that Prussian patrols had reached the vicinity of La Malmaison. On June 29 Napoleon consented to move at last. His destination was Rochefort, a minor naval base between Nantes and Bordeaux, and like them a river port. In the neighboring roadstead, two frigates were waiting, among the fastest in the French service. They were to take him to America. The party made good time; it reached Rochefort on July 3. On the road, Napoleon was recognized, but neither insulted nor cheered. Joseph, who had joined him on the way, embarked at once with a few friends and sailed off unimpeded. On the same day, July 3, H. M. Louis XVIII, the Unwanted, entered his good city of Paris "in the baggage train of the enemies."

Again a tantalizing vista of the Might-Have-Been! Imagine Napoleon, instead of Joseph, reaching the Western Hemisphere at the very moment when the Spanish colonies were shaking off their yoke! But Napoleon was still reluctant to go. For days he showed that fatalistic and fatal indecision which was as much part of his nature as his power of swift intuition and action. As in the Spanish affair, as in the Russian campaign, he saw the perils of procrastination, yet he could not make up his mind. He still vaguely hoped, without daring to hope, for a sudden twist of fate: a falling out among the Allies, an uprising of the French people. The one thing that reached him was a formal order for his arrest. The trap, half open ten days before, was closing inexorably. The British squadron patrolling the coast, aware of his presence, was fully alerted. His very last chance now was to escape in disguise on a small coastwise vessel. Napoleon could face any gamble, even the maddest, provided it was of a heroic nature, but not a gamble with the ridiculous. The fallen titan could not be discovered sneaking among barrels: that farcical possibility was ruled out.

So, on July 14, he determined at last to face the inevitable. He had moved to the small island of Aix. He penned a letter to the Prince Regent of England:

"Your Royal Highness: Exposed to the factions that divide my country, and to the enmity of the powers of Europe, I have closed my political career, and I come, like Themistocles, to claim hospitality at the hearth of the British people. I place myself under the protection of their laws, which I request from Your Royal Highness as the most powerful, the most constant, and the most generous of my foes."

A grand gesture: Alexander, who had a fine sense of sentiment and drama, would have played up to it. Posterity applauded that dignified exit. Again, the gesture was theatrical, but not histrionic. Napoleon was playing his part in all sincerity, with a touch of swagger like the heroes of Corneille. A gambler and a fighter, he was ready to shake hands as soon as the bout was over. Before we condemn the British for their icy lack of response, we should remember what the game, the fencing bout, had been. After ten years of aggression, Napoleon had been treated by his victors with great consideration; and he had broken loose to start on the same mad career again. This time no drunkard's promise would avail. France was to shoot Labédoyère and Ney for becoming his accomplices: the principal could hardly have expected leniency. And Murat, who staged a pitiful little return from Elba of his own, was summarily shot as a matter of course.

This surrender winds up the strange interlude known as the Hundred Days. Where glamour, not reason, is the guide, it seems incredibly mean to inquire into the cost. Napoleon himself once said: "One can't make an omelet without breaking eggs." When the omelet goes up in smoke, one may be pardoned for regretting the waste of eggs. Some fifty thousand lives blotted out or crippled; a harsher treaty lopping from France Savoy and a number of northeastern places; an indemnity of seven hundred million francs; the Restoration more bitterly committed to reaction than ever—such was the bill, and it was not light. For that heavy price, France added a colorful episode to her checkered history, including the memory of the most complete rout in her long military annals.

The die was cast: on July 15, Napoleon donned his uniform and had himself rowed over to the British man-of-war *Bellerophon,* Captain Maitland. He was taken to Torbay, then to Plymouth Sound, and transferred to H.M.S. *Northumberland,* under the command of Admiral Sir George Cockburn. The ship sailed on August 8 and reached St. Helena on October 15. Napoleon's active career was over; his most astounding and most successful campaign was ahead.

CHAPTER ELEVEN

EPILOGUE

ST. HELENA, 1815–1821. PARIS, 1840

ST. HELENA is a small island, some forty-seven square miles of crags and vales, ten miles across at its widest. Lost in the solitude of the southern Atlantic, twelve hundred miles from the African coast, it belonged in 1815 to the East India Company and was much used as a port of call for fresh water, vegetables, and fruit. Steam navigation did away with the necessity of revictualing, and the population has greatly dwindled: from six thousand to barely three. It is neither the barren rock nor the green hell of popular imagination: the landscape is varied and attractive, the climate temperate and healthy. It may be that in Napoleon's time some poorly drained parts bred malaria.

After a short stay at the Briars, the home of a wealthy merchant, Napoleon was moved to Longwood, where he remained until his death. It was an unpretentious but acceptable abode: it had been built for the lieutenant governor.

The material conditions of Napoleon's captivity— the number of rooms at his disposal, the retainers allowed him, the budget of his household, the range of his walks, rides, or drives—are of little importance. Most political or military prisoners, the field marshals of the Third Reich for instance, would have considered Napoleon's lot an enviable one. The source of Napoleon's complaints is found in his letter to the Prince Regent: he had expected to be treated as an honored guest, and found himself a distinguished prisoner. It was the plain fact of captivity that rankled.

So there was a minor St. Helena campaign directed against Perfidious Albion in the person of the Governor. Sir Hudson Lowe was an officer with a modest but creditable record. Oddly enough, he had commanded a brigade of Corsican Volunteers. Montholon, a member of Napoleon's little court, found Sir Hudson able, courteous, and not unfriendly. Still, he had been appointed as a jailer, not as a master of ceremonies. After the experience at Elba it was natural that some precautions be taken. Every one of these restrictive measures, however, reminded Napoleon that he was a captive. Then the British Government had never acknowledged the Empire. To Sir Hudson, his charge was officially General Bonaparte. Napoleon could not admit that the fabric of his dream had dissolved: "But I really *am* an Emperor!" Between the two men no social contact was possible: they negated each other's basic assumptions. They met five times only, each time with smoldering animosity. The representatives of France, Austria, and Russia would have been as "rude" as Sir Hudson: they kept out of trouble by never meeting the prisoner at all.

Napoleon won and lost this guerrilla of pinpricks. He made his own lot harder: the officers of the *Northumberland* had proved that polite intercourse with the enemy was not impossible. But he had the satisfaction of creating the legend of Sir Hudson Lowe as a brutal tormentor clanking his keys and glaring at his victim with a satanic sneer. The legend survives in popular tales and tinges even a few serious studies. On the other hand, Napoleon lowered his stature by engaging in peevish squabbles with a commonplace and conscientious official.

Napoleon's retinue was neither large, nor distinguished, nor congenial: no happy band of friends. The only one who was a natural choice was General Count Bertrand, an officer of engineers who had succeeded Duroc as Grand Marshal of the Palace, and who had inherited his devotion. General Count de Montholon, one of Napoleon's many chamberlains, had played no conspicuous part either in the army or at court. Both Bertrand and Montholon had their wives with them; both remained until the end. General Gourgaud, only thirty-two years old, one of Napoleon's aides, vainglorious and irascible, was soon at loggerheads with the rest. He sulked even with Napoleon, and had to be humored like a spoilt child. He left in 1818 after a duel, faked or real, with Montholon. The best was Las Cases, chamberlain, and secretary to the Council of State, a man of ability and culture, with exquisite manners. In 1816 a letter severely criticizing the Governor led to his arrest and deportation, as perhaps he had hoped it would. He was not allowed to return to France until after Napoleon's death.

Because of some misunderstanding at Rochefort the Emperor had with him no physician of his own. He attached to himself Dr. O'Meara, surgeon on the *Northumberland*. Sir Hudson Lowe found O'Meara something of a nuisance, and had him removed in 1818. After an interim his place was taken by Dr. Antommarchi, a young Corsican picked out by Mme Letizia and Cardinal Fesch. Napoleon had a very poor opinion of his abilities. Strangely enough, the second Constantine, the new Charlemagne, anointed by the Pope, had no chaplain in his little court. Finally Cardinal Fesch sent him, at the same time as Antommarchi, the aged Abbé Buonavita, who could not stay to the end, and Abbé Ange Vignali, who was described as "low-born and illiterate." But Vignali was a Corsican, and Uncle Fesch may have thought that Corsican blood was sufficient qualification for the care of bodies and the cure of souls. Like a true Corsican, Vignali was to perish in a vendetta.

Most of these men, and some of the servants too, were to write accounts of their St. Helena experiences. Antommarchi's is considered flagrantly mendacious, Gourgaud's thoroughly unreliable. The best by far is the *Memorial* compiled by Las Cases. The Master himself was dictating furiously—once fourteen hours at one stretch—between periods of apathy. He composed his Memoirs, Cæsar-like, in the third person. They are something of a disappointment. Every reader is struck by the fact that Napoleon had supreme gifts of style. He was a master of Roman eloquence, *à la Corneille,* preserved from ranting by the restraint of military brevity. He had flashes of imagination ranging from the familiar to the sublime. He was a master of pungent phrase: his description of Talleyrand is not easy to forget. The picture of a wreck in a storm (in a letter to Josephine, July 21, 1804) is worthy of Chateaubriand: "My soul was in communion with Eternity, the Ocean and Night!" Yet Napoleon has never attained classic rank in French literature, as have his fellow general Choderlos de Laclos, his constitutional adviser Benjamin Constant, and a rather erratic minor officer in his Quartermaster Corps, Henri Beyle by name, who was to become Stendhal. The key to that disappointment is that every page of Napoleon's except his early letters to Josephine is sheer brazen propaganda. The man, who had undeniable elements of greatness, is obliterated by the immediate purpose. Among the innumerable writers on the Napoleonic theme, Napoleon may well be the ablest: he is far from the favorite.

But in his dictations and in his talks at St. Helena, he did achieve his purpose, which was to recast for posterity his own character and the nature of his reign. It was a wheeling movement of incredible daring, his strategic masterpiece, his most astounding victory—a victory wrenched out of utter defeat. In 1815 he was still posing as the champion of conservative order in France and in Europe. He alone could protect Western civilization from the double menace, the Cossack and the Jacobin. He was still pleading with the other crowned heads: "Do you not realize that I alone have curbed the Revolution and saved you from the rebellion of the masses?" And even in his first years in St. Helena his attitude suffered little change. He still had some hope, if not for himself, at any rate for his son. And he wanted the throne of Napoleon II to be worth having.

Philippe Gonnard [1] has studied in a most thorough and convincing manner the change that came over Napoleon on the island. Material power was gone; the dynasts among whom he had attempted to force his way had cast him out. Even the bourgeoisie was forgetting that he had been the faithful sword protecting the moneybags. So he boldly went over to the people. He turned himself into the apostle and the martyr of that democracy he had so long despised. He did not call it a conversion: he had never been wrong. It was the inner meaning of his whole career that he was at last revealing: he had admirably kept his secret. His democratic Napo-

---

[1] Philippe Gonnard: *Les Origines de la légende napoléonienne: L'Œuvre historique de Napoléon à Sainte-Hélène* (Paris, 1906). *The Exile of St. Helena: The Last Phase in Fact and Fiction* (London and Philadelphia, 1909).

leonism is another *Additional Act:* there again he pretended that there had been no change. The apparent
contradiction between the old Napoleon and the new
did not destroy their permanent unity.

The plea was plausible. After all, he had been something of a Jacobin in his early career, and *The Supper
at Beaucaire,* which was radical enough, sounded sincere. He never had any faith in legitimist nonsense,
though he toyed with it about 1810. He despised titles
while scattering them like crumbs to the hungry. Above
all, as a soldier, he loathed the profiteers whose buckler
and shield he had been for fifteen years. At bottom he
had kept in all things an ambivalent attitude: religion or
free-thought, monarchy or republic, the common people
or the moneyed interests, what did it matter to him as
long as he had power, and power absolute? His sole
enemies, man, class, or nation, were those who refused
to bow down. *Debellare superbos.*

Napoleonism was a genuine religion with him—that
religion of which Victor Hugo vowed to be the priest.
So his solipsism assumed forms that must sound crazy to
the free-thinker, blasphemous to the Christian: *Sum qui
sum,* "I am the way." He spoke without strain in
Messianic terms. He was the Man, the Man who stood
for the whole people and for all peoples, the supreme
incarnation of our common humanity. He alone could
have redeemed mankind, so long held in bondage by
the oligarchs. The oligarchs were crucifying him, but
he would rise again in the spirit and confound them.
And the oligarchs were giving him a splendid chance:
after rejecting him, they had double-crossed their peoples. As in many campaigns he had hurled his battalions
against the weak point of his enemies, the spot where
they had failed to establish or maintain contact, so he

now directed the massive columns of his propaganda against the point where dynasties and national sentiment had drifted apart. This masterly move was prophetic: when Napoleon was dictating to Gourgaud and Montholon, the bitter feud between the Holy Alliance and democratic aspirations was not yet evident. There was a brief flare-up of liberalism and nationalism just at the moment of Napoleon's death: but the great popular storm did not come full-blast until 1830.

Napoleon was forty-six when he reached St. Helena. But the tension of twenty incredible years had sapped a constitution that perhaps never was robust. In the leisure of his captivity, when it was no longer necessary to assure the world that "Never has His Majesty been in better health," he indulged in almost every kind of disease: according to O'Meara's report in 1818, "indigestion, catarrh, headache, rheumatism, swollen legs, inflamed gums, biliousness, and constipation." He had no good doctor at hand: he long refused the services of the British medical men on Sir Hudson's staff. Even if his advisers had been as good as Corvisart, he would have spurned their suggestions, partly out of fatalism, partly out of willfulness. A doctor is a dictator, and Napoleon was unable to brook any authority.

The medical record of his six years in St. Helena is uneven and confusing: Raoul Brice, a French army surgeon with the rank of lieutenant general, managed to make that confusion worse confounded.[2] The patient had moments of tolerable and rather torpid well-being, none of sparkling health and vigor: his mental activity, which was intense, appears all the more creditable. His

[2] Raoul Brice: *The Riddle of Napoleon* (New York, 1937).

principal disease was not properly diagnosed: there were squabbles between Antommarchi and the British surgeons. The one certain fact is that he was afflicted with a variety of diseases which his physicians failed to recognize in time, let alone cure or even alleviate. In the spring of 1821 he felt that the end was near, and he worked feverishly on his elaborate Testament. On May 3 he received the Last Sacrament. Early in the morning of May 5 he made unintelligible sounds, which Montholon, with the ears of faith, interpreted as *"France . . . armée . . . tête d' armée . . . Joséphine . . ."* He expired the same evening before six o'clock.

The autopsy failed to clear up the ambiguity that clouded his last battle with disease. Dr. Arnott, appointed by the Governor, gave the cause of death as cancer of the stomach in an advanced stage: it was the disease that had carried off Carlo Buonaparte and was to kill Pauline. The Napoleonists claimed there were only ulcers of the stomach, with adhesions and perforations; the deeper trouble was with the liver, and had been induced by the deadly climate of St. Helena: thus England had slowly tortured her victim to death. The British maintained that the liver, though large (or enlarged?), was perfectly sound.

The Emperor's body was clothed with the uniform of the Mounted Chasseurs of the Guard. A first coffin of zinc was sealed and enclosed in one of mahogany. This was enclosed in its turn in a sealed leaden coffin, and the whole in an outer box of mahogany. The work was well done, without embalming: when the body was exhumed in 1840, the Emperor's features were recognizable. The burial took place at Hutsgate, near Longwood, a spot he had loved and had himself selected.

England was bound to deny him imperial honors, but she granted him the highest accorded to British army officers. The little colony soon scattered, and Napoleon remained alone in a grave that needed no name.

On May 5, 1821 Napoleon was very dead indeed. Talleyrand could say, when apprised: "An event? Hardly. Just an item of news." But a great life does not end with death.

There was at that time little trace of Napoleonic sentiment: imagination loved to dwell on the remote and storied past. Sir Walter Scott found avid readers. Chateaubriand was the monarch of French literature; and after his example the rising romantic generation— Lamartine, Vigny, the "sublime child" Hugo—were ardent Catholics and royalists. They strove to view the Bourbons in a magic medieval light. This orgy of anti-quarianism culminated in the sedulous will-to-make-believe of Charles X's coronation in 1825. Even the phial of Holy Chrism was miraculously found again. The Voltairians tittered.

The turning-point came just after that elaborate pageantry. Public opinion was aflame with enthusiasm for the cause of Greek independence: that the great Lord Byron had espoused it gave it an irresistible halo. Chateaubriand quarreled with his masters. Romanticism evolved swiftly from an aristocratic mood, enamored of the past, to a faith in the divine right of the people. And as it so moved, it discovered the figure of Napoleon. Not the Sword of Thermidor, not the martinet, not the efficiency manager, not even the conqueror, but the latest avatar, the Napoleon of St. Helena, the Prometheus of Democracy.

As against the dusty and senile Bourbons he was as vivid as a flame. By 1830, as against the shrewd profiteers of the bourgeois monarchy he offered an escape into a world of epic glory. So the Napoleon of the 1830's became one of the gigantic myths of the time. He assumed his place in that teeming Pantheon by the side of Prometheus, Don Juan, Faust; and he possessed very much the same kind of reality. A myth is far more dynamic than plodding common sense; it opens infinite vistas which, even though delusive, have a deeper appeal than a blank wall encircling a neat vegetable garden. So long as you are willing to suspend disbelief, the magic preserves its glow.

There were ten full years (1830–40) of militant Napoleon-worship. The craze was rife especially among bourgeois writers; Thiers, Balzac, Hugo, Béranger. The aristocrats—Chateaubriand, Lamartine, Vigny—held aloof: what they saw in the Napoleonic saga was the exaltation of brute force. A true man of the people like Michelet could not be deceived; the Parisian masses, profoundly democratic, resented Cæsarism as a travesty of their ideal. But the craze continued to spread: on every stage in Paris there was a Napoleon strutting proudly, striking attitudes, mouthing historic words. The Vendôme Column became a place of pilgrimage. The Arch of Triumph was completed to his glory.

This tumultuous movement I have attempted to study in my *Reflections on the Napoleonic Legend*. It was Napoleon's second life, far more poetic than the first. In the minds of most readers, and even of many well-qualified scholars, it has substituted itself for the checkered earthly career that ended in 1821. Historians even today piously accept the essence of the Legend—the epic sweep, the miraculous achievements, the apocalyptic catastrophe, the ultimate Golgotha. They do not challenge the saga of the Hero, the Genius, the Titan, the Demigod: all they do is investigate details which, however damaging, do not affect the total impression. Theirs is a glowing Fundamentalism, so deep-seated that the results of dispassionate research are never allowed to interfere with the Faith. If we seek *biography*, not hagiography, the story of a great life as it was actually lived, if we strive to understand Napoleon the human being, then we must bear in mind that Napoleon the Demigod was conceived in St. Helena, came of age in 1830, and was solemnly canonized in 1840.

For reasons of its own, the bourgeois government of Louis-Philippe deliberately adopted and fostered the Legend: it shed reflected glory on that stodgy regime. In 1840 the remains, poetically termed the Ashes, of the Emperor were brought back from St. Helena by the son of Louis-Philippe, the Sailor Prince, Joinville. The ship was called *La Belle Poule*, the Beautiful Hen. Transferred to a barge, the bier went up the Seine as far as Courbevoie. Thence it was carried on an ornate chariot along the great avenue which, under various names, leads to the Place de la Concorde. It was the 15th of December, "a day as dazzling as glory, as cold as the tomb." Hundreds of thousands thronged the long route of the procession. Canvas and cardboard monuments everywhere; banners fluttering; crippled veterans in their historic uniforms; martial music; tolling of bells; booming of guns. The catafalque, a shrine on wheels, a car of Juggernaut, proceeded with majestic slowness amid shouts and tears.

At the Invalides the King, in the name of France, received the sacred relics from his son the Sailor Prince.

A Presence filled the church and struck every heart with awe. And now, under the marvelous gilded dome shaped like a spiked helmet, Napoleon reposes in his tomb of red porphyry "on the banks of the Seine, among those French people he had loved so well."

NOTE ON SOURCES

IT is commonly accepted that no man in history has been the subject of so much writing as Napoleon I. It has even been asserted, more dubiously, that Napoleon fascinates the German reader more than Barbarossa, Frederick the Great, or Bismarck; the English reader more than Elizabeth, Cromwell, Marlborough, Chatham, or Wellington; the Russian reader more than Ivan the Terrible, Peter the Great, or Catherine II; the American reader more than Washington, Jefferson, Jackson, and perhaps even Lincoln. Napoleon is not in the same class as other world heroes in modern history: he alone belongs to the fields of scholarship, epic, romance, legend, and contemporary politics: for all modern dictators have a Napoleonic complex. F. M. Kircheisen attempted an exhaustive bibliography of the subject: *Bibliographie des napoleonischen Zeitalters* (Berlin 1902); *Bibliographie du Temps de Napoléon comprenant l'histoire des Etats-Unis* (Paris, 1908–12). It reached one hundred thousand titles. It was not completed, and for the last half century the flood has swept on. It shows some signs of slackening, owing to World War II and its aftermath. Hitler has not displaced Napoleon in popularity, but certain resemblances are too obvious for comfort (Hitler's *imperium* was far more extensive than Napoleon's). And the atomic age has at last relegated Napoleonic warfare to ancient history.

I. BACKGROUND WORKS

If we desire to escape dithyramb, satire, and romance, the first step is to place Napoleon in his historical setting by consulting general books on the whole period. They are as a rule parts of series intended for the student as well as for the general reader. They are provided with bibliographical aids. Among the best-known and most easily available may be mentioned:

Lavisse *et* Rambaud, editors: *Histoire Générale du 4ème Siècle à nos jours*, Vol. IX, *Napoléon*. (I have been using the third revised edition, Paris, 1925.)

The Cambridge Modern History, Vol. IX, *Napoleon* (1906). (The later popular editions omit the bibliographies.) In these two great collective works, the separate chapters are by different authors; the general impression is therefore slightly blurred—as perhaps it should be. Ernest Lavisse, editor: *Histoire de la France Contemporaine*. Vol. III. G. Pariset: *Le Consulat et l'Empire* (Paris, 1921). William L. Langer, editor: *The Rise of Modern Europe*. Geoffrey Bruun: *Europe and the French Imperium* (New York, 1938); the one book I would single out for the American reader. The preceding and following volumes in the same series have some bearing on the Napoleonic theme: Crane Brinton: *A Decade of Revolution* (New York, 1934); and Frederick B. Artz: *Reaction and Revolution* (New York, 1934). L. Halphen *et* Ph. Sagnac: *Peuples et Civilisations*, Vol. IX, Georges Lefebvre: *Napoléon* (Paris, 1935). The richest in facts and thoughts; indeed, a masterly piece of work. But, intended as a guide for the professional student, it may be found too highly condensed for the general reader.

II. GENERAL WORKS ON NAPOLEON

They are innumerable, and many have achieved a high reputation. In many respects, Adolphe Thiers's will never be surpassed. Among the best-known: A. Fournier (Viennese): *Napoleon I*, edited by E. G. Bourne (New York, 1903); Holland Rose; William Milligan Sloane; of recent years, Fletcher Pratt, very lively, and notable for a clear presentation of military events. The most practical one-volume history is F. M. Kircheisen: *Napoleon* (New York, 1932); a condensation of his enormous labor in that field. Emil Ludwig: *Napoleon* (New York, 1926), remains the most readable. Ludwig acknowledges the aid he received from Kircheisen, Driault, and Pariset, all three excellent guides; as well as from Wildhagen, for whom I could not vouch.

The most ambitious modern work about Napoleon is that of Louis Madelin, the Thiers of our days. He did some excellent research work (*Fouché; La Rome de Napoléon*). In his more general books, in spite of his extreme bias, Napoleonic and nationalistic, and of his old-fashioned academic eloquence, he remains well informed as well as lucid. His *Histoire du Consulat et de l'Empire* comprises twelve substantial volumes. At the end of each there are very full *Notes et Références*. As a sort of pilot work, he also published in Fr. Funck-Brentano's *L'Histoire de France Racontée à Tous* two volumes on *The Consulate and the Empire* (New York, 1934–6). There are notes on Sources and Bibliography at the end of each chapter.

Hubert B. Richardson: *A Dictionary of Napoleon and His Times* (New York, n.d.), was very well conceived, and a revised version would be greatly welcome.

III. original sources

The most essential is Napoleon's *Correspondence*, edited in magnificent form, but with unfortunte excisions, under the Second Empire. Numerous additions and corrections have been made since that monument was completed. It is too bulky and all-embracing to be of use to the general reader; but J. M. Thompson has given an excellent selection and translation of three hundred typical letters: *Napoleon Self-Revealed* (New York, 1934). Napoleon's *Letters to Josephine* have been published separately in a pretty edition that inspires little confidence (New York, 1931). Also those, more sedate, to Marie-Louise (New York, 1935).

The second great source is the St. Helena literature. The best is: E. Las Cases: *Mémorial de Sainte-Hélène* (1823), often republished and translated, in full or in abridgment; and *Mémoires pour Servir à l'Histoire de France sous Napoléon*, dictated by the Emperor himself to Generals Gourgaud and Montholon. These can be used only with the greatest caution, and are too bulky for the general reader. Many writers have been tempted to offer "autobiographies" of Napoleon, combining the St. Helena literature with fragments from letters, proclamations, speeches, conversations. Among them: R. M. Johnston: *The Corsican: A Diary of Napoleon's Life in His Own Words* (New York and Boston, 1910); F. M. Kircheisen: *Memoirs of Napoleon* (English edition); *Napoleon's Autobiography* (American edition, New York, 1931); Somerset de Chair: Napoleon, Emperor of the French, *Memoirs*, (1950), changing the Cæsarian third person to the first. J. Christopher Herold's *The Mind of Napoleon* was issued in 1955. Of these, *The Corsican* was the most successful. But the work still remains to be done in a critical spirit and with brief but adequate references.

IV. MEMOIRS BY CONTEMPORARIES

It is greatly to be lamented that the memoirs of the protagonists should be of such doubtful value: Talleyrand's are disappointing, Fouché's wholly unreliable. Practically all members of the imperial connection and most marshals wrote their memoirs or had them ghostwritten at the time of the great Nalopeonic vogue under Louis-Philippe. Few of them are of commanding value, with two exceptions, both edited by Major Jean Hanoteau: *The Memoirs of Queen Hortense* (2 vols., New York, 1927), and *the Memoirs of Caulaincourt*, abridged American edition in two volumes: I. *With*

Napoleon in Russia (New York, 1935); II. *No Peace with Napoleon* (New York, 1936).

The minor contemporaries come out rather better. I can specially recommend:

For Napoleon's early career: L. A. de Bourrienne.

For court gossip: Duchess of Abrantès (Laure Permon, Madame Junot); and Mme de Rémusat.

For the political and administrative world: A. C. Thibaudeau.

For army life: J. B. de Marbot. (There is a charming abridgment, with sprightly illustrations: *Adventures of General Marbot*, by John W. Thomason, Jr., New York, 1935.)

For the life of the common soldier: the fullest and most engaging: *Cahiers du Capitaine Coignet*, edited by Loredan Larchey (Paris, n.d.).

V. LITERATURE

The Napoleonic saga is pictorial rather than literary. It lives in monuments, statues, paintings, popular prints, and bric-à-brac rather than in epic poems, novels or dramas. As a guide (for French literature only) see my *Reflections on the Napoleonic Legend* (London and New York, 1924), part III. The results of many seminars on the Napoleonic legend in Western literature have not been published.

Among the headliners: F. R. de Chateaubriand: *Mémoires d'Outre-tombe* (1849–50). A whole book devoted to Napoleon, surprisingly fair, magnificent in style. Reprinted separately in Collection Nelson. The Battle of Waterloo in Victor Hugo's *Les Misérables* (1862); in sharp contrast with the account of the same battle, totally unrecognizable, in Stendhal's *La Chartreuse de Parme* (1839). (Stendhal never completed a long-projected *Life of Napoleon.*)

H. de Balzac: the first chapter in *La Femme de Trente Ans* (*The Woman of Thirty*) (1831). *Le Napoléon du Peuple:* story of Napoleon told in a barn, in *Le Médecin de Campagne* (*The Country Doctor*) (1833). *Une Ténébreuse Affaire* (*A Dark Mystery*) (1841). Alfred de Vigny: The Life and Death of Captain Renaud, in *Grandeur and Servitude of the Soldier* (1835). A fine study of *séidisme* or fanatical hero-worship; with the famous scene between Napoleon and Pius VII at Fontainebleau.

Leo Tolstoy: *War and Peace* (1865–9). The impact of Napoleon upon Russian society. The campaigns of 1805 and 1812. Long disquisitions against the "heroic individual" conception of history.

Thomas Hardy: *The Dynast* (1904–6): a great epic and philosophical drama of the Napoleonic age; with proper roles assigned to the Spirit Ironic and the Spirit of the Years.

Joseph Conrad left unfinished a novel, *Suspense:* the uneasy lull while Napoleon was in Elba; and in retrospect, the crushing dullness of society under the Empire (this chiefly from the Memoirs of Countess de Boigne).

INDEX

This book was set on the Linotype in a face called *Eldorado*, so named by its designer, WILLIAM ADDISON DWIGGINS, as an echo of Spanish adventures in the Western World. The series of experiments that culminated in this type-face began in 1942; the designer was trying a page more "brunette" than the usual book type. "One wanted a face that should be sturdy, and yet not too mechanical. . . . Another desideratum was that the face should be narrowish, compact, and close fitted, for reasons of economy of materials." The specimen that started Dwiggins on his way was a type design used by the Spanish printer A. de Sancha at Madrid about 1774. Eldorado, however, is in no direct way a copy of that letter, though it does reflect the Madrid specimen in the anatomy of its arches, curves, and junctions. Of special interest in the lower-case letters are the stresses of color in the blunt, sturdy serifs, subtly counterbalanced by the emphatic weight of some of the terminal curves and finials. The roman capitals are relatively open, and winged with liberal serifs and an occasional festive touch.

This book was composed, printed, and bound by The Plimpton Press, Norwood, Massachusetts. Paper manufactured by S. D. Warren Company, Boston. The typography and binding were designed by the creator of its type-face—W. A. Dwiggins.

WAD

50 THINGS YOU NEED TO KNOW ABOUT THE PROSTATE

C. A. Whitney

with an introduction by
Arnold M. Kwart, M.D.
Clinical Professor of Urology at
George Washington University Medical Center

ST. MARTIN'S PAPERBACKS

50 THINGS YOU NEED TO KNOW ABOUT THE PROSTATE

ISBN: 0-312-95357-7

Printed in the United States of America

St. Martin's Paperbacks edition/October 1994

10 9 8 7 6 5 4 3 2 1

In memory of
Frank L. Whitney
1911–1991

Contents

A Personal Note

This is not the first medically oriented book I have written. As always, I was struck by the personal nature of this project. When we think about medicine in the abstract, it can seem very dry and technical. But when it touches us personally, there's nothing in the world that has such a passionate force. Medicine, we are reminded, is about people living and dying and struggling against odds. It's the most human story there is.

From the start, my editor at St. Martin's, Jennifer Weis, realized that this important medical story was above all a human story. She was determined to create an easily accessible lay guide about the prostate—a subject that has been mired in complexity, misinformation, controversy, and fear. My literary agent, Jane Dystel, was equally passionate about the goal of this book. Both Jennifer and Jane have had their lives touched by this issue, and such personal encounters are powerful motivators.

I also want to express my great appreciation to Paul Krafin, whose assistance in medical research, interviews and writing was invaluable.

Most of us know someone who has been affected by prostate problems, including cancer. When we face it in our own lives or in those of our loved ones, we find that our questions quickly move beyond the technical to the human. I have tried to use this book to raise the real questions that ordinary people ask.

Illness is a challenge to dignity, and it's always an inspiration to encounter people who refuse to let disease rob them of their self-esteem. I have dedicated this book to Frank L. Whitney because during the painful course of his illness, he was a special inspiration to those who knew him. Frank was a Methodist minister by vocation, but his spirituality was always down-to-earth and practical. He was loved and admired by many people during his eighty years of life, but I think it was in his illness that some of his family and friends truly came to appreciate what a quietly profound man he was.

In fact, Frank Whitney expected to live many years longer; men in his family have impressive strains of longevity. When he developed an especially virulent form of prostate cancer, he fought it vigorously. As it became clear that he was losing the battle, Frank openly expressed his deep disappointment that he would not have the ten or more years of living he had expected. Having done that, he made his peace with dying, and his death was a dignified moment, attended by the family he had loved and nurtured.

I imagine Frank Whitney would be a bit bemused to find himself heralded as an inspiration. But he would no doubt have welcomed the chance to use his illness to good purpose, since he always believed that life's opportunities should be fully explored and its gifts recycled. He was frugal in that way.

Most of the men who contract prostate cancer do not die from it. But they are surely reminded of their mortality in a most jarring way. Maybe it's not such a bad thing for us to be reminded of our mortality now and then—to grapple honestly with life's challenges and celebrate its victories. Which is why this book is more than just a factual presentation of medical information. It is a conversation that you and I will have together as we work through some of the issues that most concern you.

Introduction

A Hopeful Outlook
by Arnold M. Kwart, M.D.

By the time a man walks into my office, he is usually experiencing a number of deep concerns. No doubt he's also feeling somewhat betrayed because prostate problems often appear just when everything else is under control. I've seen it happen many times: A man is at the peak of his career, his kids are raised, he's achieved a measure of achievement and security—and boom! He's got a prostate problem, maybe cancer. And the first thing he thinks of is death. It's a rude awakening.

If you're reading this book it's because you've experienced something like this—or it's happened to someone you love. You're looking for information and for hope—a way to make the prospects seem less scary. Listening to the ominous-sounding media reports about prostate cancer can be both confusing and discouraging. I hope you find something different in this book—straight talk and optimism.

I feel strongly that there is good reason for optimism when you compare our current situation with that of twelve years ago. Then, the American College of Surgeons reported that only fifteen percent of the men diagnosed with prostate cancer could be cured. Today, that statistic is almost completely reversed.

Why? There are two reasons. One is the wonderful advances made in diagnostic technology that allow us to catch prostate cancer in its early stages. The other is public awareness, which brings men in for screening even before they experience symptoms. In the last five years, men's awareness of the risk factors and screening recommendations for prostate cancer has reached a level equivalent to that of women and breast cancer. I can't stress enough how important this is. The most sophisticated technology in the world is meaningless if people aren't educated to take advantage of it. I'm always delighted when a man schedules a PSA test on his own. It means the word is getting out and people are becoming educated.

Having said that, it's also true that prostate conditions can be very confusing to understand. And while I applaud the increased media coverage on the issue, it has also opened the way to misinformation and unnecessary scare tactics. The problem is, when data becomes available from a research study, the average lay person has no way to evaluate it. It usually appears beneath a headline that boasts a "new finding," leading most people to assume this is the total picture. But these published pieces of research are only fragments of a very complex picture. They may illuminate an aspect of the problem, provide clues to prevention, suggest a promising new treatment, but usually they are in the early stages and can't be relied upon with any certainty. So, it's good to read the latest news, but don't make too much of it. Especially since prostate problems, more than many other conditions, seem to carry a very individual signature. It has been my experience that if you have twenty people in a room who have all been diagnosed with prostate cancer, you're looking at twenty different diseases. The same holds true for noncancerous prostate conditions.

Let me give you a simple example, using two men who recently came to my office. They were both in their late fifties. The first man, Ken, had what he called a "minor problem." He'd sometimes have the urge to urinate, but would only produce tiny amounts of urine. He wasn't too worried about it since he didn't feel sick.

The second man, Richard, was very worried. He spoke with great fear about his symptoms. Chief among them was a frequent urge to urinate, including at least twice during the night. The process of urinating seemed to take a long time. "I think I'm finished, then there's another dribble, then another," Richard said. He told me miserably that Ken was resigned to the probability of surgery.

As it turned out, Ken was the man I scheduled for surgery, not Richard. A residual urine ultrasound test showed that Ken had two liters of urine in his bladder. The guy was barely urinating at all! He needed an immediate operation.

Richard, on the other hand, was not in danger. Tests showed an enlarged prostate, but it wasn't harming him, only making life less comfortable. I put it to him this way: "Look, Richard, you've got a problem that's shared by about eighty percent of all men over fifty. It's very annoying, but at this point it's not dangerous. What you're facing is a quality of life decision, not a medical one. Is your discomfort great enough to warrant treatment? It's up to you to decide." Richard was so relieved, he opted for a program of ongoing observation rather than any treatment at the time.

Another man might have found the urinary problems intolerable and chosen immediate treatment with drugs or surgery. The point is, it often boils down to a person's decision about what makes sense for his own life.

The same range of options exists even when cancer is present. Our current technology allows us to detect cancer cells in the early stages and to track them over time. We have a clinical scale that essentially measures the architecture of the tumor—and shows its rate of growth. A very slow growing cancer, especially in a man over seventy, may suggest no treatment; a more rapidly growing cancer might require more aggressive treatment. Even then, surgery is not always the first course of action. Although I am a surgeon, my personal philosophy is that you only operate if you have to, since an invasive procedure in a hospital environment carries its own set of risks and costs.

Like everything else in life, treatment is relative. The bottom line is this: Know yourself and know your options. And know your support system; you'll need one. When you have a prostate condition, it's very much a partner issue, if you're married. When a couple has good communication between them, it can make all the difference, and I always encourage a man's wife to be involved.

Regardless of your marital status, a support system is essential. That might include family members, friends, or a structured group. The need for support is hard for many men to accept. They're not used to being vulnerable and asking for help, and it's a new experience for them—one that has unexpected rewards.

This book won't tell you absolutely what to do if you're diagnosed with a prostate condition or cancer. What it will do is clear up the confusion and give you more power in your situation.

- We'll teach you to distinguish between benign and cancerous conditions.
- You'll learn the difference between a condition that requires immediate assertive action and one that can be watched for further developments.
- We'll explain what the new research data really means.
- We'll provide a straightforward course of screening that every man should follow, adjusting it to account for age and other risk factors.
- You'll learn about the latest screening technology, especially the PSA Test, the best diagnostic tool we've ever had to detect prostate problems.
- We'll give you a checklist of treatment options you can ask your doctor about—including laser surgery, radiation, and hormone therapy.
- You'll learn the truth about drug therapy.
- We'll warn you about the treatment gimmicks you should avoid.
- We'll give you straight talk and good news about sexual potency.
- You'll learn how to take care of yourself and live more healthily—including what is known about the role of diet in preventing prostate cancer.
- We'll give you information about support groups and educational organizations that you can access no matter where you live.

In my years of practice, I've seen thousands of men confront their mortality, compliments of this tiny little gland to which they'd never given a moment's thought. It's a humbling event when you run up against your human condition and discover, in a very tangible way, that you can't control every aspect of your life. That's not such a bad lesson to learn; sometimes the jolt of reality leads to an important reevaluation of self and priorities. But the message with which I leave you is this: An essential aspect of the human condition is our ability to think, judge, and take action. So, while you may not be able to avoid prostate problems altogether, especially as you get older, you can vastly improve your chances by knowing your risks, getting early screening, and understanding all of your options. We no longer live in a time when your doctor tells you what to do and you go along without question. Your best care comes when you and your doctor are partners.

Arnold M. Kwart, M.D.
Clinical Professor of Urology,
George Washington University Medical Center
Washington, D.C.
February 1994

PART I

What's All the
Fuss About the Prostate?

Case Study: Charles K.'s Revelation

Charles K. knew something was wrong, but he kept it to himself. That's the way the men in his family handled things, and he was no different. Charles had little patience for the way some people walked around spilling their guts and grievances to anyone who would listen. He figured, whatever was wrong, he'd manage to handle it himself.

If Charles had been inclined to share his problem, he would have called it a mix-up of male plumbing. Not that he really understood what that meant. Although he was a bright guy in his mid-fifties, Charles knew relatively little about how his innards worked. He'd never had to pay much attention because everything had always seemed to be okay. His last full physical was thirty years before on the occasion of his induction into the Navy.

So, here was Charles, going along trying to cope on his own, when one night a piercing yowl of pain sent his wife racing to the bathroom. She pounded ferociously on the closed door. "Charles! Are you okay?"

Her beloved husband of twenty-six years groaned in a half sob and finally admitted, "No, I'm not okay."

That was a big moment for Charles—a turning point. Physically, his problem wasn't too serious—an early and very treatable case of an enlarged prostate. The turning point was Charles's realization that the stoic pattern of manhood he had subscribed to religiously since youth was just a crock. Why suffer pain when he could get help? Why pretend to be a loner when he had a wife who loved him so much?

Like many people, Charles was changed by his encounter with physical vulnerability. That happens a lot with prostate patients because nothing makes a man face the truth of his humanity more starkly than a breakdown in the very stuff of his maleness.

1. Why is everyone talking about the prostate?

The panic about prostate seems to have arrived out of the blue. During the past five years the prostate—a topic once thought unfit for polite company—has emerged from the closet to be featured in men's magazines, newspaper health columns, and television reports. It is casually discussed at dinner parties. Men of a certain age, suddenly taken ill, are asked without a blink of embarrassment, "Is it prostate?"

Of course, of all the various afflictions that can be associated with the prostate, cancer is the most widely discussed and feared. Prostate cancer does not discriminate. Rich or poor, famous or unknown, it's an equal opportunity disease. Only recently musician Frank Zappa and actor Bill Bixby died of the disease—both were young men in their fifties. Luminaries who are currently battling prostate cancer include comedian Jerry Lewis, Senator Bob Dole, former financier Michael Milken, ABC News president Roone Arledge, former quarterback Len Dawson, and French president François Mitterand. Former president Ronald Reagan has had two prostate surgeries. And for some reason, prostate cancer is particularly hard on Supreme Court justices; it has stricken John Paul Stevens, Harry Blackmun, William J. Brennan, and Lewis E. Powell.

Are we in the middle of a prostate disease epidemic?

The statistics aren't very encouraging. Since the 1960s there has been a 17 percent leap in cancer incidences—pretty substantial by clinical standards. This year, an estimated 200,000 men will be diagnosed with prostate cancer, and about 35,000 of them will die from it. Prostate cancer has achieved the dubious distinction of being the number-one cancer to afflict men, and it's the second most deadly—the first being lung cancer.

Noncancerous conditions like infections or enlargement produce symptoms ranging from mild discomfort to severe problems. As they age, most men will encounter some troubles with the prostate.

If it seems like the prostate dilemma has taken us by surprise, that's because prostate problems of the scope we're encountering today are a relatively new phenomenon. Why? Because living beyond the age of fifty is a relatively new phenomenon. This is not a young man's disease; men under age fifty usually don't need to give their prostates a moment's consideration. Historically, prostate problems have been rare. For example, at the turn of this century there wasn't much talk about prostate disease because most men didn't live long enough to have it. Like other body parts, the prostate ages, and with aging comes complications. With the average male life expectancy climbing into the seventh decade and beyond, it's not so hard to figure out why this is an issue now.

What makes prostate treatment so deeply frustrating for medical professionals is that in spite of long and aggressive research and clinical studies, the prostate remains such a mystery. Research has examined prostate disease from every angle, searching for links with sexual activity, venereal disease, race, diet, and environment. The results have been inconclusive, even though the evidence is building that there's a relationship between prostate cancer and high-fat diets. We'll talk more about that later. The point is, no one is quite sure what causes the various prostate conditions—for example, how bacteria invades the prostate, how the prostate becomes inflamed, what makes the prostate enlarge as men age, or how cancerous cells suddenly appear on the scene.

Having painted this gloomy picture, it may surprise you to hear that this is really a book about hope. It's about a concept that is perhaps overused but nevertheless valid—empowerment. It's about helping you to replace panic with knowledge, and paralysis with action.

I'm fully aware that even if you have no symptoms and have never had any family history of prostate cancer, it's easy to get caught up in the hysteria once you start reading about it. A forty-five-year-old friend of mine, after perusing my research material one day, later confessed that every time he felt an unfamiliar twinge or had to get up at night to urinate, he thought, "This is it!" He admitted, "I walked around with aching balls for two weeks before I realized that I was just being paranoid."

In a category of human suffering that seems weighted toward the downside, it helps to stress the good news. And the good news about prostate problems, including cancer, is that they are very often controllable. They don't have to destroy the quality of your life. If you want to take charge—and since you're reading this book, I assume you do—you can begin to accomplish that by becoming a knowledgeable owner of your body and a savvy utilizer of the medical system. The human condition leaves us without control over many things. But why not use our knowledge and common sense to control the things we can?

2. What exactly is the prostate?

Let's back up a bit and describe this troublesome little gland. Actually, it's not always so troublesome. In fact, when your prostate is healthy, it's pretty much an invisible player on the male anatomical team.

The prostate is a small gland about the size and shape of a walnut, weighing no more than an ounce, which is located below the bladder and in front of the inner wall of the rectum. Its only known function is to provide part of the fluid for semen, the milky white substance that helps transport sperm cells during ejaculation—which usually amounts to between one-fourth and one-half teaspoon. Prostatic secretions increase the semen's bulk and help keep sperm alive by providing an alkaline environment.

Most men have a rudimentary understanding of how their "equipment" works, but they're often amazed at the true intricacy of the system. As you'll see in the illustration below, a tube similar to a drinking straw passes from your bladder to your penis. It's called the urethra. Along the way, the urethra travels through the center of your prostate. During sexual excitement, fluid is produced in the glands and emptied into the prostatic urethra. It is joined with the spermatozoa that have arrived from the testes. There they mass and wait for the spasmodic contractions that will signal ejaculation.

3. What can go wrong?

The human body is miraculous, but it is also baffling. As one man whose prostate grew enlarged in his sixties

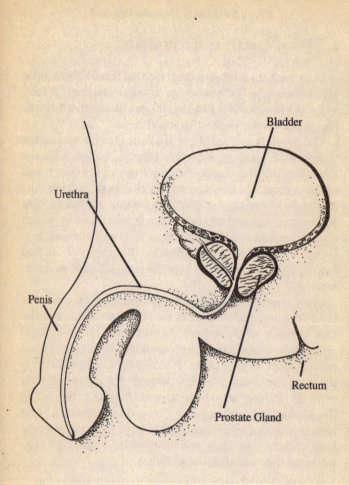

Bladder

Urethra

Penis

Rectum

Prostate Gland

asked, rightfully so, "Why does something natural automatically get screwed up? Who designed this machine, anyway?" Philosophers could, and do, have a field day with such questions. Our focus is more practical.

As you'll learn, there are many different types of prostate problems, and they're not always going to be signaled by overt symptoms. Some are silent, especially cancer. That's why regular checkups are absolutely essential. Current recommendations are that all men over fifty get annual screening; and high-risk men should get screened yearly after age forty. Generally speaking, if you're not sure about a symptom, get tested. The most common signs of a prostate problem include:

- painful, frequent, urgent, or hesitant urination
- trouble fully emptying your bladder
- frequent need to urinate during the night
- sluggish urine flow
- frequent urination during the day
- sharp pain in the pelvic region or rectum
- blood in the urine

Some of these symptoms mimic other conditions, but don't make any assumptions. Have symptoms checked out—for your health and your peace of mind. And be sure to follow the screening guidelines for all men, since prostate cancer is usually asymptomatic in its early stages. Sometimes, other prostate conditions will exist for a time without being noticeable. Silent prostatism is an enlargement of the prostate that is not accompanied by symptoms. This can be dangerous since, over time, the flow of urine may become increasingly obstructed until you experience a dramatic failure that can land you in the hospital.

4. What are my risk factors for prostate problems?

The biggest risk factor of all is being a male and having testosterone! In fact, if you're looking for a simple set of risks which you can eliminate, thus protecting yourself from ever having a problem, you'll be disappointed to learn that there's no such magic formula. All prostate owners are at risk. Having said that, it's also important to put the matter of what constitutes "risk" into some perspective. I'm sure you hear the terms high and low risk tossed around all the time. But having a risk is not the same as having the inevitability of getting a disease. You may have none of the risk factors and still get a disease. I once knew a thirty-five-year-old man who had never smoked, didn't grow up around smokers, and was never exposed to any toxic chemicals. To the bafflement of everyone, he developed lung cancer and was dead six months after the diagnosis. So, go figure. The point is, don't get overly panicked by the idea of risk. It's just a piece of information that helps you calculate a wise strategy.

Prostate disease, especially cancer, is a somewhat confusing picture since even the known risk factors are so poorly understood. For example, it is known that black Americans have a higher incidence of prostate cancer than whites, but this may be environmental, not genetic, since black Africans have a low incidence. (Latinos and Japanese also have a low incidence of prostate cancer.) Cadmium miners have a higher rate of prostate cancer than the general population, but the reason is not known. It's also a mystery why men who have had vasectomies seem to have more prostate cancer than the general population. So, you see, knowing one's statistical risk isn't always so helpful.

YOUR RISK FACTOR CHECKLIST

Keep in mind that nobody is quite sure why the following factors affect prostate cancer risk. But knowing the risk helps you take informed action. If you fall into a high-risk category, you'll want to start screening practices by the time you're forty.

1. Do you have a family history of prostate cancer? Your risk is doubled if your father or brother have the disease; it's even higher if family members were stricken before age fifty.
2. Are you an African-American? Statistically, African-Americans get prostate cancer at a 40 percent higher rate than whites.
3. Have you had a vasectomy? This may or may not be a factor. Although there seems to be a higher incidence among men who've had vasectomies, it may just be because they make more frequent visits to their doctors, so diseases are detected earlier.
4. Do you eat a high-fat diet? We'll be exploring this factor in much greater detail later, but suffice it to say that new research provides compelling evidence that men who typically consume high-fat diets are far more likely to have prostate cancer. More startling, their cancer is more likely to be fatal.

> 5. Along with a high-fat diet, a sedentary lifestyle may also increase the risk. One reason might be that exercise tends to lower testosterone levels. We'll take a closer look at this factor later too.

5. What should every man do?

The most important thing you can do is to get regular checkups and prostate screening. That might seem like a simple enough instruction, but it's really not. Studies repeatedly show that men tend to make limited use of health care services, often seeing a doctor or visiting a clinic only when they absolutely have to. Unlike women, who are conditioned to undergo regular screening procedures like Pap smears and mammograms, men take the attitude that if their equipment seems to be working, everything must be okay. I urge you to get into the habit, especially as you move into your forties, of getting regular checkups. It can make the difference between vitality and frailty as you age.

What should you look for in a doctor? How do you choose one whom you can trust? People tend to seek the same qualities in their doctors that they do in their auto mechanics, as though illness was simply a matter of finding out what's broken and fixing it. Certainly, technical proficiency is important, and all doctors are not equal in that regard. Your regular internist or general practitioner should be competent for general prostate screening. If you are diagnosed with a prostate condition, however, you'll probably be referred to a urologist, a doctor who specializes in urinary tract and prostate disorders. Beyond the objective realm of credentials, consider whether the doctor's philosophy of treatment squares with your own. For example, will the doctor work in close collaboration with your general practitioner or internist to assure well-rounded care? Does the doctor have a surgical bias, or is he or she more inclined to try other therapies before surgery? Does the doctor tend to see you as an individual and base treatment recommendations on your personal profile? This is a very important consideration because very few prostate conditions have absolute treatment protocols. Many factors are involved in decision-making, including who you are and what you require for a good quality of life.

Today, the average layperson comes to the doctor equipped with some knowledge of his own. Books like this one, magazine and newspaper articles, and television reports have educated the public, and this education has changed the dynamic between doctor and patient. The fact that you're reading this book is a good indication that you want to be treated with respect and dignity—to be a knowledgeable member of your own medical team. You probably won't be happy with a doctor who takes an authoritarian approach.

Should your doctor be a male? Most men would probably express some initial discomfort with the idea of seeing a woman urologist for a prostate problem, although there are certainly many fine women urologists who treat male patients. It really depends on what works best for you. You might feel more at ease describing intimate symptoms with a male doctor, and you may also feel he is better able to empathize than a woman doctor would be.

Before you make a visit to your doctor, spend some time preparing. In other words, get ready to be a partner in your care. Doctors aren't mind readers. They're not magicians. They need you to help them get to know you so they can place your symptoms and medical conditions in context. In many respects, a doctor is only as good as his or her patient.

Make these notes:

- Jot down everything you know about your family's health history, starting with your grandparents. Do the same for your parents, aunts and uncles, and siblings. Has there been cancer of any kind? Heart disease? Hypertension? Diabetes? (Include both males and females; certain hereditary factors are passed through both.) Is there a history of alcohol, drug abuse, depression, or mental illness? If your grandparents, parents, aunts, uncles, or siblings are no longer living, what were the causes of their deaths? How old were they when they died?

- Make notes about your own health history. Any surgeries? Allergies? Injuries? Special problems? In particular, have you had a history of prostate infections, urinary tract infections or other related problems? Have you ever had cancer?

- Give an honest account of your lifestyle and habits. Do you smoke? Do you drink alcohol? Do you use illegal drugs? How often, how long? Are you currently taking or have you recently taken prescription drugs? Name them and state the reason. Also include nonprescription drugs like cold medications.

- Your doctor will want to know about your sexual history and current activity. For example, do you have a regular partner, multiple partners, any history of sexually transmitted diseases? Do you use condoms, engage in anal intercourse, masturbate regularly? These sound like pretty embarrassing questions, but it's important that your doctor know as much as possible about your lifestyle and related conditions. Choose a doctor whom you trust and can speak to in confidence.

One other thing: If you have symptoms, avoid using the words, "Oh, it's nothing." Or, "It's probably not important." Let your doctor help you make an informed decision about that. Some men are very stoic about their symptoms. They don't want to appear to overreact, to sound like wimps. But a symptom is a symptom. A pain is a pain. Your body is talking to you. Listen, and share the information with your doctor.

There's another reason many men procrastinate about getting help. That reason is denial. Since prostate disease is an age-related affliction, it might be hard to face the reality that age is upon you and that suddenly you're getting the diseases of the old. That was the way Bert F. felt.

Case Study: Bert's Battle With Age

At fifty-two, Bert F. was a vigorous, athletic man who looked and felt great—as he liked to say, in the peak of health. He ran three miles every morning, worked out at the gym a couple of times a week, and enjoyed active sports like tennis and racquetball.

Bert was also proud of his virility. All his life he'd heard stories about how men's sexual ability faltered as they reached middle age, but that certainly hadn't been true for him. Divorced from his first wife when he turned forty, Bert had enjoyed an active social life before marrying for a second time at age forty-eight. He was crazy about Sue, and he thought their sex life was everything he could have wished for. Sue made him feel young again.

Then one night while they were making love, Bert felt a terrible seering pain just as he ejaculated. He hollered and leaped off the bed. Alarmed, Sue cried, "What's wrong?" She was afraid Bert was having a heart attack. After a great deal of prodding from Sue, Bert admitted that lately he'd sometimes get a burning sensation when he urinated—and now this. He couldn't even make love to his wife without being in pain! "This shouldn't be happening to me," he moaned bitterly. "I do all the right things. I take care of myself. I'm in better condition than men who are half my age!"

Bert's prostate enlargement—for that was what his doctor diagnosed his problem to be—was easily controlled with medication, but Bert never felt the same again. "It was like I crossed the line between youth and age—the point of no return. I may have been in great shape and looked ten years younger. But I was getting old people's diseases. And the realization shook me up."

With time, Bert gained some perspective on his condition, and on the natural inevitability of aging. He even started joking about it. "The way I carried on, you'd think I was the first guy on earth to grow old or have a physical problem. Fact is, I'm darn lucky to have the life I have and the health I have. A little prostate enlargement isn't going to set me back. It just woke me up a little, that's all."

PART II

Not Every Prostate Problem Is Cancer

Case Study: Jimmy D., Reluctant Expert

Jimmy D. was a healthy, hardworking construction engineer, and a very social guy. He was an after-work regular at Moonie's Tavern in the small southern town in which he'd grown up. Jimmy and his wife Shirley had a son in college, a little money in the bank, and they agreed that life was good.

It was during his forty-sixth year that Jimmy began to have problems with what he called his "water works." He found that he was getting up three or four times every night to urinate, and sometimes he couldn't quite get the job done. He felt like he was spending an awfully long time getting rid of his beer. After a few weeks of this, Shirley convinced him to see their family doctor. When the doctor suggested Jimmy go to a urologist, he was surprised. "I need a specialist?" he asked. "Come on, Doctor, what's up?"

His doctor explained that he was showing the first signs of a prostate condition known as benign prostatic hyperplasia—or enlargement of the prostate gland.

Jimmy was too embarrassed to admit that he didn't even know where his prostate was, much less what size it was supposed to be, but he'd heard enough to be alarmed. "Are you telling me I have prostate cancer?" he gulped.

"No, no," his doctor assured him. "Prostate enlargement has nothing to do with cancer. It's a benign condition that happens to just about everyone. Turns out, it's happening to you a little early. Go see the urologist. He'll tell you what to do."

The urologist gave Jimmy a thorough checkup, which included a rather indelicate finger prod. Later, in his office, he gave Jimmy a sympathetic smile. "I have some good news and some bad news," he said.

"Oh yeah? What's the bad news?" Jimmy was feeling somewhat grumpy from this ordeal.

"No more beer."

Jimmy frowned. "Ah, come on . . ."

"Okay, maybe once in a while," the doctor allowed. "But we've found that beer seems to irritate the prostate, and you don't need that right now."

"Yeah, okay," Jimmy said reluctantly. "So, what's the good news?"

The doctor grinned and clapped Jimmy on the back. "You're going to be just fine."

Jimmy switched from beer to club soda, but he still socialized with his friends at Moonie's, and he became something of a local expert on prostate problems. He'd had a big scare, and he'd come through, and he felt good about it. Only when it was over did he even admit to Shirley how scared he'd been.

By the following year, he'd talked most of his buddies into having their prostates checked out. He considered it a public service.

Jimmy's prostate is still enlarged, and he has it examined annually to be sure it stays in check. So far, there's been no additional enlargement. Some of the initial symptoms are still there, though lessened, and there's a good chance that he'll be able to maintain things as they are for some time.

To anyone who is willing to listen, Jimmy preaches the miracle of his new lease on life. That's what he calls it. He feels on top of the world, and he plans to stay that way for a long time.

6. What are the most common prostate afflictions?

As Jimmy D. learned, not every prostate problem is cancer. Nor does every condition require immediate aggressive medical treatment. In fact, there are four medical conditions associated with the prostate, and each of them has various levels of severity. Each will be described in greater depth. But simply put, the conditions are:

- Benign Prostatic Hyperplasia: Commonly referred to as BPH, this is a noncancerous enlargement of the prostate gland, common in 80 percent of men over age fifty.
- Infectious Prostatitis: A condition caused by the invasion of bacteria into the prostate.
- Noninfectious Prostatitis: Irritations to the prostate that have no known cause.
- Prostate Cancer: The development of abnormal cells in the prostate which multiply at an uncontrollable rate.

Any one of these conditions might have varying degrees of severity—from watch-and-see, to urgent action required. In this section, we're going to focus on noncancerous prostate conditions.

7. Is there an all-purpose test to detect prostate problems?

The good news is that screening methods for prostate conditions have grown more accurate and easily available in recent years—making a big difference in men's ability to catch problems early on, before they become serious. Screening is the number-one action you can take to offset problems.

There are several tests that measure the relative health of your prostate. Even if you have no symptoms, it is recommended that you be screened for prostate conditions after age fifty—earlier if there is a family history of prostate problems or cancer. These are the recommended screening methods:

Urinalysis: A standard urinalysis should be part of every exam. It will rule out urinary infections or the presence of blood in the urine that could signal prostate cancer.

Digital Rectal Exam (DRE): Just to be clear, "digital" refers to the digit of a finger, not a machine. Most men hate the very thought of this exam, but it's not painful or even very uncomfortable. The idea is probably worse than the reality. During this exam, you lean over the examination table or a chair so the doctor can get clear access to your rectal area. Then, the doctor carefully inserts a gloved, lubricated finger up into the rectum. The prostate is adjacent to the rectum, no more than an inch and a half from the anal opening, so it's a fairly easy reach. By palpating the prostate through the wall of the rectum, the doctor can quickly determine two essentials: Is your prostate its normal size, and does it have the smooth, elastic feel that indicates health?

The National Cancer Institute recommends the DRE as the only regular screening exam necessary for men who are not in a high-risk category. But the position is controversial—which brings us to our discussion of the PSA test.

Prostate-Specific Antigen (PSA): This is a relatively new procedure that is quickly becoming widely used as the first prostate screening test—even before the DRE. The PSA is a simple (inexpensive) blood test that works this way: There is protein in the seminal fluid, which is made in the prostate but circulated throughout the body. When PSA levels are elevated in the bloodstream, there's the possibility of a problem. Doctors who favor using the PSA test even before the DRE say that it's far more accurate.

The reading shows how many nanograms (one billionth of a gram) of PSA are present per milliliter of blood. As a rule, up to four nanograms is considered acceptable, although doctors also watch for rapid changes in the PSA over short periods. For example, if your PSA reading is 2.5 one year, then 3.5 the next, it might raise a red flag, even though it is within the normal range.

Some experts believe the PSA test should precede the DRE since a manual exam can potentially upset the hormone level of the prostate and result in a false reading.

Since the PSA is so obviously a wonderful predictive test for prostate problems, what's the controversy? Some doctors worry that the PSA is overly sensitive, detecting cancer cells too early to be of any real concern—that is, at stages when aggressive treatment would not be appropriate. More disturbing, the test has a false positive rate of 60 percent, and you can imagine the havoc this can create. Men get alarmed that they have cancer, and maybe undergo desperate medical or surgical measures that screw up their lives and provide little benefit.

Furthermore, although the PSA is sensitive when it comes to finding out that a problem exists, it's not so hot about identifying what that problem might be. It's impossible to tell from a PSA whether the higher antigen levels are caused by a tumor, an infection, or a noncancerous enlargement.

If your attitude is, "So what? I'd rather have the test and be aggressive than sit back and wait," consider this: Prostate cancer progresses so slowly that up to 75 percent of men who have cancer cells detected in their prostates die of other causes before prostate cancer ever becomes a threat.

So, where does that leave you? Unfortunately, there's no sure answer. But at least you know the terms of the debate, and that will help you to make a more fully informed decision. Like it or not, science moves at a snail's pace, and this is no exception. This issue may not be fully resolved until the end of a sixteen-year national screening study. Maybe the best approach is one of educated caution. Go ahead and get the PSA, along with the other tests your doctor recommends. But don't base further action on one test or even a single PSA reading. Repeat the process before taking action.

If screening tests indicate the presence of a cancer, the next step is a biopsy, since cancer can only be confirmed with a tissue sample. We'll talk about cancer-detecting biopsies in the following part. If the tests indicate a noncancerous problem, such as prostate enlargement, there are two diagnostic tests:

Ultrasound: This is a noninvasive procedure during which sound waves allow the visualization of many different structures of the body. It's used in many screening as well as treatment conditions, replacing the previous method of using a catheter. Ultrasound is safer and far more comfortable than previous methods. It's also diagnostically superior since it allows a clear view of the area in question. An ultrasound can also measure residual urine— that is, urine left in the bladder. Any amount over ten ounces requires immediate action.

Peak Flow Test: This is a test that is designed to determine your urine flow pattern. It measures urine flow at its highest rate to see if you are voiding properly. Less than ten milliliters per second can indicate trouble since it means that your urine is being retained in the bladder. Sometimes your doctor will use a stop watch and time your flow as you urinate into a glass. This test can be a little embarrassing. A sense of humor helps!

8. What is prostatitis?

Prostatitis means literally "inflammation of the prostate." It is actually a collection of disorders that account for as many as three million visits to urologists every year. There are two types of prostatitis—infectious and noninfectious. Infectious prostatitis will probably let you know it's there. Symptoms include swelling, redness, tenderness, and a feeling of heat in the infected area.

How does the infection occur? The correct answer is just about any way. Sometimes we fail to appreciate just how delicate our systems are; the slightest things can set them off.

Bacteria can get into the prostate through urinary tract infections, anal or vaginal intercourse with someone who has an infection which is passed along, the insertion of a catheter or other instrument into the bladder, or even by drinking too much alcohol, eating high-fat foods, or just about anything else that might insult this delicate gland.

Noninfectious prostatitis is a condition that is possibly related to sexual activity, but not caused by a known bacterial infection. It may be related to the activity itself—or, in some cases, the lack of activity. One suspected cause of noninfectious prostatitis is a condition commonly referred to as "blue balls." Most men understand what that means: intense sexual arousal without release. Essentially, the prostate is signaled to produce fluid that will move the sperm along. But when the release is aborted, the fluid causes a feeling of congestion or tightness in the scrotal area. This condition is sometimes seen in men whose frequent sexual activity is interrupted. Again, the prostate continues to produce fluid, but there is no release. Noninfectious prostatitis can cause lower back pain, pelvic soreness, a burning sensation during urination, painful ejaculation, and sometimes blood streaks in the semen.

Another form of inflammation can be related to stress. A stress-related flare-up can sometimes be treated with muscle relaxants, nonsteroidal anti-inflammatory drugs like ibuprofen, as well as biofeedback or regular warm baths.

In spite of its frequency among men between the ages

of twenty and forty-five, the exact cause of noninfectious prostatitis has yet to be determined. Some experts believe it may in fact be bacterial—caused by an organism that has not yet been defined. This belief is based on clinical experiences that show many men with so-called nonbacterial prostatitis getting better when they are given antibiotics.

More frustrating still is a similar condition called prostatodynia, which causes pain like other forms of prostatitis, but lacks any specific signs of inflammation or infection. Its origin is unknown, but it is usually treated with the same methods as other forms of prostatitis.

9. What are the treatments for prostatitis?

Since infectious prostatitis is caused by bacteria or other microorganisms, most cases are cleared up with antibiotic treatment. In more severe cases that do not respond to antibiotics, hospitalization might be necessary until normal urine flow can be restored. (Never take this lightly! If you can't pee, you can't live.) The usual course of antibiotic treatment is between two weeks and three months. Have repeat tests to be sure the infection is cleared.

Some men have a condition of chronic bacterial prostatitis, which is difficult to eradicate with standard antibiotic treatments. This may be caused by the so-called blood-prostate barrier—a part of the prostate that prevents certain substances from entering the prostate. While the barrier is designed to maintain prostate health, it can also impede the action of antibiotics. If you have chronic bacterial prostatitis, you'll probably need to make some lifestyle changes to prevent continued flare-ups. Many men have discovered that substances like alcohol, caffeine, and spicy foods cause problems, as do heavy exercise and stress. Sometimes over-the-counter cold medications or antihistimines can be the culprits.

As far as treating noninfectious prostatitis, that's a little less clear, especially since its cause may sometimes elude detection. Believe it or not, masturbation to orgasm might be a good way to get relief. Occasionally, prostatic massage is recommended if antibiotics or anti-inflammatory agents haven't worked. Many men might feel squeamish about the procedure, not to mention embarrassed. It involves the doctor placing a finger up the rectum and massaging the prostate until the congested fluid is expelled through the urethra and the penis.

Be aware that your symptoms may be related to other than prostate problems. For example, bladder or kidney complaints can produce similar symptoms. Don't just assume that the prostate is the cause. Help your doctor investigate the source of your problem by being knowledgeable about your personal and family history, honest about your lifestyle habits, and as descriptive as possible about your symptoms.

10. What is benign prostatic hyperplasia, known as BPH?

BPH is a noncancerous prostate enlargement that accompanies aging. After a rapid growth spurt at puberty, your prostate pretty much remains the same size until around the age of forty-five, when it commonly begins to enlarge, due to the activity of a key hormone called dihydrotestosterone (DHT). More than half of all men have some degree of BPH by the time they reach age sixty, and 90 percent of men have BPH by the age of eighty. Jimmy D., our friend in the case study at the beginning of this section, developed BPH much earlier than the average man. If you're lucky, even if you get BPH, the enlargement won't be that severe, and it won't substantially interfere with your quality of life. Some men who have minor BPH deal with it by using common sense—for example, avoiding liquids a few hours before bedtime, planning rest stops on long car trips, and cutting down on alcohol and caffeine.

There are two ways in which BPH can cause real damage: *static,* referring to the size, and *dynamic,* referring to the muscular motion. A static problem is caused by an enlarged prostate interfering with the urinary flow from the bladder. A dynamic problem is caused when the smooth muscle around the prostate is affected, causing contractions that squeeze the channel and make urination difficult.

11. Are there early warning signs of BPH?

It's entirely possible to have a slightly enlarged prostate with no real symptoms. More often BPH makes itself known. The most common three early warning signs are:

- a decrease in the force and stream of urine;
- a hesitation when beginning to urinate, as if there is something blocking the flow;
- a need to get up to urinate several times during the night—a condition called nocturia.

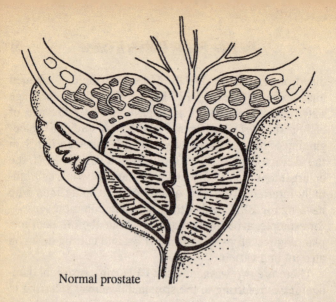

Normal prostate

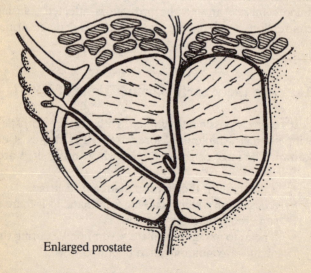

Enlarged prostate

There are other bothersome signs as well—all having to do with urination. There might be a problem stopping urination. You tighten the urinary sphincter muscle to stop the flow and prevent any more urine from discharging, but instead there is a series of continuing dribbles.

You may also experience the feeling that your bladder is not completely empty, although you think you're finished urinating. Or you may have a strong urge to urinate but find that you can't.

Not only do you get up several times during the night to urinate, you also find yourself needing to urinate frequently throughout the day.

Obviously, this is inconvenient, not to mention maddening. But it can be worse than that. Over time, BPH can compromise your most vital organs. The ultimate result of untreated BPH can be damage to the kidney. That's because when urine is left in the bladder, a backup of pressure on the kidneys can lead to kidney failure.

SELF-TEST FOR BPH

The American Urological Association has prepared the following symptom index to help diagnose BPH. Answer the following questions, then take the completed survey to your doctor. He or she will help you evaluate your status. The American Urological Association refrains from scoring this test since it believes an accurate score can only be determined by your personal physician. But your answers to the following questions can provide valuable information.

1. Over the past month or so, how often have you had a sensation of not emptying your bladder completely after you've finished urinating?

   not at all _____ (0)
   less than one time in five _____ (1)
   less than half the time _____ (2)
   about half the time _____ (3)
   more than half the time _____ (4)
   almost always _____ (5)

2. Over the past month or so, how often have you had to urinate again less than two hours after you finished urinating?

   not at all _____ (0)
   less than one time in five _____ (1)
   less than half the time _____ (2)
   about half the time _____ (3)
   more than half the time _____ (4)
   almost always _____ (5)

3. Over the past month or so, how often have you found that you stopped and started again several times when you urinated?

   not at all _____ (0)
   less than one time in five _____ (1)
   less than half the time _____ (2)
   about half the time _____ (3)
   more than half the time _____ (4)
   almost always _____ (5)

4. Over the past month or so, how often have you found it difficult to postpone urination?

> not at all _____ (0)
> less than one time in five _____ (1)
> less than half the time _____ (2)
> about half the time _____ (3)
> more than half the time _____ (4)
> almost always _____ (5)

5. Over the past month or so, how often have you had a weak urinary stream?

> not at all _____ (0)
> less than one time in five _____ (1)
> less than half the time _____ (2)
> about half the time _____ (3)
> more than half the time _____ (4)
> almost always _____ (5)

6. Over the past month or so, how often have you had to push or strain to begin urination?

> not at all _____ (0)
> less than one time in five _____ (1)
> less than half the time _____ (2)
> about half the time _____ (3)
> more than half the time _____ (4)
> almost always _____ (5)

7. Over the past month, how many times did you most typically get up to urinate from the time

you went to bed at night until the time you got up in the morning?

none _____ (0)
one time _____ (1)
two times _____ (2)
three times _____ (3)
four times _____ (4)
five or more times _____ (5)

Add your score: _____

TAKE THE TEST RESULT WITH YOU
WHEN YOU VISIT YOUR DOCTOR

12. What should I do if I have symptoms?

Don't ignore them. Infections or an enlargement of the prostate won't simply go away if you will them to. See your doctor.

Having said that, it's pretty understandable that you'd be tempted to ignore the symptoms as long as you could stand it. If you're an otherwise healthy man in your prime, with a good quality of life and a normal sex drive, the very idea that your prostate might be acting up could send you reeling. Of course, there's the big fear of cancer, which appears like the monster in most people's closets. But there's also the challenge to your self-esteem and image of manliness. If your prostate, that tiny little gland that you probably weren't even aware of, suddenly betrays you, you might think you're facing the end of your manhood.

It will comfort you to know that in most cases, BPH isn't the boogeyman in the closet. More often, it's controllable, rarely drastic, and almost never fatal. And it has nothing to do with cancer!

13. Are there non-medical treatments for BPH?

In the early stages of BPH, most men don't have to worry about surgery or even medical treatment. Rather, there are a number of lifestyle changes that can greatly relieve the symptoms of BPH. A high-fat diet has been isolated as the biggest single factor in the eventual development of prostate cancer, and it is also a risk factor for BPH—a conclusion that was reached after all of the other risk factors were weighed.

For most BPH sufferers, common sense is the best treatment—like watching your fluid intake, especially in the evening. But there are other simple ways to alleviate the symptoms. Since alcohol is believed to irritate the prostate, cut down on your alcohol level. (If you must have an occasional beer, avoid drinking it late in the day.)

Caffeine is another substance best avoided. It stimulates the urinary tract and increases the urge to pee—not exactly what you need in your condition. In addition to coffee, tea, and caffeinated colas, check over-the-counter medications that might contain caffeine.

If it's sometimes hard for you to urinate—that is, you feel the urge, but nothing comes out—it might help to sit down on the toilet instead of standing up. The relaxation of muscles can encourage the flow.

14. What if my condition gets worse?

You may have lived for many years with only minor problems from BPH. But it's not going to go away, and usually it's a matter of time before your enlargement will require more assertive intervention. You've got a few options, so investigate them thoroughly. I'll warn you in advance that you're going to experience some frustration. A lot of people assume that science is, well, science—containing the imprimatur of certainty. Actually, science is more like art—a touch here, a highlight there, let's try this, now that. You get the idea.

Science is also highly personal. Assembly line medicine simply does not work. You're not just a set of body parts, and your prostate is intimately connected with who you are as a total person.

With that in mind, let's look at some of the treatments available for advanced BPH.

The Turp: Transurethral resection of the prostate (TURP) is currently the procedure of choice. Ninety percent of prostate surgeries performed today use this method. There are good reasons. Instead of cutting into the abdomen or the perineum—the bridge that connects the anus and the scrotum—the prostate is reached through the urethra, where it is resected. There is a low rate of complications from TURP, and it also allows a tissue sample to be sent to a pathologist to check for malignancy. So, it's a good way to test for cancer too.

Now let's look at the downside. When you have a TURP, it changes the way you ejaculate. Don't worry—you're still going to have orgasms, just like before. But instead of the ejaculate coming out the head of the penis, it backfires into the bladder. The technical term is retrograde ejaculation. The most straightforward consequence of retrograde ejaculation is that it makes you infertile. This isn't a problem for the majority of men who undergo the procedure, since they're usually older. However, let's not downplay the dramatic change in sexual experience. I urge you to engage your doctor in a thorough discussion about what retrograde ejaculation is like so you can prepare yourself and your partner. No question is off limits, and there's no such thing as a "silly" question when it comes to your sexual experience. This is a time when a "buddy" might come in handy. Check out one of the organizations or support groups listed later in this book, or ask your doctor to introduce you to another patient who has been through the procedure. Generally speaking, most men report that once they get used to it, it's not a problem—especially when their doctors fully explain what they should expect.

Like any surgery, the TURP requires a period of recovery during which time you're not going to be feeling a hundred percent. There will be discomforts and inconveniences; be ready for them. Expect to have some urinary difficulties—urgency, incontinence, unusual frequency. These will usually resolve within a few weeks. Small percentages of men suffer long-term or even permanent effects from the TURP. Incontinence is relatively rare—about one-half of one percent; up to 8 percent of men can't have erections, although they can still achieve orgasm and have satisfying sex lives. (We'll talk more about this later.) In any event, severe problems following TURP are rare. Focus on the positive.

Of course, the TURP isn't your only option, but most experts agree that once treatment becomes necessary, it's the most reliable. Doctors at the University of Minnesota have introduced a balloon insert which dilates the urethra, but that method is not yet widely used and it's still the subject of controversy.

15. How about drug therapy?

Efforts to treat severe BPH with drugs have often left men feeling that the "cure" was worse than the disease. Drugs that blocked the production of testosterone, or female hormones that shrank the prostate, might have solved the immediate problem, but in the process they created many miserable fellows. Since the prostate—and its related problems—are so hormonally driven, it's always been very hard to find treatments that do not diminish the sexual quality of men's lives.

Fortunately, the research continues. There are currently two drugs on the market—one that shrinks the prostate if it is enlarged (a static condition), and another that relaxes the muscles around the prostate (a dynamic condition).

The most hopeful new drug is called Proscar, manufactured by Merck & Co., and approved by the FDA in late 1992. To date, Proscar is the only drug that shows promise in reducing enlarged prostates. It does this by blocking the conversion of testosterone into dihydrotestosterone. Proscar isn't a miracle drug. It normally takes several months to show any results, and once on it, men must use it permanently. Proscar can also lower PSA levels, making it hard to detect early stage cancers. Like any drug, Proscar's ultimate benefits have to be weighed on an individual basis. It isn't suited for all men, but it might be a perfect solution for some.

Hytrin, manufactured by Abbott Laboratories, is an alpha blocker that relaxes the smooth muscle tissue around the prostate, lessening pressure on the urethra. It was first approved by the FDA in 1987 as a blood pressure medication. Many doctors favor Hytrin because its results are seen immediately. There are side effects, however, which make it intolerable for some men. The worst of these include dizziness, light-headedness, fatigue, and occasional fainting spells.

16. Will BPH or prostatitis put me at risk for prostate cancer?

BPH is not a risk factor for cancer. Having an enlarged prostate is not related to the development of cancer. Nor is there any relationship between the development of BPH and previous infections or sexual activity. In fact, some people believe that the early diagnosis of other prostate conditions might avoid later problems because of the established habit of getting regularly screened for prostate problems.

Case Study: Barry's Snow Emergency

Barry Z. was sure he was going to die of pain right there in his car. It was almost seven P.M. and Barry had been sitting in traffic for almost an hour and a half now. The snow was coming down so hard that he couldn't even see the shoulder of the road he was waiting on. What a nightmare! And to top it all off, that familiar urgency had been pressing on him for some time and it was getting excruciating. The traffic, the snow, the pain—come on, people, let's move here! He couldn't take this anymore. He was honking his horn, his window was down, he was yelling for everybody to move, and nothing was happening. He was almost ready to get out of the car and urinate on the side of the road.

Barry finally made it home an hour later, and by this time he felt very sick—sweaty, nauseated, his bladder in agony. Almost running and hunched over, he pushed past his wife in the kitchen and made a beeline for the bathroom. Shaking, he unzipped and prepared to relieve himself of his painful burden. Nothing happened. He waited, tried to relax. Still nothing. He was panicking. Come on, come on . . . finally a few drops, the beginning of a stream, and . . . nothing. Stopped again. He felt a wave of nauseating heat welling up from his gut. Then Barry remembered what his urologist had told him a couple of years before, about the urinary sphincter muscle and how to relax it. He sat down on the toilet and in a couple of minutes experienced sweet relief. He also knew it was time to get back to his urologist.

Barry, fifty-nine, had first noticed his problem in his early fifties, but like most men, he'd tried his best to ignore it. It was his family doctor who had discovered his prostate problem during a routine digital rectal exam and had sent him to the urologist, who confirmed the initial diagnosis of early BPH. Barry had been one of those lucky few whose symptoms—frequent urination during the night, some trouble starting and stopping urination—were controllable with careful attention and a change in his diet and drinking habits. He'd had few real problems in the years since. He'd been happy to avoid drugs, surgery, or other treatments, but now he was ready. He knew one thing: He never wanted to be in that kind of "snow emergency" again!

Barry's urologist agreed that what had happened to him was a BPH sufferer's worst nightmare. But he put Barry's fears to rest with his easy manner and calm matter-of-fact explanations. He suggested that they start with Proscar and see what happened. "Don't you worry," the doctor said, "I'm going to work with you on this every step of the way. No more emergencies."

Within six months of starting Proscar, Barry was seeing a big difference. He felt almost normal again. It was a great feeling. Considering how lousy he'd felt before, it was like getting a new lease on life.

PART III

When the Diagnosis Is Cancer

Case Study: Phil's New Lease on Life

At fifty-seven, Phillip G. was on top of the world. Not only did he look and feel great, thanks to a good diet and exercise program, but now his business smarts gave him the edge to become president of his company. He was a bit taken aback when he received a call from his doctor, Jeff P. He'd been in to see Jeff a week ago for his annual checkup. What was the problem?

"Phil, I'd like you to come in and see me at about four-thirty today. Can you manage it?"

There was something in Jeff's tone of voice that Phil didn't like. "Gee, Doc," he hesitated, "I'm right in the middle of twenty-seven things. Can we clear this up over the phone?" As he spoke, Phil's mind rapidly recalled the recent visit. Jeff had done all the usual blood work, urine sample, the routine stuff. What could possibly be wrong? He'd never felt so great.

"Phil," Jeff's voice softened, "I'm asking you to come in. Trust me. It's important."

Phil's stomach plummeted three feet to his toes. "Okay," he croaked. "Four-thirty. I'll be there."

Phil's day dragged by as he tried to run an internal audit on his health. His heartbeat felt fine, no aches or pains. He'd run his usual three miles after work last night. What on earth could this be about?

He swept into the doctor's office at four-thirty on the nose, and for the very first time in his memory was ushered directly into Jeff's office. No cooling his heels with the ancient magazine stack. It didn't comfort him.

Jeff P., a large, shambling fellow with a somewhat distracted air, came into the room ten seconds later and sat down across from Phil. He grinned. "So, how are you doing?" he asked, as though they were engaged in a social visit.

Phil was growing impatient with the subterfuge. "How the hell can I tell you how I'm doing until you tell me how I'm doing?" he asked in exasperation.

"You've got a point there, Phil. I'm sorry. Look, I got your tests back from the lab and we've got a positive read on your PSA. I want to do another test, and then I want you to see a urologist. I'll give you a couple of names."

Phil's face flamed. "What the hell are you telling me?"

Jeff shrugged—not unkind, just businesslike. "With levels this high, it could be cancer. We've got to repeat the test. I'm going to send you to a top-notch urologist. He'll take it from here."

Phil was ashen. Shocked. Prostate cancer. He could barely think straight. But he heard his voice speak, sounding surprisingly calm and in control. "Cancer, huh? Okay, Doc. What are my chances with this?"

"First, Phil, there's no way to know you even have cancer without a tissue biopsy. If you do have cancer, you have a lot of options. You've got to get to this urologist." Jeff scribbled a name on his pad. "Fred's the best. Only the best for you, my friend. Meanwhile, try not to worry."

Phil grimaced. "Isn't that like saying there's an elephant in the room but I should try not to notice it?" They both laughed, but uneasily.

Phil left Jeff's office feeling dazed and apprehensive. He made his way home on automatic pilot, paced, tried to eat, worried, and even cried a little. Finally he fell into a fitful sleep.

In the following days, Phil learned as much as he could about prostate cancer so he could weigh all of his options carefully. He made an appointment with Fred S., the urologist Jeff recommended. Fred confirmed the initial PSA finding and performed a biopsy right in his office. Phil was impressed with that.

The tissue came back positive. Fred tried to break the news gently, but by now Phil was ready for it. Phil listened carefully as Fred laid out the options. Frankly, Phil thought the guy lacked charm, but Jeff had said he was the best. "It's my opinion," Fred told Phil, "that the best strategy for you is the radical retropubic prostatectomy. Your cancer is fairly advanced, and you're a relatively young man."

"Radical . . ." Phil murmured.

"We can remove the lymph nodes, send them to a pathologist, and make sure the cancer hasn't spread."

Phil wasn't ready to make a decision. He got a second opinion, did more reading, talked to Jeff, and finally came to the conclusion that Fred was right. He called him up. "I'll do it," he said. "Let's go ahead."

Fred sighed with relief. "I'm glad," he said quietly. "You're generally healthy, Phil. I think we can make you well. But I have to tell you one thing. Listen very carefully. It may be necessary, just to be sure all the cancer's out, that we remove the nerves that control your erections."

There was barely a beat of silence. "Are you saying what I think you're saying?" Phil asked.

"Umm . . ."

"Shit—excuse my French. How many surprises like that one do you have up your sleeve?"

Fred didn't answer right away. Phil took a heavy breath. "Look," he said, with more bravery than he felt, "we'll cross that bridge later. Right now, to be perfectly honest, I just want to live."

The surgery was done quickly, and Fred said he was very pleased with the results. He was sure that he had removed all of the cancer, but only time would tell. There was no way of knowing for certain whether the cancer had already escaped the prostate and spread, but the lymph nodes removed and examined during the operation had disclosed no trace of cancer.

Five years later Phil was going strong. "I'm not problem-free," he said philosophically, "but who is? I'm alive. I feel good." Every year for those first five, Phil had sent one bottle of champagne to Jeff and another one to Fred. He called it "our anniversary champagne."

17.   What if my doctor says it's cancer?

Cancer can be one of the scariest words in the language, especially when it's being used by a doctor to describe something that's happening to you. It wasn't that long ago when the very word *cancer* was rarely spoken, except in a whisper. People were ashamed to admit they had cancer; it seemed to imply a fundamental inadequacy, a failure of life force, and most surely a death sentence.

We've come a long way from those dark ages. But the fear persists. When you are told you have cancer, you are very aware that you are embarking on a journey whose course is uncharted.

But cancer isn't a single illness. If it were, it wouldn't be so elusive. Rather, cancer is a term we use to describe literally hundreds of different cell abnormalities. Some of these are deadly; others are treatable. Still others are so slow-growing that their impact might be virtually nonexistent for many years. This is very often the case with prostate cancer. Therefore, when your doctor tells you that you have cancerous cells in your prostate, don't think you've just been introduced to the Grim Reaper.

One out of eleven American men will get prostate cancer, and the statistics are higher for black men. Most men, if they live long enough, will die with some cancerous cells in their prostate gland. These cells have been developing slowly for decades, but have not yet reached the point where they escape the gland and become engaged in destruction elsewhere. Most men who have cancer cells in their prostates ultimately die of some entirely unrelated cause.

Prostate cancer is considered a primary cancer. That is, it always originates in the prostate itself, rather than spreading from other sites. It is often silent in the early stages—a creeping, invisible disorder whose presence might go undetected until it is discovered in a standard checkup.

18.   What causes prostate cancer?

No one knows for sure what causes prostate cancer, although some new theories have been gathering steam. The most promising has to do with the relationship between the development of prostate cancer and a high fat diet.

In 1993 a study was published in the *Journal of the National Cancer Institute* suggesting that men whose diets are rich in animal fats run an 80 percent higher risk for developing potentially fatal prostate cancer than do men with a low intake of animal fats. The study, begun by the

Harvard School of Public Health in 1986, followed the dietary habits of 47,855 men between the ages of forty and seventy-five. Of the 300 men who developed prostate cancer, those whose cases were most advanced had consumed diets high in animal fats.

These results supported what scientists had already discovered from laboratory tests conducted with animals. Why animal fat? One reason might be that animal fat boosts the production of sex hormones, which can trigger the production of tumors.

An interesting example of the potential role of diet is seen when we study Japanese men. Prostate cancer is very rare in Japan. Yet, when Japanese men move to the United States, their incidences increase substantially. This would suggest a strong dietary link.

19. How does prostate cancer progress?

The words, "You have prostate cancer," are chilling. They summon up a sense of ultimate defeat. Hearing that you have cancer may sound like hearing a death sentence —or at least the knowledge that life will never again be the same. The first thing that happens when you hear a diagnosis of cancer is that your brain shuts down. That's normal. But then, take another look and you may find that the prognosis is not as grim as you originally suspected.

In fact, prostate cancer usually takes its time, advancing very slowly through four stages.

Stage A: The cancer is microscopic, there are no symptoms, and it can't even be detected by a digital rectal exam. A PSA test might show elevated antigen levels, as will a biopsy performed in conjunction with another procedure, such as a transurethral resection.

Stage B: There are probably no notable symptoms, although a doctor performing a digital rectal exam can normally detect a lump or an unnaturally hard area on the prostate's outer lobes. At this point, there has been no spreading beyond the prostate itself. Stage B cancers are usually divided into two subgroups. Stage B-1 means that the cancer is contained to one lobe of the prostate; in Stage B-2 the cancer has spread over two lobes.

Stage C: By this stage, there's a good chance that the cancer has spread beyond the prostate and initially invaded surrounding tissues. There might be some urinary problems. Stage C prostate cancer can be detected by a DRE or other standard exam. Stage C-1 is the less severe of the two C stages because the cancer's involvement with other tissues is still minimal. In Stage C-2 the cancer has caused some blockage of the urethra and has made its presence known by impinging on the flow of the urine.

Stage D: By now the cancer has spread widely throughout the body, potentially infecting the lymph nodes and bones. This is the most serious stage of all. It has four subgroupings. In Stage D-0, other than elevated prostate enzyme levels, there are no signs that the cancer has progressed. In Stage D-1 there is clear evidence that the cancer has spread to the lymph nodes in the immediate area surrounding the prostate. In Stage D-2 the cancer has metastasized or spread to other sites of the body, notably the other lymph nodes, the bones, or other organs. Stage D-3 refers to men with Stage D-2 cancer that has not responded to treatment. In Stage D-3 there are major problems to be dealt with, including extreme fatigue, weight loss, and pain.

20. What tests does your doctor do to make sure it's cancer?

There are several tests that are designed to evaluate not only the presence of cancer, but also the stage and character of the cancerous cells or tumors. The PSA blood test, described earlier, shows a rise in antigen levels that indicate the possibility of cancer.

To assure that there are cancer cells present, the doctor needs to perform a biopsy. Cancer can only be detected with absolute certainty when there is a tissue sample that can be examined under a microscope. Prostate biopsies used to be invasive procedures, conducted in the hospital under anesthesia. Today, noninvasive methods allow biopsies to be easily done as office procedures.

What does the biopsy involve? One method is to use what is called a "biopsy gun" to shoot a needle into the rectum in the blink of an eye. This method is so quick that it's virtually painless.

Another technique is the fine needle aspiration, which is used to procure tissue samples for various kinds of cancer. For prostate tests, a very fine needle is passed through the rectum, which removes cells from several different locations. To help the doctor view the area more specifically, an ultrasound probe can also be placed in the rectum to provide a picture of the area. Ultrasound probes are not at all painful, and they are now the favored approach among doctors.

A more invasive biopsy procedure, preferred by some doctors, uses a core needle which is as thick as a pencil and requires some form of sedation. This method yields a larger tissue sample than the fine needle aspirate.

The biopsy tells the doctor whether or not cancerous cells are present and which kind of cells they are. About 95 percent of cancerous cells found in the prostate are adenocarcinoma—a type of cancer that originates in the lining of the inner surface of an organ; in this case, the prostate.

Your doctor will also look into your urethra with an instrument called a cystoscope to see if there is a tumor pressing on your urethra and if there is cancer in the bladder. A bone scan will detect cancer spread to the bones, and the CT scan will show the presence of cancer that may have spread to surrounding organs. Magnetic resonance imaging is a somewhat new technique that allows the doctor to view an image of the prostate on the screen. The technique is similar to CT (CAT) scanning, but there is no exposure to radiation because a magnetic field and radio signals are used instead of radiation.

Doctors use physical examinations and laboratory tests to "stage" a cancer. Some use what is called a Gleason Score, a system that essentially traces the architecture of a tumor and shows how aggressive the cancer cells are. A score of between one and five is given to the two largest clusters of cancer cells; the number one denotes the least aggressive type, and five the most aggressive. When the two numbers are added together, the result can help your doctor gauge the status of your tumor.

21. What are the survival rates for prostate cancer?

The strongest argument for regular screening, especially the PSA test, is that when it is detected early, there is a 90 percent cure rate for prostate cancer. If the cancer is contained in the prostate and the prostate is removed, you have an excellent chance of leading a healthy, cancer-free life.

The key (I'll say it again!) is early detection. Since there are rarely any symptoms in the early stages of prostate cancer, only about 30 percent of all cases are caught before they've spread. This is an entirely preventable situation. If we were to characterize it in salesman's terms, the cost-benefit ratio would be off the charts. Men would be lining up outside urologists' offices at the same rate women show up for their annual Pap smears.

22. Can prostate cancer be treated without surgery?

One common misconception about any kind of cancer is that surgery is always the best option. This is the "out damn spot" theory of cancer treatment—as though excising the troublesome area will ultimately make you better.

A responsible doctor will always present you with the full range of choices, which include:

1. watchful waiting
2. surgery

3. radiation
4. hormone therapy or chemotherapy

Surgery can actually be an undesirable way to deal with prostate cancer. It might surprise you to know that a highly recommended form of "treatment" for prostate cancer is no treatment at all—what is known as "watchful waiting." Increasingly, watchful waiting is being recommended as a reasonable strategy, especially for older men, since prostate cancer tends to be slow-growing. By all means, don't rush into surgical solutions before you investigate other options.

Most Stage A cancers are easily cured. In 85 percent of all cases, there is no recurrence of cancer in the future. (This is a good argument for avoiding panic at the mention of cancer. Not all cancers are equal!) The 15 percent that resist early treatment are more vigorous and may require the same aggressive treatment as Stage B cancers.

At Stage B, the cancer is still highly curable. Lymph nodes surrounding the prostate will be removed to make sure the cancer has not spread. If it's found to be contained to the prostate, the most common treatment is complete removal of the prostate gland.

By Stage C the prostate has been consumed by cancer, but it can still be treated if it has not spread to other parts of the body—a fact determined by biopsies of surrounding lymph nodes. The usual course of treatment is hormonal or radiation treatment.

If Stage D cancer has spread only to the surrounding lymph nodes, there's still a chance that the cancer can be contained. Although Stage D cancer is not curable, it can be controlled. There are different attitudes about the best course of treatment at this point. Some doctors believe that a radical prostatectomy and a bilateral orchiectomy are necessary. These terms are as intimidating as they sound; they mean removal of the prostate and both testicles.

There's no gentle way to break the news of this procedure. It's an ugly reality, and the common term for it—castration—is even uglier. But this is very late-stage treatment, and there's some disagreement about whether or when it's necessary to go this far.

Currently, the surgical operation of choice is the radical retropubic prostatectomy, which is the removal of the entire prostate gland, the attached seminal vesicles, and a small portion of the bladder.

First, the surgeon makes an incision that extends from the belly button to the pubic bone. The lymph nodes are then removed and sent for a biopsy to find out very quickly whether or not the cancer has spread. If it has spread, the surgery does not continue. The prostate remains. If the cancer has not spread, the prostate is removed, then the urethra and bladder are sewn back together.

There's also a very new procedure that might be promising for early stage prostate cancer. It's cryosurgery. Intensely cold liquid nitrogen is used to kill sections of the prostate where the cancer is detected. Used in conjunction with ultrasound, which allows a precise reading on the location, cryosurgery may someday become state of the art. For now, it is totally experimental, and most surgeons don't recommend it.

23.   So, the prostate is gone, but so is my sex life?

This is a myth: Prostate surgery means good-bye sex life. We'll be talking about this in greater detail later, but here's a bit of good news to cheer you on. Dr. Patrick Walsh, director of the Brady Urological Institute at Johns Hopkins University, has invented what he calls a "potency sparing prostatectomy." This surgical method has been widely acclaimed. The procedure essentially preserves the nerves that control erections. According to Dr. Walsh, this surgery allows up to 75 percent of men in their fifties to regain potency after healing. For younger men, the percentage is higher—up to 90 percent. Even men in their sixties have a 60 percent chance of regaining potency. It's important to know if your surgeon has training in Dr. Walsh's method.

If you're like most men, the sexual implications are at the front of your mind—which is why we'll examine the issue thoroughly in Part V.

24.   Is it true that some men are given female hormones?

At first gasp, this sounds like the worst of all possible scenarios. "I'd rather be dead than be a woman," one patient remarked when his doctor suggested hormone therapy. But take a deep breath and relax. It's not really as bad as all that. Hormone therapy is usually a late stage therapy, and it's often the only alternative to removal of the testicles. It is important to remember that each cancer produced in the body has a unique method of development and a unique way of attacking—and destroying—its host environment. On the one hand, there are cancers so virulent that they are virtually unstoppable. Patients who develop them inevitably succumb. For example, many brain tumors, liver, and pancreatic cancers remain beyond the scope of medical understanding or treatment.

Prostate cancer is one of the diseases that has yielded some information about its course. Though the prostate itself may always remain something of a mystery, specialists agree that its tumors are composed of the following types of cells:

1. Those that depend on testosterone, the male hormone, to act as fuel for a tumor's growth.
2. Those that partially depend on testosterone, but not entirely, for their growth.
3. Those whose growth is not dependent on testosterone.

In most cases of prostate cancer, testosterone is the singular element that spurs the continued growth of the malignancy. This knowledge, combined with an understanding of how testosterone is produced in the body, has led to the development of testosterone-inhibiting drugs that, either alone or with surgery, disrupt the hormone's ability to feed the growth and spread of the cancer.

There are several options in hormone therapy. One of these involves taking a small estrogen pill called DES—only about three milligrams a day. Taking female hormones doesn't make you feminine, although you may feel some uncomfortable side effects like swelling of the breasts, edema, and sometimes nausea. Some men find that their body hair grows more slowly and they notice slight changes in their physiques. But these are minor enough to be unremarkable to observers. Of greater concern is the link between estrogen and cardiovascular disease in men. Oddly enough, although estrogen seems to protect women against heart disease, it has the opposite effect when it is administered to men. If you have heart disease, estrogen treatment is probably not advisable.

Another hormone treatment involves compounds that prevent the stimulation of testosterone. These compounds, or agonists as they are called, stop the luteinizing hormone releasing hormone (LHRH) which controls sex hormones from doing their work. LHRH agonists do not have the same effects as estrogen, but there are reports of hot flashes and impotence.

Unlike estrogen and LHRH agonists, which essentially inhibit the production of testosterone, another drug, flutamide, blocks the interaction between testosterone and the prostate. It is sometimes used in combination with LHRH.

Unfortunately, hormone therapy does not cure cancer, although there are physicians who claim that it has thrown some cancers into remission for years. The best scientific evidence at this point is that hormone therapy can push prostate cancer into remission for an average of a year and a half. Even as you are reading this, advances are being made on this front. It is vital that every man facing prostate cancer be kept as current as possible on the latest research and treatments available.

Hormone therapy is worth trying because, though it may not significantly effect your life expectancy, it may offer other substantial benefits. For instance, hormone therapy may:

1. Shrink tumors growing in bones and muscle.
2. Reduce the size of any tumor directly affecting the prostate, thus making the act of urinating much easier.
3. Have a major impact on the pain caused by the cancer and its spread, allowing the reduced use of narcotics and other pain-relieving medications.
4. Allow you to regain lost strength, perhaps regain lost weight, and move about with less discomfort.

25. How about chemotherapy?

There is some controversy among specialists about whether chemotherapy is effective against prostate cancer. Prostate cancer cells grow and divide very slowly, and some experts say a course of chemotherapy has little chance of doing away with many cells. The slow reproductive rate of prostate cancer provides an immunity against the action of chemotherapy, which works best on those cancers that are distinguished by malignant cells that divide often. Also, because tumors that have become large have an unusual blood supply system, chemotherapy may be able to reach some parts of the cancer while leaving other areas unscathed.

So, on the one hand you have many cancer specialists who feel that chemotherapy will achieve little while exposing the patient to a wide range of unpleasant side effects. On the other hand, some oncologists will argue that chemotherapy hasn't been given a real opportunity because it is so often the therapy of last resort, used somewhat reluctantly after the cancer has not responded to hormone treatment or radiation. But there are insufficient studies to demonstrate any real certainty about this, and many patients and their doctors will opt for a course of chemotherapy, figuring it will at least have some positive benefit. Perhaps chemotherapy would yield more satisfactory results if it were administered earlier in the course of treatment. Chemotherapy is believed worth trying by its proponents because there has been some evidence of success in shrinking tumors if it's given at the proper time.

Chemotherapy can be administered in pill form, which you take at home, or intravenously in a hospital or clinic setting. Any decision to enter this course of treatment should be investigated thoroughly because there are many side effects. You see, although chemotherapy kills the "bad" cancer cells, it can also kill healthy cells too. All things considered, it is not the treatment of choice for prostate cancer.

26. Is radiation treatment an option?

In early stage cancer, radiation is sometimes used as an alternative to surgery, although there is a lower cure rate. For later stages it might be used to control the spread of cancer. The goal of radiation is to destroy the ability of cancer cells to reproduce and survive.

The best current method of radiation treatment is the linear accelerator, which has a very precise ability to target cancer cells, minimizing the damage to normal cells in the area.

However, doctors are experimenting with internal methods, especially for early stages. One outpatient procedure is called seed implantation. Small radiation-charged "seeds" are implanted directly into cancer tissue, using ultrasound to show the exact position. These "seeds" do their work for between 17 to 35 days before they are passed off by the body. Not all radiation oncologists perform this procedure; many believe there is not sufficient evidence that it works. However, studies conducted at the Memorial Sloan Kettering Cancer Center have shown a ten-year survival rate of 70 percent among men using the implants.

Does radiation work? Does it make a difference in long-term survival? This is a topic of great dispute, and the answer depends on which expert you ask. However, like other decisions you make about treatment, this one depends on your personal profile—your age, the stage of cancer, your willingness to undergo the procedure, and so on. As you investigate your options, treat it as one in a series that you consider.

Some prostate cancer patients opt for radiation as the first course of action because they want to avoid the complications and risks that come with surgery. They figure if radiation doesn't work, they can then have surgery. But it's not that simple. Even in the most skilled hands, radiation therapy is bound to affect healthy tissue as well as the target area. If radiation therapy fails and you then must have your prostate removed, the damage caused by presurgical radiation will make postsurgical complications like impotence and incontinence more likely. For this reason, many doctors say flat out that the advisability of prostate surgery is not great for men who have had a course of radiation.

Even men who have radiation after surgery to kill cancer cells that might have escaped the prostate often have urinary complications and other side effects. Radiation is never a completely benign treatment. Nor does it affect every person the same way.

Case Study: Harry's Choice

Harry O. peered at his doctor through wire-rimmed glasses and said stiffly, "I'm really very sorry that you find me intractable, Doctor, but there is really nothing you can say that will dissuade me from what I believe to be the proper course. I think we should design a treatment plan and implement it as soon as possible. I'm afraid if I have any more time to consider it, I'll forego any treatment whatsoever." He leaned back in his chair, readjusted his glasses, straightened his tie, and tried to look far more nonchalant than he felt. Despite his studied air of calm, cool rationality, Harry was scared. And it wasn't the cancer that scared him as much as it was the surgery. He'd come to this meeting armed with everything he could find on alternatives to prostate cancer surgery, and although he knew the doctor was disturbed by what he had decided, he was sure in his heart of hearts that this was the right decision for him.

Dr. Charles G. had been practicing urologic medicine for almost thirty years. He'd seen his share of prostate cancers, and he admitted to a surgical bias, simply because it had always been the most effective method of treatment. However, he tried to be open-minded, knowing that ultimately a treatment's success was dependent, in large part, on the optimism and commitment of the patient. And Harry, underneath his professorial pose, had a desperate fear of surgery.

"Harry," Charles said in an even tone, "I'm always open to what my patients think best, and it certainly isn't as though you are making this decision in an offhand manner. But I think you're wrong. I'd even say you are dead wrong, but, considering the circumstances, that phrase may turn out to be far too precise. I'm just the expert here. I want to see us attack and destroy this cancer with every means available to us. But I can't make someone have surgery if they don't want to have surgery. My question to you is this: What is it you want me to do? How am I supposed to treat your condition when you won't let me do what I know I should do?"

He paused to let his words sink in. At least he'd said his piece. It wasn't even that Charles was so opposed to radiation as a surgical alternative. He simply felt that Harry's cancer had progressed beyond the point where radiation was a viable option. In many respects, the doctor found Harry a baffling character. It simply amazed him that a man with Harry's intelligence would throw up such roadblocks to successful treatment. The fact that Harry had avoided seeing a doctor for almost fourteen years was extraordinary enough, but to come in and find yourself facing a Stage B-1 prostate cancer, and to then refuse to consider your doctor's recommendation . . .

Harry could see that Charles was disturbed, but what could he do? He had only come in for an exam at his wife Edith's insistence, and now this. As soon as the diagnosis of prostate cancer had been confirmed, Harry had gone to the local university's library and thoroughly researched the topic, hoping to find an alternative. He carefully studied the pros and cons of radiation before deciding he was going to give it a try. He had discussed his choice with Edith, and she had, as always, told him to do as he thought best. He was deathly afraid of any sort of surgery, having lost his mother to a surgeon's scalpel while still a young boy. And besides, he didn't feel that surgery could guarantee a renewed quality of life. These doctors were always so eager to cut! Why not just have the radiation and be done with it? In his reading on it at the library, he had been encouraged by the differences between surgery and radiation.

"So you are willing to have radiation treatments?" Charles asked.

"I feel as though you were reading my mind, Doctor," Harry responded. "I can't say I'm wildly enthusiastic, but it does seem to be the way to go."

"You understand, of course, that there are potentially serious side effects," Charles said.

Harry adjusted his glasses and read from the notes he had brought with him: " 'Possibility of diarrhea, edema in the legs and feet, urinary frequency and urgency, skin rash, erectile dysfunction' . . . that about cover it?"

Charles had to smile. "I don't want to discourage you from being well-informed, Harry, but I want you to know that not all of those side effects are likely to occur. And even if all or some of them do occur, the symptoms brought on by the radiation often weaken over time. It's an individual thing. Different people have different responses. Since this is your decision, I suggest we get you set up with a radiation oncologist right away. You can't afford to wait on this."

Harry soon learned that reading about a procedure was a long way from having it done. He realized immediately that he would have to fight every step of the way to maintain his dignity and sense of individuality.

Within a week he had spent hours being prepared for the first of his many radiation treatments. First, his radiation target point was established by a series of "dress rehearsals" that allowed the radiation oncologist to determine precisely where the muzzle of the machine would be placed. Then the "target" was carefully drawn on Harry's body with a semipermanent ink. This would be the "Ground Zero" for the radiation.

In the following weeks—seven in all—that Harry underwent radiation treatment, he found the process to be far less uncomfortable than he had expected. He was one of the lucky ones, experiencing few side effects from the treatments—just a little diarrhea. He didn't feel much like having sex either, but who would?

Did radiation work for Harry? Only time would tell. Tests done after his treatments indicated that the cancer had been eradicated. But his doctor wouldn't give him a clean bill of health for some time—maybe never. Even so, Harry was glad he'd decided against surgery. Even if the cancer came back, he wouldn't regret his decision not to have surgery. It was a choice he had made for his quality of life.

27. Will prostate treatments sterilize me?

Procedures that involve removal of all or part of the prostate will sterilize you. Hormonal treatments and radiation can also have this effect. However, the question of sterility isn't the first thing on most men's minds when they're facing prostate problems, since they usually occur later in life.

The one surgical procedure that doesn't rule out fertility is the TURP, performed for BPH. Remember, with a TURP there is retrograde ejaculation—that is, your semen backs up into the bladder and is excreted along with your urine. But if semen is separated from urine right after an orgasm, your partner can sometimes be successfully artificially inseminated.

28. How do I know whom to trust and how to get the best care? It seems like there's so much confusing information!

When you are sick—especially if you're facing cancer—it's a very vulnerable period. It doesn't help that there seem to be so many differing theories about treatment. You need to investigate the available information as though you were a journalist delving into a scandal. For indeed, cancer is a scandal on your body. If you don't have a doctor whom you trust, begin your investigation by checking out the groups and organizations at the end of this book. You are not alone. You're not the first man on earth to face this, and it should give you some comfort that much of the groundwork has already been laid. Resist the temptation to be stoic. Now is the time to ask for help!

29. I've never been in a hospital. Any tips to help me through it?

There's no such thing as a "minor" hospital stay. It's one of the most foreign environments you're likely to encounter. From the instant you walk through the door, you're barraged by forms, tests, pricks, pulls, questions, decisions. One of the advantages of prostate surgery is that you can schedule it in advance so you're not in a position of having to make rushed decisions about life-and-death issues.

Medical issues aside, many men have said that the worst thing is the indignity of it all. "This sounds silly," one man recounted, "but nobody ever told me about the shaving. I mean, I can see the reason for it. But nobody told me. This little girl appears in my room, all chipper and bright, and bammo. Dry-shaved me right down the front. It itched for weeks too."

Another procedure that novice hospital patients find distasteful is the obligatory enema. The colon and bowels must be clear before surgery, but the procedure can feel like one more miserable moment added to so many others. Likewise, many men are baffled by the need for additional blood and urine tests, when it seems they've already donated their fair share. Some get annoyed by new faces showing up to take medical histories they've repeated many times before. This seeming duplication of effort actually serves a purpose, but it's annoying—especially for someone who is facing the big moment of major surgery.

Perhaps the best way to prepare for your hospital stay is to get both your mind and body ready. Prior to surgery, stop smoking and cut back on substances like alcohol and caffeine. Eat a nutrient-rich diet—plenty of fruits, vegetables, grains, beans, and low-fat protein. If you choose to do so, you can set aside some of your own blood in advance, in case it's needed during the surgery. This process should be started a few weeks before the surgery.

It may not make you feel any better knowing what to expect. Hospitals are an insult in a dozen big and small ways. The best I can suggest is that you try very hard to keep your focus—which is on making yourself well. A growing body of evidence shows that there really is a direct link between healing in the body and what's happening in the mind.

Case Study: A Course of Watchful Waiting

Kevin G. felt a wave of heat rising to his cheeks as his doctor continued discussing possible treatment options. "Treatment options," Kevin mused. "This guy has basically told me I've got prostate cancer, and he's talking options. How about the option of blowing my damn brains out now, Doc? What about that option, huh?"

Kevin knew the doctor would be shocked to hear what he was thinking, but he couldn't help himself. He'd been a little boy when his grandfather had been transformed from a loud, brawny man to a wizened, shuffling skeleton in what seemed no time at all. He remembered overhearing his parents late at night in the kitchen of their little ranch house talking softly to each other about Big Jim's (that's what they'd called his granddad) sickness, the "cancer." Twenty years later he'd seen his dad go through the same thing, watched him slowly eaten away by the ravages of that horrible disease. And now it was his turn. Kevin wasn't sure he could go through it. He felt an acrid taste in his mouth as he contemplated what looked like a very grim future. His reverie was broken when he realized the doctor was silent across the desk, staring at him.

"Did you hear a word that I've been saying, Kevin?" the doctor asked. "You look like you're a million miles away. I know this seems shocking to you, especially considering your family history, but you really have a lot of reasons to feel optimistic."

Kevin shifted in his chair and slowly shook his head. "Tell you the truth, Doc, I sorta feel hopeless, you know? I guess it was inevitable, but it's a real kick in the balls, literally and figuratively. I'm scared. I don't want to die like this."

"Kevin, you make me feel like I've been talking to the wall. We have caught this cancer at the top of its cycle. If it weren't for the PSA test, we wouldn't have had any reason to even suspect that you had cancer. The biopsy we took confirmed the diagnosis, and frankly, I wish you were as happy about this as I am. This is a Stage A cancer, Kevin. You've got an almost microscopic tumor growth on one lobe of your prostate, which at this point we are going to leave alone. You are a sixty-year-old man in excellent health, no prostate enlargement to speak of, and now that we are aware of your problem, we are going to monitor you very carefully. Down the road, we may want to think about some radiation or hormone treatment, but for now I think we'll just do some 'watchful waiting.' What I want you to do is to take a deep breath, listen to what I'm telling you, and relax. You're in a hell-uva lot better shape than you think. Okay?"

Kevin tried to absorb the information the doctor had just provided. Why did he feel so damn uneasy? "I hear you, Doc," he said finally. "It's just, uh . . . well, me and Mary have always had a really good life together. I mean, sex has always been real important to both of us. Am I not going to be able to . . . you know? Because if that's the case . . . well, we'd both be pretty unhappy."

"Kevin, the only way this is going to effect your sex life is if you let it!" the doctor exclaimed. "You are one of the healthiest sick men I know. Now get the hell out of here, go home and tell your wife you're going to be watched like a hawk, and make an appointment to see me in a few months. Okay?"

Kevin slowly rose to his feet. He and the doctor shook hands, and a smile crept upon his lips. "I'll keep in mind what you said, Doc. Thanks. I do feel a lot better about this." Maybe I can beat the odds, after all, Kevin thought. Maybe I'm going to be okay.

PART IV

Living Well After Prostate Surgery

Michael's Lifesaving Disease

Michael H., sixty, lay in his hospital bed staring at the TV high up on the wall. His favorite team had just been knocked out of the playoffs by the current world champions, so he had lost a pretty nice bundle on the game. All he really wanted at that moment was a cigarette and a beer. Nah, what he really wanted was a carton of cigarettes, a case of beer, and that incredibly hot nurse who had just come in to check up on the old geezer across the room.

He shifted slightly in his bed and felt a swirl of hot pain rise up from his crotch. He lifted the sheets to take a peek once again. Geez! They had shaved him clean as a whistle down there, and he had a tube coming out of his penis, along with a row of staples from his belly button down. It was a ghastly sight—almost inhuman. But he couldn't resist the urge to look. God, he thought, I hope they got everything.

When the doctor first told Michael he had cancer, he was pretty shook up. When he told him it was prostate cancer and what they proposed to do about it, he was damn scared, humiliated, betrayed, you name it. He and his wife Annie had always had a pretty active sex life, though things had slowed down some the last few years. He figured it was mostly the drinking that did that, though all the smokes and maybe forty pounds of gut hanging over his belt hadn't helped either. But to think that he and Annie might never . . . well, it was too damn depressing to imagine. He couldn't wait to find out if his "equipment" was ever going to work again. His doctor had performed the potency-sparing operation, but he said they wouldn't really know for a while. Now, if only they got all the cancer . . .

Six and a half months later, Michael's recovery was going remarkably well. "You're my prostate poster boy!" his doctor beamed. There had been an initial bout with incontinence, which had shaken Michael up a bit, but at his doctor's urging, he started practicing exercises every day to tighten his sphincter muscle and give himself more control, and he was doing pretty well.

The doctor had insisted on no beer and no cigarettes, and Michael had succeeded there too—except for one fall from grace. He had gone out one night with some of the guys—his first such foray since the operation. One thing led to another, and he ended up having two beers, a few cigarettes, and getting sick as a dog.

That was it for him, he'd vowed after that experience. And he'd stuck to it. He realized that without all the smoking and drinking, he was feeling better than he had in years. He could take a deep breath without coughing—imagine that! And he'd dropped twenty pounds. A good part of that had to be the beer. Also, since the operation, Annie had been cooking a lot different. Low-fat city, he called it. It wasn't so bad, though.

He and Annie had messed around a few times in the last couple of weeks, but nothing had happened in terms of him getting excited. It was pretty much what he'd expected, so it didn't upset either of them. The doctor had said these things take time, so he was determined to be patient.

In the meantime, Michael decided to try and get into better shape. He and Annie began walking every day, just a few blocks at first. And he discovered an old set of weights down in the cellar that had belonged to one of the kids. He cleaned it up and began using that too. In less than a year Michael was looking and feeling healthier than he had for most of his adult life. The sex problem had cleared up and everything was back to normal. Better than normal.

"Geez," he said to Annie one night. "Who would have thought an old fogey like me could feel this good? Maybe getting sick saved my life." He laughed heartily at the idea.

Annie just smiled. She happened to believe it was true.

30. How long will it take to get back on my feet after surgery?

That depends on your age, physical condition at the time of surgery, what was done to you, how well you endured it—and on and on. I want you to keep remembering that you're not a machine. You're an individual. Your friend George may have been up and out in three days. Your experience may be very different. There are no "shoulds."

Prior to surgery or any serious treatment for BPH or prostate cancer, you should have a heart-to-heart talk with your doctor about some of the side effects you might expect from the treatments. Don't expect that your doctor will necessarily volunteer the information on his or her own. Unfortunately, doctors often practice the policy of the least said, the better. I think the opposite might be true.

In any case, here's a short list of big questions to ask before any procedures are done. (You might think of others. Remember, there's no such thing as a silly question!)

- Describe the surgery. Do you use Dr. Walsh's potency sparing surgery?
- How will you know if the surgery is successful?
- What method do you use to find out if the cancer has spread beyond the prostate?
- Describe the way I'll feel after surgery. What will be the discomforts? Intrusive procedures? For example, will I have to wear a catheter, and if so, for how long?
- What will be used to treat any pain I might experience? Will I be comfortable and pain-free?
- Will I need radiation after surgery? How will you know? If I need it, what is it supposed to accomplish? What kind will I be getting? What type of routine is involved? What are the risks and potential side effects of radiation?
- Will I need chemotherapy? What type of medication will be used and how will you know if it's effective?
- Will I need hormone therapy? Explain why female hormones can help me. Will they make me seem feminine? Is this a short-term treatment, or do I have to take the hormones forever?
- How do each of these treatments affect me? How sick will they make me? Can I work? Will I throw up a lot? Will I lose my hair?
- Are there drugs I should be taking? Drugs I should be avoiding?
- Can I ever have sex again? If you do the potency-sparing operation, how long will it be before we know it worked? Will my recovery be complete?
- How long will it take to recuperate?

- Does having prostate cancer mean I can get other cancers too?

And so on. It might help to make a list in advance so you don't forget any of your questions.

31. Will I be incontinent?

Dr. Walsh's potency-sparing surgery has also diminished the incidence of postsurgical incontinence because its precision removal avoids damage and scarring of surrounding tissues and organs. Although many men will experience temporary incontinence after surgery, only a small percentage should experience long-term or permanent incontinence, if the procedure is done properly.

Men don't always report problems with incontinence because, frankly, they're ashamed. Incontinence is the ultimate loss of control—the return to a state reminiscent of childhood. It can be extremely depressing, especially when it's coupled with poor sexual function and other side effects of surgery.

Another reason incontinence is often not reported is that people aren't always sure they have it. You see, it isn't necessarily a constant experience. Many men report only occasional leakage, and they don't want to start complaining to the doctor about such a "silly" thing as a few odd urine stains on their trousers. But I think it's always serious if it is disrupting your life in any way, or even just existing as a possibility you have to worry about at work or in social situations. As Dr. Katherine Jeter, editor of the *HIP Report* (Help for Incontinent People) points out, "Some health professionals refer to a person as being 'slightly incontinent.' That is like being 'a little pregnant.' The unexpected loss of urine in any amount, on a regular basis, in an inconvenient place is incontinence."

Why is incontinence a problem associated with prostate procedures? The reason is simple. An enlarged or cancerous prostate can interfere with the bladder's ability to empty itself normally, causing an ongoing loss of urine. Prostate surgery does create a temporary trauma to the bladder.

Incontinence can be described as a problem if you have any of the following symptoms:

- the urge to urinate, followed by leakage before you can make it to the bathroom
- urinary leakage caused by coughing, sneezing or laughing
- nocturnal wetting

A number of things may trigger an episode of incontinence. You might leak urine when you laugh, sneeze, or cough. It might happen when you're nervous. You might suddenly feel the urge to urinate and leak before you can make it to the bathroom. Cold temperatures can sometimes trigger the urge to urinate.

32.   Can incontinence be reversed?

Often, urinary incontinence is manageable and responds well to behavioral treatment—including biofeedback, pelvic muscle exercises, and scheduled voiding.

If you have incontinence, there are several effective

ways to reduce its impact on your life—and potentially eliminate it.

Practice Biofeedback. This is a learning technique that can help you exert better control over urine storage and release. It utilizes visual or audio aides to give you moment-by-moment information on how well you are controlling your muscles. Over time, you learn to better control your muscles automatically. Biofeedback has been shown to produce complete control of incontinence in 20 to 25 percent of patients and to provide substantial improvement for an additional 30 percent.

Practice Pelvic Exercises. Here's an exercise program that has been shown to be very effective. It is adapted from the *Pelvic Training Manual* produced by HIP. If you do these exercises every day, you'll be amazed at what a substantial change they make.

Step 1: Identify the two different muscle groups: the muscles around your anus, and the muscles around the base of your penis and urethra.

> Muscles around the anus: Tighten the area around your anus as if you are trying to stop a bowel movement. The muscles working are the ring of muscles around your anus.

> Muscles around the urethra: Tighten the muscles around the base of your penis and urethra, as if you were trying to stop the flow of urine. (If you're not sure which muscles these are, practice while you're actually urinating, stopping and starting the flow.)

Step 2: Lie comfortably on the floor or bed, breathing steadily and deeply. Place one hand on your lower abdomen; it should remain still while you are doing the exercises.

Tighten the anal muscles, pulling inward and upward. Hold tightly while counting slowly to ten. Relax.

Tighten the urethral muscles, pulling inward and upward. Hold tightly while counting slowly to ten. Relax.

Repeat five to ten times, several times a day.

33. Will a low-fat diet really make a difference?

In recent years, evidence has been mounting that links high-fat diets to several kinds of cancer—among them, colon and breast. Now there are new studies that demonstrate a direct relationship between diets high in animal fat and the development of prostate cancer. Dr. David Rose, who conducts diet-cancer studies at the American Health Foundation in Valhalla, New York, explains it this way: "A number of different fatty acids drive prostate cancer cells once they've developed. Fats can accelerate the growth of tumors and increase their propensity to metastasize."

In studies linking animal fat intake and prostate cancer, red meat was found to be the most damaging. In one study, those men who consumed the most red meat were two and a half times more likely to be found with advanced cancer or to die of prostate cancer.

Scientists readily admit that there is a long way to go in fully understanding the diet-cancer risk. But it is a matter of common sense to say that there is a connection between nutrition and wellness. In some cases, that connection is vibrantly clear. For example, diet is certainly a factor in the development of the arterial plaque that signals coronary artery disease—the number-one killer of adult men. In other areas, the connection between diet and disease is less clear. However, researchers are growing more and more convinced that there are dietary links to some cancers.

Current data suggests that as many as 40 percent of cancer deaths in this country are associated with nutrition. And all too often, the nutritional culprit is fat. But let's put the picture into perspective.

Most meat and dairy products are high in fat. Fat has received a bad reputation because it has been associated with a variety of health problems, including coronary artery disease and cancer. But in itself fat is not bad. Your body needs fat to operate, just as it needs protein and carbohydrates. More accurately, your body needs lipids, which not only become storage fats but are also made into hormones and other substances such as cell membranes.

Here's the problem with dietary fat. While your body needs protein, it does not need the kind of fat that comes with animal foods, since it has the capacity to produce that kind of fat itself. What it does not produce—and therefore must have through your diet—is polyunsaturated fatty acids. These are essential to your diet, but only in very small amounts. It's almost impossible to suffer from a deficiency.

When you compare this picture with the average American diet, the difference is clear. The high protein, high-fat American diet is in direct opposition to our nutritional needs.

34. So, what is the right diet?

According to most dietary guidelines, a healthy diet should include between 10 and 15 percent protein, and no more than 30 percent fat (two-thirds of it unsaturated). Newer guidelines even suggest that fat intake should not excede 20 percent of daily calories. At least 50 to 60 percent of your diet should be composed of carbohydrates. There are two forms of carbohydrates: simple sugars and starches, known as complex carbohydrates. Simple sugars are the basic elements of all carbohydrates; starches are formed by complexes of simple sugars called polysaccharides. When you eat starches, your gastrointestinal system breaks them down into the simple sugar glucose that is used for energy. Good sources of complex carbohydrates include all vegetables, cereal, rice, pasta, bread, nuts, grains, and legumes. Fruit is not a complex carbohydrate since it is composed mostly of the simple sugar fructose and water. But it is important to health by virtue of its vitamin, mineral, and fiber content.

There is substantial evidence that fiber, a substance found in plant foods, has many health benefits. There are two types of fiber. Water insoluble fiber is made from the structural parts of plants and is found in wheat bran, whole wheat, fruit and vegetable skins. Water soluble fiber comes mostly from fruit, vegetables, beans, and oats. Insoluble fiber is a potent digestive aid which improves the process and adds bulk to the stool for easy elimination. It is one of the primary preventive measures to guard against colon cancer. Soluble fiber is believed to play a role in decreasing blood lipid levels, offering protection against coronary artery disease. And all kinds of fiber seem to help lower blood sugar.

A well-balanced diet will also ensure that you're getting the necessary vitamins and minerals.

Ask your doctor to recommend a nutritionist who can help you devise a healthy meal plan. You can also get information from the American Cancer Society regarding their dietary recommendations.

35. I'm on chemo and I'm having trouble eating at all.

Various treatments associated with prostate surgery—including radiation, chemotherapy, and hormone treatments—can have a dramatic effect on your appetite. They can also cause side effects that make you nauseated or unable to eat. This puts you in a double bind because you need to eat in order to regain your strength and help your body fight the disease.

If this is your dilemma, you may get some good advice from a nutritionist or by contacting one of the cancer support societies listed in this book. Here are a few basic tips if you're suffering nausea, appetite loss or other problems eating:

- Eat small, frequent meals instead of the standard "three squares."
- Dry toast, crackers, or cereal in the morning helps combat nausea.
- Eat food very slowly in a relaxed environment.
- Keep healthy snacks available and munch on them in small amounts throughout the day.

- Avoid foods with strong smells or flavors, or food whose temperature is too hot.
- Avoid eating before a treatment, or eat only dry toast or crackers.
- If you're nauseated, you might get relief by sucking on ice cubes or Popsicles made from fruit juices.
- Be sure to get plenty of liquids. Drink cool, clear beverages and clear broths.

Treatments can also cause constipation or diarrhea, or both at one time or another. If you're constipated, try to solve the problem by adding fiber to your diet and drinking plenty of water. Don't take laxatives unless you've consulted your doctor. If you have diarrhea, temporarily maintain a diet of clear liquids, avoiding both high-fat and high-fiber foods. The water loss that accompanies diarrhea will also drain your body of important nutrients like potassium and calcium. In addition to drinking plenty of fluids, make an effort to restore potassium after the diarrhea has passed by eating foods like bananas and potatoes, which are rich in this nutrient.

36. Is it true that taking zinc supplements will help treat prostate problems?

Zinc is an essential mineral that is necessary for immune function and growth. Among the many other functions this mineral performs, it aids the production of testosterone and sperm. The reason it has been suggested as a prostate curative is that there is a high concentration of zinc in the seminal fluid and the prostate gland itself. Scientists who have studied the results of zinc deficiencies have learned that they can impair many normal functions, including male sexual function. However, studies have not yet established any benefit from taking zinc tablets; indeed, too much zinc can impair the function of white blood cells, the cells that fight infection.

For now, the best advice is to try and maintain zinc in your diet. It's plentiful in meat, poultry, oysters, eggs, and beans. If you're a vegetarian, you'll probably need to take supplements. You can also avoid a zinc deficiency by limiting or avoiding alcohol, which speeds the rate of nutrient loss from your body.

37. What's the best way to get better?

If you were about to undertake a major business project, I'll bet the first thing you'd do would be to organize your files, establish a strategy, and start keeping a diary. I'd suggest that this is going to be the most important "business project" of your life.

A lot of men have said they don't like to keep diaries; they consider them "girlie." But this is more like a war plan than a gushing journal. It's also a medical log. Many people still believe that their health outcomes are determined by the knowledge and skills of the doctors they choose. Indeed, the choice of a doctor is very important. But the true measure of long-term health is your own commitment to stay on top of your condition, monitor physical changes as they occur, and be prepared to be your doctor's partner. In the appendices of this book you will find some guides to help you do that—a Personal Medical File to fill out in preparation for doctors' visits;

and a Daily Health Journal to support you during the period of your recovery.

Case Study: The Gift of Years

When seventy-two-year-old Gabe learned he had advanced prostate cancer, his first thought was, "This is it." What a year it had been, losing his wife Claudia to breast cancer, and now learning he had cancer himself. He almost wondered if it was worth fighting. In his mind, he visualized himself curling into an unresisting ball—giving up. But as a Protestant minister, despair was against everything Gabe believed in. He vowed to put his faith in God, as he had during his wife's long illness. He thought of his daughter Elaine and his new little grandson, Jack, and his resolve strengthened. He was scared, but also determined to take on this challenge with every bit of fight he had in him. His doctor had the same attitude.

"We doctors are fools by nature," Gabe's oncologist told him cheerfully. "Kind of like you clergy. We keep believing, against all odds. But you know what? Sometimes we're right."

Gabe had a radical prostatectomy, and tissue samples showed the cancer had spread beyond the prostate. It was not unexpected news, and Gabe agreed to the next step, which was radiation. He joined a support group and started talking about himself and his feelings—for the first time in his life. Gabe realized that he had always been focused on giving counsel and support to others. It was a new experience learning to lean on others, and not such a bad one at that.

Gabe lived four years after he was first diagnosed with cancer, and he didn't regret a single one of them. "Not many men have a chance to prepare leaving this world," he said shortly before his death. "I've made my peace with myself, my family, and with God. I'm content." Gabe viewed the four years as a gift from God. He died in peace, his daughter and grandson near his side, his house in order.

PART V

A Return to Good Sex

Case Study: Love
Makes the Difference

It was three-thirty on a cold January morning. Steve B. sat at the kitchen table drinking a cup of hot chocolate and smoking his fourth cigarette in half an hour. He knew he shouldn't be smoking, shouldn't be drinking cocoa—the caffeine, of course—but he just didn't give a damn.

Eighteen months ago his doctor had discovered the prostate cancer. What a kick in the butt that had been. He was only fifty-eight, and overnight he had changed into an old man. Steve stubbed out his cigarette and rose from the table. Ellen had been great about the whole thing, he thought as he walked into the study and flicked on his desk lamp. He slumped down in the chair, still thinking about Ellen. What a doll, a beautiful woman, still fabulous after thirty-five years. He felt a familiar wave sweep over him. He'd never lost that initial thrill when he thought about Ellen—the thrill that had kept him a one-woman-man all these years. But now, along with the familiar thrill, Steve felt an equally strong wave of frustration and bitterness.

So, how do I let her know how I feel? he wondered. Pat her on the back? Tell her what a swell buddy she is? He put his head in his hands and ran them through his hair. It seemed this was to be a night of encountering demons.

Yes, he was alive. Yes, he had recovered. The surgery had been pretty rough, but so far so good. No cancer. Beat the incontinence. And just when he was feeling good again and his doctor was giving him the go-ahead for sex, poof! Nothing.

He remembered the first time they tried. It was sweet,

romantic, like a honeymoon night. It felt so good to touch Ellen again that he could have buried himself in the sensation. But nothing happened "down there." It was as if his male equipment was disconnected from the rest of him.

The doctor had told them to be patient, to relax. "This happens," he assured them with a confident smile. "You've had a trauma to your system, Steve. An insult."

Well, months later Steve was beginning to understand the meaning of the word insult. Nothing had changed. Not a stir, not a movement, not an anything. He was deeply depressed.

He had been getting up in the middle of the night for at least two months now, restless and frustrated. Was his whole life supposed to pass him by? Were he and Ellen to become warm companions and nothing more? Would she give up on him and find someone else? Who could blame her? He opened his desk drawer and took out the brochures the doctor had given him at his last appointment. Penile implants. Oh God, the stuff of office jokes. Well, let 'em laugh. Maybe it's funny when all your stuff is working right. This was no joke to him, not now. Rigid, semirigid, inflatable pumps. How the hell did you choose one of these things?

"Can't sleep, honey?" Ellen asked from the doorway.

"Oh, Ellen, I'm sorry. Did I wake you?" Steve gathered up the brochures and began putting them away, almost furtively.

"Whatcha got there, Steve? Top secret documents?"

"Uh, no, stuff from the doctor." Steve reluctantly handed the brochures to Ellen.

Ellen perused them for a moment, then came around to Steve's side of the desk and knelt down next to his chair. "Is this something you want, honey?" she asked quietly.

Steve reached out and stroked Ellen's cheek. "What I want is you."

Ellen's eyes filled with tears. "You've got me, stupid. And always will. But I know what you mean. I want you too. I just don't know if I want you to go through any more pain, any more surgery."

"Ell, look, it's driving me nuts. I just want things to be more like they used to be."

Ellen rose and adjusted her robe, then took Steve's hand in hers. "Come to bed now, baby. Let's get some sleep. When we get up, we'll call the doctor, make an appointment, and find out the best way to go about this. Okay?"

Steve got out of the chair and put his arms around his wife. "You're the best thing that ever happened to me, you know that? Let's go back to bed. We'll call tomorrow."

38. How will prostate surgery affect me sexually?

There are two ways to answer this question—from a psychological standpoint and from a strictly physical standpoint. I'm sure you realize that having sex is more than a "mechanical" process of stimulation leading to erection. Your sexual function is highly influenced by your state of mind. And if you've just had surgery for BPH or for prostate cancer, your mind may be busy with other matters. Any number of things can affect you sexually:

- tiredness or lack of energy during the recovery period
- feelings of fear and uncertainty that are natural to those confronting cancer
- postsurgical depression—a common experience
- a single-minded focus on getting well that sets aside everything else
- your partner's fears, concerns, and feelings of nervousness
- anxiety about not being able to make your penis hard, which becomes a self-fulfilling prophecy

And so on. The power of the psyche is so great that some men need only to hear that they might have sexual dysfunction for it to happen.

From a physical standpoint, you have every reason to be optimistic about a return to sexual functioning if you've had a potency-sparing prostate operation. However, don't expect to be instantly okay. It can take up to a year or more after surgery before full function is restored. If you know and accept this in advance of surgery, you'll save yourself a lot of anxiety during your recovery period.

39. Can I ever again be a normal man?

I don't think anyone has ever figured out a believable way to convince a man that he's still sexual even when he can't have an erection. Or that his "manliness" is in no way compromised by the failure of his semen to come out of his penis. Or that unexpected bouts of incontinence won't ruin a romantic mood. Or that never again experiencing an orgasm is the least bit tolerable.

Let's not pretend.

A study conducted by researchers at the universities of Chicago and Toronto asked fifty men between the ages of forty-five and seventy who didn't have prostate cancer what kind of treatment they'd prefer if they developed the disease: a treatment that guaranteed survival for five years but made them impotent; or a treatment that gave them a smaller possibility of survival for a shorter period of time but preserved full sexual capacity. Does it surprise you that most men preferred the latter?

Sex is important. It's fundamental.

However, if we're going to talk honestly about sex, especially as it relates to the prostate, we have to start by acknowledging that as a culture, we've created a grand myth about male sexuality and potency. Among the most prevalent (and most blatantly false) stereotypes:

- "Real" men are high performance machines.
- "Real" men always want sex.
- A man without an erection is no man at all.
- "Real" men "shoot" voluminous quantities of semen.
- Women are more attracted to men who have large penises.

If you've just had prostate surgery, or are having problems that interfere with your sexual performance, these myths can drive you to despair. It doesn't matter that rationally you know they're not true. Cultural myths are emotion-based.

But trying to define yourself by arbitrary standards of normalcy is always a trap. Instead, ask yourself what you want. How do you define quality of life? What is sexually normal for you? If that has changed, what adjustments can you make? If you have a partner, how does your partner feel about it?

Your sexuality is too precious and too private to be judged against somebody else's standards. When you feel shame about your human condition, it gets in the way of living well. It's impossible to feel this kind of shame and thrive as a man. If prostate disease has changed your experience of sex, in a sense you must reinvent your sexuality. And you have to get past the shame to do that.

There is another side of the coin too. Being a sex-obsessed society, we tend to believe that everyone wants it pretty much all of the time. Especially men. Research has shown that couples are more ashamed to admit that sex is unimportant than they are to admit they crave it all the time. But studies have also shown that many Americans, male and female alike, are simply not very interested in having sex. They find great pleasure and intimacy in other ways.

Here again the problem is the arbitrarily defined norm that suggests there's something wrong with people who don't want frequent sex. That same myth encourages an impotent man to believe that an essential part of his life force has died. But that might not be true.

Remember, too, that human beings are more than merely erotic creatures. Our complex natures allow us to experience fulfillment, beauty, satisfaction, and exquisite pleasure from a wide range of experiences. Our sensitive intellectual and emotional abilities also allow us an unlimited ability to experience a depth of intimacy that transcends the physical. I would never suggest that impotency is not painful; it is equivalent to the death of a meaningful part of one's life. But it might also awaken another vista.

40. Can I still have an orgasm after a TURP?

If you have a TURP and now experience the resulting retrograde ejaculation, which we discussed earlier, the sensation of orgasm does not change, regardless of the change in direction of your semen. You may, however, experience an initial psychological adjustment that has an effect on the frequency and sensation of your orgasms. Once you get adjusted to it, your sexual activity should feel quite normal and satisfying.

41. Can I have intercourse if my testicles are removed?

The removal of your testicles—called an orchiectomy —will halt the production of sperm and greatly diminish your testosterone levels. Even so, about half the men who have their testicles removed are able to resume sexual intercourse with time. Furthermore, almost 80 percent of men taking female hormones for prostate cancer report being able to have sexual intercourse.

42. I'm not sure if I'm impotent. Can a doctor tell for sure?

Your doctor can perform some basic tests to determine if your penis still has the nerves to respond to sexual stimulation. He'll feel for a pulse in your penis, then test what is called a bulbocavernosus reflex. If all is well, your anus should contract when the doctor squeezes the tip of your penis.

Another way to find out if you are able to function sexually is to test your sleep patterns. As you know, most men have erections off and on throughout the night as a normal part of the sleep cycle. There are special monitors that can be attached to your penis; if erections occur, all is probably well—at least mechanically speaking.

If your penis is able but still not "willing" to have erections, you may need to devote some time and attention to the matter. The key is to relax and be patient. Some sex experts recommend what they call sensate focus exercises, which gradually reintroduce you to sex—and also give you pleasurable alternatives to actual intercourse. The exercises are done with your partner and involve lengthy sessions of touching, caressing, and gentle stimulation without intercourse. Eventually, the goal is to achieve orgasm without intercourse, then, if possible, to resume normal activity. Many couples find that these exercises have the happy advantage of reestablishing the physical intimacy that may have been lost amidst medical concerns. They can also reveal new sensations and pleasures, even for longtime partners.

43. What about prosthetic devices?

Modern technology can be miraculous, and certainly the advance made in sexual prosthetic devices is an example of our ability to restore meaningful activity where it once seemed impossible.

But any man who has reached the point of considering a prosthetic device is dealing with a wide range of emotional and psychological issues. I won't trivialize the issue (nor would most medical professionals) by presenting this as an option that is always in a man's best interests.

First, let me describe what's available. Then let's talk about some of the considerations that might help shape your decision.

There are essentially two types of devices: One type remains rigid or semirigid at all times; the other type is an inflatable device.

The semirigid model basically involves an implant that gives a man a permanent hardened penis. It includes a flexible silicone rod that allows the penis to hang naturally when it is not being used for intercourse. Still, many men find it disconcerting, sometimes uncomfortable, and potentially embarrassing to be in a constant state of hardness.

The basic concept of an inflatable device is the implantation of a hollow cylinder on each side of the penis, where blood gathers during an erection. A rubber pump placed under the scrotum (not visible above the skin) fills these cylinders with fluid when a man squeezes it. The result is the same as the normal effect of blood being pumped into the area. A deflation valve is pushed when the man desires the penis to become flaccid.

A new device seems promising—combining the best of both worlds. It achieves an erection without a surgical implant. It's called the Erect Aid Suction Device for Potency, and here's how it works: A hollow tube fits over your penis, held tightly in place with hand pressure. A small pump exhausts the air in the tube, causing blood to rush into the penis and create an erection. Once there is an erection, the tube is removed and replaced with a rubber device that keeps the blood in place so intercourse can occur. The advantage of this method is that there is no surgery, it's easy to obtain and use, and it ultimately feels more "natural" than the other methods.

If you are thinking about penile prosthetics, I strongly urge you—and your partner, if you have one—to seek counseling, and to investigate some of the organizations and resources mentioned in the following part. It's important for you to clarify your reasons for making the choice—and to determine whether your expectations are realistic. This is a time for total self-honesty, and I know that's very hard because a vital aspect of your identity is at stake here. But take a private moment and consider some of these questions:

- Do I want to do this because I'm worried about my wife's sexual satisfaction?
- Am I afraid no woman will want me if I can't have an erection?
- Do I feel unbearably ashamed by my "unmanliness"?
- Do I believe that there's no replacement for the kind of intimacy full sexual intercourse provides?

And so on.

These are all valid points, by the way. There's no right or wrong answer to the question of whether you should consider a device. However, this might be a good opportunity for you to examine some of your attitudes, as well as your partner's attitudes.

Whatever your decision, remember that you are not just a set of mechanical body parts. You're not a performance machine. You are a human being. Make your choice based on where you find pleasure and dignity.

44. Will sex feel the same if I have a pump?

After prostate surgery, you may never again recover the same sensations you once had. A lot depends on the nerve damage you've suffered. Some types of surgeries allow men to retain orgasmic sensation; more radical procedures in cases of highly advanced cancer do not. The issue of regaining sexual function is not just about having an orgasm. Nor is it just about doing your partner a favor. It's more complicated than that. The ability to participate in the act of intercourse—the insertion of penis in vagina —is associated with a deeply felt sense of intimacy. It is primal. It feels good. It is a closeness between two people unlike any other. But it is not necessary for a complete and satisfying romantic partnership. Nor is it necessary for the expression of love.

So, while an implant may not restore sex the way it once was, it may give you back the intimacy that is a fundamental aspect of your relationship.

45. How about potency drugs?

There are injectable drugs available that stimulate erections. Ask your doctor about them. While the idea of injecting a needle into your penis may seem like a real romantic mood-breaker, the process is really quite simple and painless, and usually produces an erection within fifteen minutes. However, not every man responds to these drugs, and there are potentially harmful side effects. Most doctors recommend them only for infrequent use, and there is much that remains unknown about their long-term effects.

How about aphrodisiacs? For the most part, these are expensive gimmicks. If you have potency problems related to physical conditions like prostate surgery, an herbal remedy to increase desire is certainly not going to get to the root of your problem. However, laboratory testing is now under way to develop a topical cream that can cause erections. This cream would be a welcome advance in the science of potency.

Speaking of drugs, talk to your doctor about the various medications, which you may be taking for other purposes, that can interfere with your potency. These include antidepressants, tranquilizers, antihistamines, cough medicines, sleeping pills, heart medications, blood pressure medications, ulcer medications, and anabolic steroids.

46. How can I explain my implant to a new woman in my life?

If you are a single man who has chosen to have an implant, you're probably scared to death of your first sexual encounter. I hope by the time that moment occurs, you're comfortable enough with yourself that you can deal with it calmly. Besides, most people these days—especially people over fifty—aren't just hopping into bed on the first date. This is a good argument for a return to the old-fashioned art of courting. By the time a woman really gets to know you, if she really cares about you, she's probably not going to be scared away. Women are swept away by intimacy—not by the size or operative technique of a man's penis. One piece of advice, however: Don't just "spring" it on her the first time you make love.

Whether the woman in question is a new love interest or your wife of many years, give her credit for appreciating the man you are. And keep in mind that the best way to help a woman be comfortable with your implant is to be comfortable with it yourself.

Case Study: A Wife's Exasperation

Julie R. sat across the desk from her husband's urologist, knowing it was sneaky for her to have arranged this private consultation. But she was totally beside herself and didn't know where else to turn. A year ago, when Gary, fifty-seven, had come through his prostate cancer surgery in good shape, she'd been elated that the cancer had not spread and he would live. In the months after his surgery, Gary and Julie had been completely focused on his getting well—whatever it took. Now he was well— better than they'd ever anticipated. But in spite of the surgical technique the doctor had used, it was becoming increasingly clear that Gary was impotent.

Her voice filled with emotion, Julie told Gary's doctor how devastated her husband was by his inability to get an erection. "He's become obsessed about it," she said, "And somehow . . . well, he's turned it on me. He keeps making these comments about how I should find another man. He said he'd understand it if I took a lover. He thinks I should leave him." Now she was crying full force. "Look at me, Doctor. I'm fifty-three years old. I love my husband. I'm not used to talking so frankly, but the fact that he can't put his penis inside me is the last thing I care about. He's still my partner, my lover, my friend. He's alive. But sometimes I'm afraid he'll leave me 'for my own good.'"

Gary's doctor promised Julie he'd have a heart-to-heart talk with her husband when he came in for his next appointment in two weeks.

"I've felt for some time that you're an ideal candidate for a penile implant," the doctor told Gary. "But one thing has stopped me from encouraging it."

"What's that?" Gary asked. He felt a little surly—wasn't sure he even wanted to consider an implant.

"Well," the doctor smiled, "you know how they say that sex is ninety-nine percent in the brain and only one percent in the genitals? I think you've got it backward. An implant can restore your sexual functioning, but it can't change the way you feel about yourself, or how you relate to your wife.

"Julie deserves better," Gary mumbled.

"Is that what she says?" the doctor challenged him.

"No, of course not. But—"

"Wake up, Gary," the doctor cut in. "Listen to this woman who loves you!"

In the end, Gary was persuaded to get couples counseling, and he and Julie came to a positive understanding of what they meant to one another. Then Gary was ready to talk about an implant.

PART VI

Ask for Help

Case Study: Benjamin's Rescue

Benjamin M., seventy-four, wanted to die. "I've lived a full life," he told his wife, Ruth. "Hey, when it's over, it's over," he joked with his horror-stricken son, Ted. He repeated these comments so frequently that his family lived in a constant state of nervous exhaustion. Ruth was convinced her husband was suicidal.

The strange thing was, Ben had survived his prostate cancer beautifully. Physically, he was in better condition than he'd been in a long time. Emotionally, it was a different matter. "I think a support group might help Ben," their family doctor suggested to Ruth. "I know of one that's run by a local doctor just for men who've had prostate cancer. See if you can get him to attend a session. This experience has shaken him in ways that you and I can't understand because we've never been there. Ben needs to be around people who've been through it."

Initially, Ben was resistant to the idea. "You know I'm not a group type," he told Ruth angrily. "I'm not going to sit around in a room with a bunch of cancer losers and hear 'em whining and moaning about being sick."

"It's not like that, Ben," Ruth said. "It's just people like you talking. Look, I know you're feeling lousy. Maybe this will help. Please, just try it once. If you hate it, I'll never mention it again."

So, Ben agreed to go. The meeting was held at another man's home, and there were six men present, plus the doctor—who was about twenty years younger than everyone else in the room.

Ben didn't do very much talking during the first meeting. But he found himself more interested in what the others were saying than he'd expected. One thing was for sure: Nobody was whining. And there was quite a bit of practical information being shared. He had to admit he liked a couple of the guys. They reminded him of himself. After the first meeting, he told Ruth he'd go back. He didn't tell her how much he had enjoyed it.

After Ben had attended three meetings and said very little, Edward, one of the guys in the group about Ben's age, nodded in his direction.

"So, what's the deal with you?" he asked. "You hardly say anything."

Ben shrugged. "Don't have much to say," he replied. "I just like listening."

Edward laughed. "Sounds like me when I first came. Now you can't shut me up. You want to know what I think, Ben?"

"Not especially." Ben couldn't help smiling, but he felt uncomfortable.

"I think your whole life you thought you had to keep everything inside because that was your job. Not to let anyone worry. Now you don't even know how to talk anymore."

"Well, there's not much to say," Ben replied.

"Ah, sure there is! There's more to say than there's ever been in your whole life. Look at it this way: What the hell do you have to lose anymore? Nothing. Look at us pitiful old guys sitting around here. We're in this boat. So, we talk. That's all. Just talk."

Ben didn't respond right away. It took him a few weeks longer to start feeling comfortable. But Edward's words had meaning for him. This man knew how he felt. For the first time, someone knew. It was a brand-new feeling.

47. Maybe older people get these diseases because humans weren't meant to live so long.

Modern medical technology has certainly put a new twist on human experience and longevity. On one hand, it has enabled us to live longer. On the other hand, it has made us vulnerable to diseases of aging. Most prostate problems are the by-product of aging. Yet, who would argue that humans were meant to live shorter lives? We are the beneficiaries of our own inventions, and we must feel grateful for them even when their outcomes are ambiguous. It's the way of life.

In the end, whether you are experiencing the gifts or the struggles of living longer, your prostate problem—or the potential for a problem—has put you in touch with your mortality. It has reminded you that every life, no matter how hearty, has an end. Most of the men who get prostate cancer survive it and go on to live very full lives. In that respect, medical technology offers a second chance. But few if any men can truthfully say they are the same as they were before they developed cancer.

48. A support group sounds depressing. Isn't it just a bunch of people complaining about their problems?

As Ben discovered, support groups don't reinforce the negatives, but give aid and comfort. When you're sick, you feel alone. It doesn't matter if thousands of other people have your disease. It's happening to you. One reason for the sense of isolation is that although you may be surrounded by people who love you, none of them can really understand what you're going through. I urge you to check out a support group—even for a short period. It will help you get your bearings and feel less alone. The organization Patient Advocates for Advanced Cancer can provide you with a list of support groups across the country. PAACT also publishes a newsletter called *Cancer Communications*. The goal of PAACT is "to educate the patient about the latest available information on the diagnosis and treatment of prostate cancer, without financial obligation." Contact the organization at:

> PAACT
> P.O. Box 1656
> Grand Rapids, MI 49504
> (616) 453-1477

Your urologist or local hospital may also be able to direct you to a support group in your area.

49. I like to keep on top of what's new in the field, and be in touch with organizations. Can you give me a rundown?

You'd probably be amazed at all the help that is available, if you know where to find it. A number of organizations are set up for the sole purpose of providing information and advice. Most are nonprofit.

Cancer Help Agencies

AMERICAN CANCER SOCIETY
National Headquarters
4 West 35th Street
New York, NY 10001
(212) 736-3030

Your local phone directory will contain the address and phone number of a nearby branch. The American Cancer Society funds its own research, and has patient and family support programs.

THE NATIONAL CANCER INSTITUTE
CANCER INFORMATION SERVICE
National Institutes of Health Building 31,
Room 1018A
Bethesda, MD 20014

The National Cancer Institute conducts research on cancer, supports other research facilities, and has an up-to-date reference and informational service for cancer patients and their families. This service is referred to as the Cancer Information Service, or CIS. CIS has a toll-free number:
   (800) 4-CANCER, in the U.S. and Puerto Rico.
   (800) 524-1234, in Oahu, Hawaii.
A call to this cancer information service will tie you in to the regional office of the NCI that serves your area.

ROBERT J. MATHEWS FOUNDATION
3435 American River Drive
Sacramento, CA 95864
(916) 972-7055

This foundation is dedicated to the research and cure of prostate cancer. It was started by the late Robert J. Mathews, who suffered from and ultimately died of the disease.

Us Too
American Foundation for Urologic Disease, Inc.
300 West Pratt Street, Suite 401
Baltimore, MD 21201
(800) 828-7866

An organization specifically devoted to providing information about the latest developments in prostate cancer treatment; also gives referrals.

Sexuality/Impotence Help

Impotence Information Center
P.O. Box 9
Minneapolis, MN 55440
(800) 843-4315

Free information on impotence, plus referrals to urologists in your area.

Impotence Institute International
Impotence Institute of America
119 South Ruth Street
Maryville, TN 37801-5746
(615) 983-6064

Patterned after Alcoholics Anonymous, this organization has chapters across the country and is the home of Impotents Anonymous (IA). There are also partner support groups. For information about programs and newsletter subscription, send a self-addressed stamped envelope.

ROMP (Recovery of Male Potency)
Grace Hospital
18700 Mayers Road
Detroit, MI 48235
(800) 835-7667

This hospital group has chapters around the country and serves as a referral and information service. Phoning the above number will put you in touch with a nurse, who will refer you to a nearby resource for help. Newsletter and other materials are available.

SIECUS—SEX INFORMATION AND EDUCATION COUNCIL OF THE UNITED STATES
80 Fifth Avenue
New York, NY 10011

This organization serves as a clearinghouse for other groups involved with sexuality and sexual dysfunction. Send a self-addressed, stamped envelope for information.

Sexual Prostheses and Devices

For information about the latest technology available in sexual prostheses, contact the following manufacturers:

Dacomed Corporation
1701 East 79th Street
Minneapolis, MN 55425

Impotence Information Center
American Medical Systems
P.O. Box 9
Minneapolis, MN 55465

Surgitek/Medical Engineering Corporation
3037 Mount Pleasant Street
Racine, WI 53404

Osborn Medical Systems
P.O. Box 1478
Augusta, GA 30903

Mentor Corporation
600 Pine Avenue
Goleta, CA 93117

Response/KSI, Inc.
889 South Matlack Street
Westchester, PA 19382

Incontinence Help

The Simon Foundation
Box 835 Z
Wilmette, IL 60091
(800) 237-4666

Referral agency for the incontinent. Has an informational service and newsletter.

The National Kidney and Urologic Diseases
Information Clearinghouse
9000 Rockville Pike
Bethesda, MD 20892
(301) 468-6345

Medical referrals and information about treatments.

Medical Research/Information

National Health Information Center
U.S. Department of Health and Human Services
Office of Disease Prevention and Health Promotion
P.O. Box 1133
Washington, DC 20013
(800) 336-4797

Information for consumers and professionals on
health-related topics; referrals and selected literature
available.

National Library of Medicine
8600 Rockville Pike
Bethesda, MD 20894
(800) 638-8480

Computer access to medical literature and research
topics.

Your Medical Team

The medical team that participates in the treatment of prostate conditions may include several players. Your family doctor or primary physician can recommend specialists; or you can research them on your own. Your local library or American Medical Association offices will have information about licensed physicians and specialists. To check on a specific doctor, contact the American Board of Medical Specialties Certification Line at (800) 776-2378. These are the types of doctors who may be involved in your care:

General Practitioner: A primary physician or family doctor, trained to screen for most medical conditions. (If you belong to an HMO, this will often be your referring doctor.)

Internist: A doctor that specializes in internal medicine. Sometimes used as a primary physician, this doctor can also screen for common conditions. For example, he or she will do a DRE and order a PSA test.

Urologist: A surgical doctor who specializes in the treatment of conditions related to the urinary tract and male sex organs.

Oncologist: A cancer specialist. There are three different subspecialties: medical oncologists, who treat the disease with drugs; radiation oncologists; and surgical oncologists.

50. How can I really live well after prostate surgery?

Don't expect too much of yourself. Keep your sense of humor. Stay fit. Accept the help that's offered. The experience is going to change your life. There's no doubt about that. But change isn't always such a bad thing. One man reflected, "Before I got sick, I never had five minutes in the day for anything. I was so busy. Now I have all the time in the world. It makes me a little antsy. I'm eager to get back on my feet. But somehow I think I'll never go back to being the driven, mile-a-minute man I used to be. It doesn't seem worth it anymore. Last week, when I told my wife I thought we should take a few weeks off and go on a cruise, she nearly fainted. That wasn't the old me talking. But I'm not the old me anymore."

Case Study: Marvin's Reflections

"I had surgery for prostate cancer two years ago last month," Marvin S. said. A smiling, fit, seventy-two-year-old internist, Marvin agreed to talk about how the experience changed him. "At the time, I had been practicing medicine for more than forty years. I had seen every ailment known to man or woman. I had sat with many people as they died. I loved being a doctor—I still do. But when I got sick myself, it was hard to let go and be on the other side of the desk. I felt restless and uncomfortable—unexpectedly betrayed by my body." He laughed. "You'd think that I, of all people, would have come to terms with the various ways age takes its toll on the human body. But I guess you're never really ready when it happens to you.

"I was fortunate because my cancer was caught in the early stages. I'd always been very careful about regular screening, and in my case it paid off. A simple prostatectomy, no spread found, and I was on my way. It changed my life, though, made me stop and think about what is really important. The only way I can describe it is as if everything around me suddenly started moving in slow motion. There were things I was seeing for the first time. Suddenly, it became terribly important that I not let a minute of my life go unnoted—that I stop and appreciate everything."

What did that mean for Marvin? In many ways his life continued as it had before his surgery. Even at seventy-two he refused to retire; practicing medicine was his life's work and his greatest love. He did, however, change his schedule to accommodate more time for his family. And every morning before he went to the office, he took a brisk four-mile walk along the river path near his home. "I had lived beside that river for forty-five years," he marveled, "and I had never walked on that path. Now my eyes have been opened to the busy, vibrant life of nature. I notice the different varieties of birds, I stop to feed the ducks, I converse with my fellow travelers along the path. We are so quick to judge our lives on their biggest moments—a wedding, the birth of a child, an important achievement. How much we miss! I know that my friends and family feel badly for me that I have been sick, and I didn't welcome it myself. But I have experienced something I've seen over the years in my patients—the discovery of a rewarding side to suffering."

Appendix A

An Easy Reference to Terms
Used in This Book

Adenocarcinoma: Cancer that originates in the lining of the inner surface of an organ.

Androgen hormone: A hormone, such as testosterone, which produces male characteristics.

Bacteria: Microorganisms that feed off living things. Some bacteria are "good" because they destroy harmful intruders. Others cause disease. Most bacteria that invades the bladder or prostate is a problem.

Benign: A condition that is not cancerous.

Benign Prostatic Hyperplasia (BPH): Noncancerous enlargement of the prostate which usually causes urinary difficulties.

Bilateral Orchiectomy: The removal of both testicles.

Biofeedback: A relaxation technique that uses sound and visualization.

Biopsy: The removal of a tissue sample for examination under a microscope.

Bladder: The muscular organ that stores urine before it is excreted from the body.

Bone Scan: The injection of radioactive chemicals to detect the potential spread of cancer to the bones.

Bulbocavernosus Reflex: A test to measure potency.

Cancer: A catchall term to describe literally hundreds of different types of conditions. Essentially, it means that cells have become abnormal and have grown and spread, taking over normal cell activity.

Chemotherapy: A form of cancer therapy that uses drugs that affect all parts of the body.

Cryosurgery: The use of cold liquid nitrogen to freeze and kill cancerous sections of the prostate.

Cystoscope: An instrument used for examining the urethra and the bladder.

Digital Rectal Exam: A manual exam, where a doctor inserts a gloved, lubricated finger into the rectum to examine the anus, rectum, and prostate.

Dihydrotestosterone (DHL): A male hormone that causes prostate enlargement later in life.

Ejaculation: The orgasmic emission of semen from your penis.

Estrogen: Female sex hormones sometimes used to shrink male testes as part of cancer treatment.

Fine needle aspiration: A biopsy technique that uses a very thin needle to take a tissue sample.

Gland: A group of cells whose job it is to secrete or excrete materials.

Hormone therapy: The use of opposing hormones (such as estrogen for men) to block the cancer-feeding activity of one's own hormones. Some cancers, such as prostate cancer, depend on male hormones for growth.

Incontinence: The inability to control one's urine flow.

Infectious Prostatitis: Prostatitis caused by bacteria in the prostate.

Impotence: The inability to achieve and sustain an erection.

Lymph Nodes: Tissues throughout the body that perform many functions, including fighting bacteria.

Magnetic Resonance Imaging (MRI): A resonance imaging procedure similar to a CAT scan.

Masturbation: Self-stimulation (or stimulation by a partner) of genital organs for sexual pleasure and release.

Metastasis: When cancer spreads from the original site to other parts of the body.

Noninfectious Prostatitis: An inflammation of the prostate that does not have a bacterial cause.

Penile Implant: A device that is surgically inserted into the penis which allows it to become rigid for sexual intercourse when that is not possible naturally.

Perineum: The bridge that connects the anus and the scrotum.

Potency-Sparing Prostatectomy: Surgical procedure that preserves the nerves that control erections.

Primary Cancer: Cancer that originates at the site itself, rather than spreading from elsewhere.

Prostate: A gland that sits below the bladder that produces fluid to enable spermatozoa to travel down the urethra before being ejaculated through the penis.

Prostate Acid Phosphate (PAP) Test: Determines whether cancer has spread to other sites.

Prostate Cancer: An abnormal growth of cells which usually forms a tumor or tumors in the prostate gland —and can spread to other parts of the body.

Prostatectomy: Surgical removal of all or part of the prostate gland.

Prostate Specific Antigen (PSA) Test: A blood test that measures the seminal fluid for high levels of a protein that might indicate a prostate problem. Although it is not strictly speaking a cancer test, it can also alert doctors to the possibility of cancerous cells.

Prostatic Massage: A finger massage of the prostate's lateral lobes to force secretions to flow through the urethra and out of the body. Therapy that relieves congested prostate.

Prostatodynia: Pain in the region of the prostate of unknown origin and treatment.

Radiation: Energy waves that kill cancerous cells.

Rectum: The end portion of the large intestine located just above the anus.

Retrograde Ejaculation: Semen that is released back into the bladder rather than emitted through the penis.

Scrotum: The external pouch beneath the penis that contains the testicles.

Semen: The fluid that gets discharged in the male ejaculate.

Silent Prostatism: Prostate enlargement that is not accompanied by symptoms.

Sperm: The mature male reproductive cell produced by the testes, which can fertilize the ovum.

Testicles (or Testes): Two reproductive male glands situated in the scrotum which produce sperm and the male hormone testosterone.

Testosterone: The primary male hormone, which is responsible for the main male characteristics.

Transurethral Resection (TURP): The removal of all or part of the prostate through the urethra.

Ultrasound: Sound waves that reveal pictures of various parts of the body.

Urethra: The tube that carries urine from the bladder through the prostate and out of the penis.

Vasectomy: The surgical removal of a small piece from the tubes that transport spermatozoa, thus resulting in male sterility.

Appendix B

Personal Medical File

Keep your own medical records up-to-date and bring them with you when you visit the doctor. Your active participation will improve the quality of your medical care.

1. Your Family Tree

Record the following information about family members:
- year of birth
- year of death (if applicable)
- cause of death
- history of: coronary artery disease, stroke, high blood pressure, high blood cholesterol, diabetes, cancer, obesity, alcoholism, smoking, drug abuse

maternal grandfather

maternal grandmother

maternal aunts

maternal uncles

mother

paternal grandfather

paternal grandmother

paternal aunts

paternal uncles

father

brothers

sisters

2. Personal Description

date of birth _____

current age _____

height _____

weight _____

race _____

marital status _____

marital history _____
_____

profession _____

3. Relevant Psychological Background

These are psychological and social conditions and experiences that have an influence on your overall health and recovery. Not all doctors are skilled in soliciting this kind of information. And male patients tend not to bring up these issues when they seek medical care. Fill out this section in advance so that relevant information won't be excluded from your medical treatment.

experiences of violence (including military) _____
_____
_____

alcoholism in family _____
_____

childhood abuse/trauma _____
_____

traumatic accident _____
_____

family suicide _____

_____

depression _____

_____

job loss/poverty _____

_____

death of loved ones _____

_____

other _____

4.   Personal Behaviors

smoking _____

drug abuse _____

alcohol use/abuse _____

sexual habits, including risk-associated behaviors ___

_____

sexually transmitted diseases _____

_____

exercise habits _____

_____

relevant dietary habits _____

_____

other _____

_____

5. History of Medical Care

Be sure to include all diagnoses, treatments, surgeries and prescription drug use.

Date   Condition   Treatment   Outcome

immunization history _____

_____

prescription drug history _____

_____

_____

toxic exposures or other relevant information _____

_____

medical screening history (heart, cholesterol, hypertension, lung and colon cancer, prostate conditions, diabetes, etc.) _____

_____

_____

_____

_____

_____

6. Preparation for Doctor's Visit

Use this space to jot down notes in advance of your doctor's visit, and to keep notes on what the doctor tells you during the visit.

What to tell the doctor:

What to ask the doctor:

What the doctor tells you:

Appendix C

Daily Health Journal

Many people find it helpful to keep track of their daily process: diet, physical activity, elimination, medications, unusual aches and pains, and general well-being. The following pages illustrate a simple method for keeping a daily journal. Feel free to add your own elements.

Daily Diet

Time	Food/Drink	Calories*	Fat Content*

*Calorie and fat breakdowns are listed in readily available pamphlets, or in the diet and cookbook published by the American Cancer Society.

Physical Activity

Time   Activity   Duration   Intensity

Heart Rate_____   Blood Pressure_____

How did you feel after completing the exercise:

Urination

(useful if you've been experiencing urinary difficulties)

Time	Urge	Amount*	Problems

*such as, full evacuation, steady stream, small amounts, dribbling, etc.

General Well Being

Symptoms (if any):

Medications taken: Medication   Time   Amount

Improvements experienced:

Unusual changes (pain, energy levels, etc.)

General reflections on the day. (Use this space to jot down any ideas you have about your care, questions to ask your doctor, thoughts about your life and health, etc.)

Self-Help Guides

from St. Martin's Paperbacks

HOW TO SAVE YOUR TROUBLED MARRIAGE
Cristy Lane and Dr. Laura Ann Stevens
_____ 91360-5 $3.50 U.S.   _____ 91361-3 $4.50 Can.

THE WAY UP FROM DOWN
Priscilla Slagle, M.D.
_____ 91106-8 $4.50 U.S.   _____ 91107-6 $5.50 Can.

IN SEARCH OF MYSELF AND OTHER CHILDREN
Eda Le Shan
_____ 91272-2 $3.50 U.S.   _____ 91273-0 $4.50 Can.

LOOK BEFORE YOU LOVE
Melissa Sands
_____ 90672-2 $3.95 U.S.   _____ 90673-0 $4.95 Can.

SELF-ESTEEM
Mathew McKay and Patrick Fanning
_____ 90443-6 $4.95 U.S.   _____ 90444-4 $5.95 Can.

Publishers Book and Audio Mailing Service
P.O. Box 120159, Staten Island, NY 10312-0004
Please send me the book(s) I have checked above. I am enclosing $ _____ (please add
$1.50 for the first book, and $.50 for each additional book to cover postage and handling.
Send check or money order only—no CODs) or charge my VISA, MASTERCARD,
DISCOVER or AMERICAN EXPRESS card.

Card number _____

Expiration date _____ Signature _____

Name _____

Address _____

City _____ State/Zip_____
Please allow six weeks for delivery. Prices subject to change without notice. Payment in
U.S. funds only. New York residents add applicable sales tax.

HELP 2/89